FOLKTALES OF *Ireland*

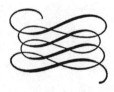 *Folktales*
OF THE WORLD

GENERAL EDITOR: RICHARD M. DORSON

FOLKTALES OF
Ireland

EDITED AND TRANSLATED BY
Sean O'Sullivan

FOREWORD BY
Richard M. Dorson

THE UNIVERSITY OF CHICAGO PRESS
CHICAGO AND LONDON

Library of Congress Catalog Card Number: 66-11885
The University of Chicago Press, Chicago 60637
The University of Chicago Press, Ltd., London
©1966 by The University of Chicago. All rights reserved
Published 1966
Printed in the United States of America
92 91 90 89 88 87 86 85 84   9876

Foreword

No nation of the world has gathered in its folktales with the fullness, the loving care, and the dazzling rewards manifest in Ireland. In the archives of the Irish Folklore Commission in Dublin rest a million and a half manuscript pages of traditions taken directly from the lips of their tellers. An international tale often has several hundred representatives in the great Irish storehouse, against a score in continental countries. Spacious stories of consummate artistry are safe in notebooks and on tape and disc recordings.

The work of the Commission only began in 1935, but it built upon a century of interest in Irish country tales. In the 1820's, '30's, and '40's, popular writers turned to peasant storytellers for characters and plots, using the conventions of the stage Irishman, until the Great Hunger turned rural comedy into pathos. At the turn of the century came the movement for a national literature, when Yeats, Synge, Lady Gregory, and Douglas Hyde uncorked the native folklore bottled in the Irish tongue. Soon Celtic scholars were finding in the humble oral traditions of the present clues to the great mythological and heroic cycles of the past. Who would know the national culture of modern Ireland must be aware of her folklore and folklorists.

In 1825 London booksellers offered for sale a slim, anonymous volume titled *Fairy Legends and Traditions of the South of Ireland*, the first collection of oral tales assembled in the British Isles. Its compiler was an admiralty clerk named Thomas Crofton Croker, born in Cork in 1798, the son of an army major. He had moved to London in his early twenties but frequently returned to the counties of Cork, Waterford, and Limerick to continue the walking trips on which he gleaned peasant songs and tales. The year before his *Fairy Legends* was published, he had brought out a handsome quarto volume, *Researches in the South of Ireland, illustrative of the Scenery, Architectural Remains, and the Manners and Superstitions of the Peasantry*, a sketchbook combining the interests of topographer, antiquary, and local collector in the synthesis that produced the Victorian folklorists. Croker thus fitted into an intellectual movement already visible. Sir Walter Scott and the brothers Grimm responded enthusiastically to the *Fairy Legends*; the Grimms translated it within a year into German, as *Irische Elfenmärchen*. Croker dedicated a second volume to Scott and a third to the Grimms, both appearing under his name in 1828. (Scott called him "little as a dwarf, keen-eyed as a hawk, and of easy prepossessing manners.") For volume three he in turn translated the lengthy essay on Irish and Scotch fairy mythology the Grimms had written for the German edition—truly a courteous exchange. Also he enriched his notes with their suggestions. In his "Dedicatory Letter to Dr. Wilhelm Grimm," Croker printed a long document sent him by Scott, which recounted the trial of an old woman in Scotland who was burned alive "for holding too close a connexion with Elf-land."

So the *Fairy Legends* opened up vistas beyond Ireland. After the long discussion of "The Elves in Scotland" by the Grimms, volume three moved to Welsh fairy legends, furnished to Croker by correspondents, while in his introduction he foraged through England for fairy beliefs. This extension of the inquiry from Irish to Celtic, English, and continental fairy traditions clearly reflects the outlook of Croker's collaborator and fellow Anglo-Irishman, Thomas Keightley, who completed *The Fairy Mythology* in 1828. Keightley claimed that he had supplied Croker with a number of the tales and most of the comparative notes. Other contributors also protested, and in later editions Croker limited his contents to legends he had personally obtained.[1] The Grimms recognized these legends as counterparts, not to their *Märchen*, or fictional tales, but to their *Sagen*, which included peasant reports of spirit beings presumably descended from the gods of

[1] Séamus Ó Casaide, "Crofton Croker's Irish Fairy Legends," *Béaloideas*, X (1940), 289–91.

an ancient mythology. Croker himself collected no *Märchen*, or any heroic tales.

At that early date Croker did not, as his accusers made plain, observe the precise methods of the modern folklorist. He inflates a kernel of spoken legend into a full story. Hence the sighting of a merrow (mermaid) by a country fellow, which could be related in a few sentences, becomes a sketch of the stage Irishman sportively conversing with the sea beauty and plighting his troth before a perplexed priest. Yet the belief in the merrow was traditional, as Croker's note testified. A whole gallery of phantasmic figures—the wailing banshee, the leprechaun (cluricaune) with his treasure secrets, the phooka or spirit-horse, the dullahan who carried his head under his arm—leaped from his pages to face a chuckling world.

After the *Fairy Legends*, various writers on Irish country scenes and characters dipped into the flowing wells of storylore. Samuel Lover in two series of *Legends and Stories of Ireland* (1831, 1834), William Carleton in two series of *Traits and Stories of the Irish Peasantry* (1830, 1833), and Gerald Griffin in *Tales of the Munster Festivals* (1827) and *Tales of the Jury Room* (1834) coquetted with Paddy, the lovable Irish scalawag who talked in a rich and circumlocutious brogue, relished his pipe and poteen, and engaged in amusing lower-class capers. Once in a while a folktale creeps into their scripts, supplying the skeleton for a droll sketch. Yeats, who would levy upon these authors in compiling selections of Irish folktales, recognized a prototype of the stage Irishman in a garrulous coachman, fisherman, or servant, who was overdrawn but existed. Closer to folk tradition was the *Legends, Tales, and Stories of Ireland* (1837), whose unnamed author, Philip Dixon Hardy, edited the *Dublin Penny Journal*. Among the usual arch scenes, such as "Paddy Doyle's First Trip to Cork," appeared chapters on "The Pooka," "The Leprawhaun," and "The Banshee," with actual descriptions of these creatures preceding imaginary episodes. One story, "Hie Over to England, or Shaun Long and the Fairies," is an early variant of a well-known folk legend in which the fairies transport a mortal to a far-off place. In this case Shaun follows the fairies to England, finds himself in a Lancashire wine cellar, is arrested and sentenced for breaking and entering, and on the scaffold whisks himself back home by donning a magic red cap.

The transitional figure in Irish folktale reporting is Patrick Kennedy, a Dublin bookseller who lived his first twenty years in county Wexford and wrote about them ever after. Those years (1801–1820) were a period of language transition in Wexford, and tales once told in the native Irish were now, for the first generation at any rate, crossing over into English. After the Great Famine of the mid-century had swept away traditional customs, Kennedy's romances, although cast in a literary frame, possessed an added historical interest.

Influences both within and outside Ireland shaped Kennedy's writings. He had read Croker, Griffin, and Carleton and followed their lead in his first work, *Legends of Mount Leinster* (1855), and such later ones as *The Banks of the Boro* (1867) and *Evenings in the Duffrey* (1869), which set forth Wexford country ways and tale-tellings in an envelope of fiction and with a touch of whimsy; unlike them, he preferred the longer romance to the short sketch. But he was also familiar with the Grimms' famous collection, with the Norwegian wonder tales of Asbjørnsen and Moe, translated by Sir George Webbe Dasent in 1859, and with the trove of Scottish Gaelic tales collected and rendered into English in 1860 by John Francis Campbell of Islay. These classics undoubtedly turned his mind to preparing a similar collection of the Irish tales he had been seeking at least since August 6, 1851, when he wrote the editor of the *Wexford Independent*: "Do not you and I and others still retain many of the traditions and legends of our native place? In the present transition state of our country they are likely to be lost, and will it not be doing some service to preserve them, however imperfectly?" And he requested readers of "our County paper" to send him such items, which he would print in his column.[2] In time Kennedy brought out three books of traditional tales, *Legendary Fictions of the*

---

[2] Quoted in James Delaney, "Patrick Kennedy," *The Past*, No. 7 (1964), p. 58. In his chap. XI, "Some Sources of Kennedy's Material," Delaney identifies Kennedy's main storytellers as his grandmother, who in turn obtained them from a wandering peddler, and the hereditary faggot cutter of the district.

Irish Celts (1866), *The Fireside Stories of Ireland* (1870), and *The Bardic Stories of Ireland* (1871).

The *Legendary Fictions* is a seminal work, parts of which the other two expand. Where Croker had noticed one segment of Irish tale-telling, Kennedy now illuminated the spectrum of oral prose traditions in Ireland. His five sections covered substantial and distinct veins of folk narrative. Part I, "Household Stories," a genre which would fill *The Fireside Stories of Ireland*, presented the international tales of magic and marvel common to all the Aryan peoples and first made known by the Grimms. Part II, "Legends of the 'Good People,'" widened the pocket opened up by Croker. Part III, "Witchcraft, Sorcery, Ghosts, and Fetches," explored the extensive lore of the supernatural apart from the fairy faith. Part IV, "Ossianic and Other Early Legends," turned to the native heroic and mythological cycles, now seen to exist in spoken as well as in manuscript form. Here was a glorious prize, a tale-tradition exclusively Gaelic, extending back over a thousand years. Part V, "Legends of Celtic Saints," considered the folk reports of miracle and wonder attached to Catholic saints that had once been fastened onto gods. Douglas Hyde would assemble a whole book of such relations.

Few forms of folk narrative escaped Kennedy. One was the humorous anecdote; he did actually compile for his final work a *Book of Modern Irish Anecdotes* (1872), but it was drawn from printed sources. Another strand he missed was folk history, still largely a folklore orphan.

Kennedy's manner was to interlard running comments between the tales rather than placing one text immediately after another. In these sandwiched paragraphs he often gives precise details about his human sources. "The narrator, Jemmy Reddy, was a young lad whose father's garden was on the line between the rented land of Ballygibbon and the Common of the White Mountain (the boundary between Wexford and Carlow counties), consequently on the very verge of civilization. He was a gardener, ploughman, and horseboy, to the Rev. Mr. M. of Coolbawn, at the time of the learning of this tale."[3] This kind of information has a professional ring. Kennedy also points out

[3] *Legendary Fictions of the Irish Celts* (London, 1866), pp.22–23.

general features linking his Wexford tales with others in the
collections of the Grimms, Dasent, and Campbell, and he sub-
scribes to the view that all emanated from a common "ancestral
household in Central Asia."

Still purer streams of story lay west of Wexford, as Kennedy
well knew, and he declared gallantly that none would rejoice
more than he when these tales were captured in their proper
Gaelic dress. Some future collector would accomplish effectually
what he had been laboring to do in the "comparatively barren
field of a semi-English country."

Various competitors for this honor could be cited. There was
the Rev. Canon John O'Hanlon, a prodigious writer of history,
poetry, and biography as well as author of *Lives of the Irish
Saints* in nine volumes and of *The Irish Emigrants' Guide to the
United States*, once a *vade mecum* for departing Irishmen. Born
in Stradbelly in 1821, he emigrated with his family to America
at the age of twenty-one and was ordained five years later in
St. Louis. But O'Hanlon was one emigrant who came back, and
until his death in Dublin in 1905 he plunged into literary labors
on varied aspects of the Irish heritage, including folklore. Under
his pen name of "Lageniensis," he wrote, in 1870, *Irish Folk
Lore: Traditions and Superstitions of the Country; with Humorous Tales*. Chapters dealt with "Fairy Mythology of the Irish,"
"Apparitions and Fetches," "Changelings, Fairy-Men, and
Fairy-Women," "Buried Treasures," and "The Merrow-Maiden
and Merrow-Men" (headed by a verse from Crofton Croker). But
these promising themes dissolved into prolix fancies. The same
year "Lageniensis" brought out *Legend Lays of Ireland,* showing his basic attitude toward folk materials, which he turned into
rhyming verse. The historical preface relates the literary use of
Irish legends in Dublin journals and magazines as well as in
books. In 1896 he returned to the subject with *Irish Local
Legends*, setting down thirty narrations he had heard from
peasant guides in different parts of Ireland, but he spun them out
according to his whim and facile pen. Had O'Hanlon's taste
and point of view prevailed—and it has enjoyed many supporters
in every country—folklore studies in Ireland would have ended
in a limbo, neither science nor literature.

Paradoxically, an American now entered the scene to establish irrefutably the worth of Gaelic oral traditions. Jeremiah Curtin, Wisconsin-reared and Harvard-educated, first visited Ireland, the land of his parents, in 1871 and returned four times during a twenty-year period. Curtin was a phenomenal learner of languages. He began by talking with the Scandinavian, German, and Slav immigrants around Milwaukee and eventually mastered some seventy tongues. As a folklorist he collected Russian, American Indian, and Irish tales, while on the side he translated Polish novels, among them *Quo Vadis*. He acquired some knowledge of Gaelic and, from reading Irish tales in print and quizzing Irish emigrants in America, came to believe he could uncover myth tales from Gaelic speakers. In 1887 he set out on his historic quest. First he stopped at the Dublin libraries to see their two thousand volumes of Gaelic manuscripts, the richest myth treasure in all Europe. Then he was off to Kerry, Galway, and Donegal, calling on Irish speakers and writing down their long tales inside miserable huts choked by a peat fire and roosting hens. His hunch paid off, and by asking for those who knew Gaelic, he found the myth tellers. In 1889 the fruits appeared in *Myths and Folk-Lore of Ireland*, a bag of twenty specimens running to four and five thousand words of poetic adventure about kings and giants, Fin mac Cumhail and the Fenians, and even one chronicle of Cúchulainn.

Curtin had advanced over Kennedy in two ways: he had collected not recollected and in Gaelic not English. Although depending on an interpreter, he could follow the speaker's thread. The laxity of his day softened Curtin's standards; he did not provide literal texts nor name his informants. In an extended introduction he speculates on questions of mythology, following the myth theories then in vogue of Max Müller and Herbert Spencer who saw, by different routes, myth tales as products of early man's confused ideas. Curtin was delighted to snare these well-preserved Celtic myths with their precision of reference and detail that denoted a clear descent from Aryan antiquity. In most European tongues the myth remnants were blurred. Among his trophies he gathered the Polyphemus episode attached to Fin mac Cumhail and related with glorious fancy.

The minute the giant closed the one eye in his head, he began to snore. Every time he drew breath into his body, he dragged Fin, the spit, the salmon, Bran, and all the goats to his mouth; and every time he drove a breath out of himself, he threw them back to the places they were in before. Fin was drawn time after time to the mouth of the giant with such force, that he was in dread of going down his throat.

When partly cooked, a blister rose on the salmon. Fin pressed the place with his thumb, to know could he break the blister, and hide from the giant the harm that was done. But he burned his thumb, and, to ease the pain, put it between his teeth, and gnawed the skin to the flesh, the flesh to the bone, the bone to the marrow; and when he had tasted the marrow, he received the knowledge of all things. Next moment, he was drawn by the breath of the giant right up to his face, and, knowing from his thumb what to do, he plunged the hot spit into the sleeping eye of the giant and destroyed it.[4]

Two more trips in 1891 and 1892–1893 brought Curtin further dividends, and he published these tales in the Sunday supplements of the New York *Sun*, whose sympathetic editor, Charles H. Dana, gave him as it were a newspaper fellowship. *Hero-Tales of Ireland* (1893) contained narratives similar to his first batch, but now he named his informants and discussed comparable tales, chiefly from the American Indians, whose animistic stories seemed to emanate from a more primitive stage of culture. In a third collection, *Tales of the Fairies and of the Ghost World Collected from Oral Tradition in South-West Munster* (1895), he turned from wonder tales and heroic legends to supernatural anecdotes. While staying in a farmhouse in the Dingle Peninsula, Curtin, having, so he thought, exhausted the Fenian tales, asked his host and some neighbors—an ex-quarry worker blinded by Italians in America, a cartman, a mason, a tinker—to tell of true experiences reflecting their ancient beliefs in the spirit world. The storytelling scene and the delineation of the group gave an immediacy and conviction to this sheaf of spectral

[4] Jeremiah Curtin, *Myths and Folk-Lore of Ireland* (London, 1890), pp. 210–11.

encounters lacking in Croker's and Kennedy's lighthearted treatment.

Recognizing Curtin's labors as part of their own legacy, The Folklore of Ireland Society reprinted sixteen of his *Sun* narrations as *Irish Folk-Tales* in 1944 in a valuable edition prepared by Séamus Ó Duilearga (James H. Delargy). Delargy described Curtin's field experiences and informants, some of whom he himself met a quarter of a century later. Still fuller details were supplied by An Seabhac in an appendix, "Notes on Some of Jeremiah Curtin's Storytellers," a mark of the modern interest in the narrator.

In the closing decades of the nineteenth century, various gifted persons, stirred by the English threat to Irish culture, developed a concern for Irish folklore. The celebrated eye surgeon, Sir William Wilde, and his equally celebrated wife "Speranza," Lady Jane Francesca Wilde, poetess, essayist, salon hostess, produced between them three books on the subject—although their even more celebrated son, Oscar, failed to inherit their common taste. The Wildes created nearly as much folklore as they recorded, Sir William with his notorious amours, one of which scandalized Dublin for months when it reached the courts, Lady Wilde with her dim-lit, intense literary teas at Number One Merrion Square. Stories gathered about them. Sir William was said to have removed the eyes of some country patients, intending to reset them promptly, but the cat ate them first. Speranza is supposed to have chided a servant by saying, "Why do you put the plates on the coal scuttle? What are the chairs meant for?"[5] As early as 1853 Wilde produced a short volume on *Irish Popular Superstitions* in which he deplored the decay of the Irish language and of the legends and notions it preserved. He gave an anecdote, later used with telling effect by Hyde, of the farmer who notched a stick hung around the neck of his eight-year-old son every time the boy spoke Irish; for those notches the schoolmaster would beat him in the morning. The doctor paid his

[5] T. G. Wilson, *Victorian Doctor* (New York, 1946), p. 307. This is a biography of Sir William Wilde. Horace Wyndham has written *Speranza: A Biography of Lady Wilde* (London and New York, 1951), and Patrick Byrne *The Wildes of Merrion Square* (London and New York, 1953).

respects to Carleton, Lover, Griffin, and above all to Croker for
his vignettes of the fairy tribe in Munster, but he recognized that
"a new set of elves, spirits, and goblin influences, with somewhat
different ideas attached to each, pervade the west, particularly
the counties of Mayo and Galway, and the isles which speckle
the wild Atlantic along their shores. . . ."[6] Actually Wilde's little
book never justified its title, for he rambled off on the ravages of
the Great Famine and the rise of fierce gangs who struck at the
English occupiers. Yet his opening set of "Queries," presumably
a finding list for items of lore he sought, covered rhymes, proverbs, charms, cures, curses, seasonal rites, corpse ceremonials,
legends of forts and raths, and opinions on fetches and spirits.
Apparently he did gather copious information on these matters
which Speranza used in *Ancient Legends, Mystic Charms, and
Superstitions of Ireland* (two volumes, 1887) and *Ancient Cures,
Charms, and Usages of Ireland* (1890), in effect a sequel. Lady
Wilde claimed that the contents came chiefly from oral communications of the peasantry in Irish or Irish-English, taken
down by "competent persons skilled in both languages, and as
far as possible in the very words of the narrator. . . ." Neverthe-
less she wrote up the entries with her own touch, paraphrasing,
commenting, moralizing. She was moved by a tradition of a
cynical priest who suffered twenty-four hours of knife thrusts
from a child to regain his soul, which left his corpse as a butterfly.

> The idea that underlies the story is very subtle and tragic;
> Calderon or Goethe might have founded a drama on it;
> and Browning's genius would find a fitting subject in this
> contrast between the pride of the audacious, self-reliant
> sceptic in the hour of his triumph and the moral agony that
> precedes his punishment and death.[7]

And she saw in the Irish taste for superstitition an instinctive
dislike for the narrow limits of common sense coupled with a
passionate yearning for the vague, the mystic, the invisible. Like
the dwellers in the fairy mansions, the "Irish love youth, beauty,
splendour, lavish generosity, music and song, the feast and the

[6] W. R. Wilde, *Irish Popular Superstitions* (Dublin, n. d.), p. 28.
[7] Lady Wilde, *Ancient Legends, Mystic Charms, and Superstitions of
Ireland* (London, 1887), I, 60.

dance."[8] Apart from these occasional flights, Speranza set down
the folk memories in scrapbook fashion. Fairy appearances, visits
of the dead, and miracles of saints abounded, but she displayed a
new emphasis, clearly the result of Sir William's interests, in folk
remedies, spells, maledictions, magical prescriptions, herbal
recipes, and odd beliefs about animals.

A long essay on "The American Irish," suddenly inserted toward the end of the *Ancient Cures,* shows that Speranza too
linked Irish folklore with Irish nationalism. She recites the
wrongs inflicted on Ireland by Elizabeth, Cromwell, and King
William that finally provoked the bitter uprising of 1798, and
deplores the Irish people's ignorance of their own history and
traditions caused by England's educational policy.

In the wake of the Wildes came a still more illustrious couple
whose joint effort in folklore, literature, theater, and the renais-
sance of national culture makes in itself a matchless tale. Lady
Isabella Augusta Persse Gregory, a plain widow in mourning
dress, met William Butler Yeats three years after her husband's
death, in 1895, when she was forty-three and he was thirty. She
entertained him at Coole, her country estate in the barony of
Kiltartan in county Galway, and took him on folklore junkets.
Yeats, also in somber garb, was often mistaken for a priest.[9]

He had already plunged into folklore. In 1888, on a publisher's
assignment for a series embracing England, Scotland, and Ireland, he prepared a selection of *Fairy and Folk Tales of the Irish
Peasantry,* following it in 1892 with a companion, *Irish Fairy
Tales.* His thoughts at this time, as his correspondence reveals,
are full of his folklore project, and he states the purpose clearly:
"It was meant for Irish poets. They should draw on it for plots
and atmosphere."[10] In his choices Yeats mixed literary and folk
tellings, although he understood the difference between "literature" and "science" and gibes at the folklorists who tabulate

[8] *Ibid.,* p. 280.

[9] Elizabeth Coxhead has written an informative biography, *Lady
Gregory, A Literary Portrait* (London, 1961). She suggests that Yeats has
been given excessive credit in his collaboration with Lady Gregory.

[10] Letter to Katherine Tynan of September, 1888, in W. B. Yeats,
Selected Prose, ed. A. Norman Jeffares (London, 1964), p. 136.

their tales like grocers' bills. So he admires the early writers, Croker, Carleton, Lover, who "caught the very voice of the people, the very pulse of life, each giving what was most noticed in his day." He praises the accuracy of Kennedy and singles out Lady Wilde's *Ancient Legends of Ireland* as "the best book since Croker's" and "the most poetical and ample collection of Irish folk-lore yet published." But it is Hyde he properly esteems as "the best of all the Irish folklorists," and he praises his simple, sincere style and thanks him for help with notes and the use of unpublished tales.[11]

During these years, Yeats was not merely reading but was also noting down folklore. In 1899 the editor of *Folk-Lore* printed a knowledgeable comment from Yeats on county Louth superstitions turned in by another collector. "I have stories about most of the things in the slip of folklore you send. I will be dealing with a good many of the subjects in a month or two." Yeats had encountered the Dead Coach driven by a headless driver and four headless horses (but in Galway they called it the Deaf Coach because it made a deaf or muffled sound); the illusion of ancient forts set afire by fairies in protest against invading workmen; the removal of persons at night by the fairies —he himself was supposed to have been transported four miles in Sligo; battles between fairy regiments, a topic about which he was seeking material. For cutting a fairy bush, a Sligo relation had been warned by the fairies, who put a black lamb in his flock, removing it after a few days. A friend knew of the death warning brought by a pigeon flying in and out of the house, while a tap sounded at the window. The poet had met four peasants who believed in fairies but not in ghosts, but never the converse, although a Roscommon man rejected both for water horses. These brief unvarnished notes show how alert Yeats was to oral lore.[12]

[11] Quotations are from *Fairy and Folk Tales of the Irish Peasantry* (also issued as *Irish Fairy and Folk Tales*, London, n. d.), pp. xix–xx; *Irish Fairy Tales* (London, 1892), pp. 8–9.

[12] Bryan J. Jones, "Traditions and Superstitions collected at Kilcurry, County Louth, Ireland," *Folk-Lore*, X (1899), 119–22: "Mr. [Edward] Clodd having shown the above notes to Mr. W. B. Yeats, the latter gentleman kindly forwarded the following memoranda upon them," pp. 122–123.

When he turned to writing pieces on folklore himself, in *The Celtic Twilight*, Yeats allowed his private feelings their rein. A first edition of 1893 grew larger in 1902, after his outings with Lady Gregory. *The Celtic Twilight* is neither pure collectors' folklore, as the opening scene of storyteller Paddy Sligo promises, nor literary sketching of folk themes, but rather a musing, introspective diary playing with the shadowy folk beliefs of fairy powers. Yeats was drawn to peasants like the Mayo woman who did not believe in hell or ghosts, but recognized fairies and little leprechauns, water horses and fallen angels.

Lady Gregory felt a kindred spirit when she read *The Celtic Twilight* in 1893. That same year brought to her Douglas Hyde's *Love Songs of Connacht*, a sampler of sensitive oral poems in prose and verse translations from the Irish. Yeats's Sligo and Hyde's Connacht roused a local patriotism for her own Galway, and she set out after every kind of spoken, sung, and recited remembrance. Afterward she recalled her sense of this experience.

> Dr. Douglas Hyde, *An Craoibhin*, had founded the Gaelic League, and through it country people were gathered together in the Irish speaking places to give the songs and poems, old and new, kept in their memory. This discovery, this disclosure of the folk learning, the folk poetry, the ancient tradition was the small beginning of a weighty change. It was an upsetting of the table of values, an astonishing excitement. The imagination of Ireland had found a new homing place.
>
> My own imagination was aroused. I was becoming conscious of a world close to me and that I had been ignorant of. It was not now in the corners of newspapers I looked for poetic emotion, nor even to the singers in the streets. It was among farmers and potato diggers and old men in workhouses and beggars at my own door....[13]

The rewards of the new discovery were rich. From the flavor of the folk speech, the Gaelicized English mirroring the syntax and thought of Irish, the mistress of Coole and the poet from Sligo found delight and inspiration. Both molded their writing

---

[13] *The Kiltartan Poetry Book* (Dublin, 1918), p. vi.

styles on the country dialect, pleased to treat Irish themes in an Irish English. Yeats declared his debt to this mode of talk which ended his imprisonment within raw conventional modern English. In the oral traditions of the country people, the two found a continuity with the mythological and heroic cycles known from medieval manuscripts. Using Gaelic English, Lady Gregory retold these cycles in *Cuchulain of Muirthemne: The Story of the Men of the Red Branch of Ulster* (1902) and *Gods and Fighting Men: The Story of the Tuatha de Danaan and of the Fianna of Ireland* (1904). Yeats wrote glowing prefaces for each; he called the Cúchulainn narrative the best book to come out of Ireland in his time, or perhaps ever. He had heard laborers and turf cutters talk of the Fenians, the magic warrior-hunters, and the Tuatha de Danaan, a shadowy pantheon of old now become the Sidhe or fairies. Rarely did one hear of Cúchulainn's exploits which, occurring around the time of Christ, and preceding the deeds of the Fenians, had passed earlier into the possession of the court poets. Yet the deeds of the Ulstermen too, he believed, must have come from an oral folklore. Lady Gregory's chronicles should restore the ancient kings, gods, and heroes to Irish youths and crowd their hills and valleys with associations once vivid before the mythologies of Greece and Rome and Judea had forced an alien antiquity on Ireland.

Soon Lady Gregory and Yeats were uncovering a wealth of living literature, and they enlarged their publishing plans to include oral as well as manuscript versions of Irish folklore. Yeats in the expanded edition of *The Celtic Twilight* in 1902 and Lady Gregory in *Poets and Dreamers* in 1903 set forth the first fruits of their Galway interviews. Yeats indulged in reverie, but the widow put together a dozen graceful essays on Gaelic oral poetry, Galway folk beliefs and tales, and the tradition-based dramas of Douglas Hyde. In the long first chapter she told about "Raftery," the folk poet whose feared satirical verses were still heard and still carried their sting, although he had been dead a generation. In a still longer chapter on "Workhouse Dreams," she offered a mixed bag of popular tales acquired in three afternoons at a country workhouse, saying "I was looking for legends of those shadow-heroes, Finn and his men, to help me in writing their

story; and I heard many tales and long poems about fair-haired
Finn, who 'had all the wisdom of a little child'; and Conan of
the sharp tongue, who was 'some way cross in himself'. . . ." But
she also encountered verses composed by Raftery and other oral
poets, stories of the kingdom of the Sidhe, episodes of modern
history, and rambling fictions about dragons and princesses.
Curiously, these international tales interested her least, perhaps
because they were European rather than Irish. Eventually she
turned her gathered hoards into books on separate themes. *The
Kiltartan History Book* (1909), which she called "the Book of the
People," isolated a species of oral narration still largely untapped,
the folk history that people choose to remember and relate, rather
than what is foisted upon them in the classroom. This oral history
centred on the mythical Finn, changed after two thousand years
in the telling from a noble hero into a cunning clown; the Goban
Saor, once a divine smith, now a master builder of Anglo-
Norman castles; patriot Daniel O'Connell, sixty years after his
death become a legendary champion and trickster; invader Oliver
Cromwell, after two and a half centuries still a devil; the modern
warrior-heroes of the 1798 uprising; and such matters which had
seared deeply into the folk memory. More conventional was
The Kiltartan Wonder Book (1910), a sheaf of sixteen magical
folktales heard at her own doorstep. She admits to splicing passages from different tales, for "folk-lorists in these days are
expected to be as exact as workers at any other science." No notes
comparing her tales with others are given, for she was never the
comparative folklorist.

Lady Gregory's finest folklore work did not appear until 1920,
the two volumes of *Visions and Beliefs of the West of Ireland*.
Yeats appended substantial essays (dated 1914) to each volume
and supplied meaty notes for the first. The *Visions and Beliefs*
deserves an acclaim it has not yet received. It deals with a form of
personal tradition, called the memorat by folklorists, just beginning to attract attention. While the subject was by no means new,
being the Sidhe or fairy race, the treatment was novel and precise.
Lady Gregory printed literal statements she had taken down
about all aspects of the fairy creed from individuals she identified
either by name or occupation. (She did not name the living or the

deceased with living relatives.) These autobiographical revela-
tions she arranged in sections of varying length, threaded around
some special element of supernatural belief or practice. In place
of the comical, literary, third-person accounts of fairy relations
with mortals customary with her predecessors, she reproduced
exactly the highly personal, shapeless, often fragmentary con-
fidences told her conversationally. In sum they testified to the
tenacious hold of the pre-Christian fairy faith upon the west-
country folk. There were sections on "Away," about neighbors
taken to fairyland by *them*; on "Forths and Sheoguey Places,"
harmful to mortals because they lay on fairy routes; on "The
Fighting of the Friends," telling of fierce struggles between
friends of a dying soul and unseen ones trying to take him away;
on "The Unquiet Dead," who come back among the living.

An arresting chapter on "Seers and Healers" introduced a spate
of folk memories about Biddy Early, dead twenty years but
flourishing in oral legends. Some said her healing powers came
from the fairies who had taken her *away* for seven years. Gentry
and common people flocked to her hideaway in spite of the warn-
ings of the priests.

Other surprises awaited the Lady and the poet. They learned
that more spirits lurked in America, where so many Irish families
had emigrated, than in Ireland. Thus they were told of an Irishman back from Boston who was in a boat steering for Aran with
three pounds worth of cable when a wave swept him overboard;
some time after a friend in Boston met the drowned man, who
gave him three guineas to pay for the cable on his next visit to
Galway.

They were informed of a new spirit. "We had, before our
quest began, heard of faeries and banshees and the walking dead;
but neither Mr. Yeats in Sligo nor I in Galway had ever heard of
'the worst of them all,' the Fool of the Forth, the Amadán-na-
Briona, he whose stroke is, as death, incurable."[14]

Yeats closed the first volume with an essay on "Witches and
Wizards and Irish Folk-Lore" and a clump of notes to the
memorats. He saw both likenesses and differences in English and

[14] Lady Gregory, *Visions and Beliefs in the West of Ireland* (2nd Ser.;
New York and London, 1920), p. 195.

Gaelic witchcraft: likeness in the universality of supernatural motif which they shared, difference in the drab matter-of-factness of English witch trials as compared with the wild passions displayed in the Scotch. Ireland escaped the witch hysteria, but Yeats shrewdly perceived in the wise woman Biddy Early a counterpart to Scotch witches burned at the stake in the sixteenth century for having knowledge acquired in fairyland. In a long, informed note on *The Faery People*, he cited the Scotch minister Robert Kirk, author in 1691 of the first autobiographical account of a visit to "The Secret Commonwealth" of the fairies, and Joseph Glanvill, the witchcraft expounder, who included in his *Sadducismus Triumphatus* of 1674 an Irish tale associating the dead and the fairies, as in modern Galway. Like Andrew Lang, the brilliant folklorist of Scottish birth, Yeats was intrigued by the family resemblance of occultists: witch, medium, seer, prophet, shaman, sorcerer, mystic. His lengthy conclusion to the second volume of *Visions and Beliefs*, "Swedenborg, Mediums, and the Desolate Places," makes the jump from the fairy creed to Swedenborgian mysticism.

In these years too John Millington Synge, persuaded back from France to his native land by Yeats, was discovering the western counties and islands and talking with peasants. He visited Inishmore in the Aran Islands in 1898 and saw Lady Gregory in the distance; later they would be partners in the Abbey Theatre. Although never so steeped in folklore as Lady Gregory or Yeats, he enjoyed the role of listener and collector, as one can see in his newspaper travel sketches reprinted as books under the titles *The Aran Islands* (1906) and *In Wicklow, West Kerry, and Connemara* (1912). Country people told him of tinkers who could witch, of plants seven feet tall that could cure any disease, of misers who took their money to their graves in their hair, of a mermaid who married a man named Shee, of fairies kidnapping children. On the Aran Islands he met a shanachie who had talked with Sir William Wilde and given a bookful of stories to "Mr. Curtin of America," who had supposedly made his fortune from them. In his book on Aran, Synge periodically inserted folktales related to him by old Pat Dirane, a daily companion. One dealt with the covenant of the pound of flesh used by Shakespeare in *The Merchant of Venice*, and Synge commented knowledgeably on its appearances "reaching from Persia and Egypt to the Gesta Romanorum, and the Pecorone of Ser Giovanni, a Florentine notary,"[15] and he knew that Campbell of Islay had included a version in his *Popular Tales of the Western Highlands.* The oldest man on the island relished telling Synge anecdotes of actual events which the playwright recognized as distinct from folktales. Such an anecdote gave him the idea for his much mooted play, *The Playboy of the Western World.*

An Englishman and an Australian also contributed to the Irish folklore movement, Alfred Nutt and Joseph Jacobs, two of the leading figures in The Folk-Lore Society founded in London in 1878. Jacobs brought out two volumes of selections adapted for children, *Celtic Fairy Tales* (1892) and *More Celtic Fairy Tales* (1894), which far surpassed his similar volumes for England, particularly in the scholarly "Notes and References" at the end. Jacobs praised the collectors in Ireland, Scotland, and Wales who, he felt, were providing the only substantial new accessions to the published folklore of the British Isles, and he urged on "the newly revived local patriotism of Ireland and the Highlands." A thoroughgoing diffusionist, Jacobs delighted in showing the far-flung wanderings of tales; he pointed out that Croker's "The Legend of Knockgrofton," about a kind hunchback whose hump was removed by the fairies while an unkind hunchback was given a second hump, was known in the United States and Japan. (Today this tale is identified as Type 503, "The Gifts of the Little People." An example is given in *Folktales of Japan*, a companion volume in this series, Number 36.)

For aid on his two books and for original research on Celtic folktales, Jacobs thanked his colleague Nutt, who used oral hero tales to cast light on the folk basis of medieval romance. The same legends told of Finn and Cúchulainn are attached to later heroes; could they not also have come from earlier ones?

Nutt differed from Jacobs in espousing the evolutionist rather than the diffusionist theory of folklore and saw in Celtic lands a splendid laboratory in which to consider the question whether

[15] *The Aran Islands* (Dublin and London, 1912), p. 27.

folktales had descended in time from prehistoric man or spread in place from one neighboring people to another. "No other Aryan civilisation," he wrote, "has developed itself so independently of the two great influences, Hellenic and Hebraic, which have moulded the modern world; nowhere else is the course of development less perplexed by cross currents; nowhere else can the great issues be kept more steadily in view."[16] He concluded that modern Celtic folklore did indeed retain ideas held by primitive Celts.

A prominent publisher, Nutt pointed his list toward folklore books and could not resist enriching the Celtic ones with his own astute commentary. He wrote a preface for Curtin's *Tales of the Fairies and of the Ghost World*, added comparative notes to Hyde's *Beside the Fire*, and amplified Kuno Meyer's edition of *The Voyage of Bran*, a medieval romance, with extensive treatises. These studies examined early Irish conceptions of the otherworld and rebirth from the folklore point of view, Nutt averring that "... what the Irish peasant of to-day fables and believes of the *good people*, his ancestors of a thousand years ago fabled and believed of the Folk of the Goddess."[17]

All the streams of interest in Irish folklore converged in Douglas Hyde. He was the friend of the writers, Lady Gregory and Yeats and Synge, and was himself a playwright and poet. He was the friend of Celtic scholars like Nutt and collectors like Larminie and was himself both scholar and collector. He knew thoroughly the work of his precursors and evaluated them shrewdly in his introduction to *Beside the Fire*. He was the one man who could, and did, link the scientific collection of Irish folktales and folk poetry to the renewal of the Irish tongue and Irish letters. As founder and president of the Gaelic League, originally a nonpolitical body, Hyde sought to reintroduce into the country towns the songs of Oisin and tales of Finn, the stepdances, fiddle music, family names, and above all the Gaelic language and its historic literature. He took the stump to dis-

[16] Alfred Nutt, "Celtic Myth and Saga," *Archaeological Review*, II (1889), 137.
[17] Alfred Nutt, *The Celtic Doctrine of Re-birth. The Voyage of Bran*, vol. II (London, 1897), p. 159.

course eloquently on the strangulation of Irish culture and the bloodletting of Irish energy and talents brought about by English schooling. As his scholarly donation to the cause, he wrote brief and bulky literary histories of Ireland and filled a whole shelf with books of Gaelic folktales in Irish and English.[18]

A "poet-scholar" and "actor-dramatist" Lady Gregory styled him. She credited Hyde with launching modern Irish drama at a school feast at Coole in 1898, when he acted in a Punch and Judy show given in Irish. Shortly afterward he began writing plays in Irish, basing them on folk memory and living tradition, particularly in the long dramatic dialogues, as between Oisin and Saint Patrick, beloved by Gaelic speakers. His play *The Marriage* was founded on a story about Raftery, and Hyde once enacted the part: "It will be hard to forget the blind poet, as he was once represented on the stage by the living poet," Lady Gregory was moved to write. Another of his plays concerned Red Hanrahan, the oral poet about whom Yeats wrote stories.

His dramatic and poetic talents in no whit softened Hyde's scholarly standards. The publication in 1890 of his *Beside the Fire, A Collection of Irish Gaelic Folk Stories* brought Irish folktale study to maturity. Hyde was collector, translator, and commentator. The first six of the fourteen tales had the Irish text as well as the English. An end note told "Where the Stories Came From," and a series of notes glossed matters in the tales and technical points of the Irish texts. A meaty preface of forty pages considered the strengths and weaknesses of the earlier collectors who had tampered with the Gaelic, discussed the intricate interrelationships between Irish bardic manuscripts and modern Irish and Highland Scottish oral tales, explained the technique of collecting, portrayed the narrators, dwelt on problems of translation, and separated the historical strata of tales. Hyde saw as originating in Ireland the longer Fenian narratives and stories marked by inflated passages or "runs," alliterative words, and poetic epithets.

Hyde thus touched on many aspects of theory and method central to the interests of folklorists. To show how folklore could

[18] A biography has been written by Diarmid Coffey, *Douglas Hyde, President of Ireland* (Dublin, 1938).

illuminate literary questions, he drew attention to a manuscript account of an ugly one-legged, one-eyed, one-handed monster. He would have dismissed this as the writer's invention had he not chanced on a similar description of the "Fáchan" in one of Campbell of Islay's West Highland tales. Having made his point, Hyde called for as intensive an exploration of Irish oral tradition as Campbell had accomplished for the Scottish Highlands, to be sparked by "a powerful national sentiment, and above all, a knowledge of Gaelic." His call would be answered.

Alfred Nutt, the publisher, added an incisive "Postscript." He supported Hyde's view that the Irish bardic authors of the twelfth to the sixteenth centuries did not invent their poetic tales but drew upon an older folklore; hence the bardic tradition was oral not literary. But he cautioned Hyde against assigning precise dates to the bardic narratives, which could easily alter from one period to another. Also Nutt added to Hyde's notes and composed a suggestive "Index of Incidents," anticipating the use of motifs.

Flaws in *Beside the Fire* are the insufficiency of comparative references to tales outside Gaeldom and the failure to divide the tales into meaningful groups. Märchen, local legends, heroic sagas, animal fables are all mixed together.

Beside the Fire set a model followed in 1893 by another first-rate collection, William Larminie's *West Irish Folk-Tales and Romances*. Larminie was a civil servant with a classical education who wrote two books of poems chiefly in praise of his native land.[19] Under the influence of his friend Hyde, he turned to collecting tales in Irish during the 1880's on his holidays in Mayo, Galway, and Donegal. He contributed two folktales to Hyde's original Irish collection of 1889 (*Leabhar Sgeulaigheachta*); one of these, marked by a distinctive, abrupt style Hyde translated into English under the title "Neil O'Carre" for *Beside the Fire*. Larminie was obviously Hyde's man in his concern for Irish texts and his attention to the narrators; indeed he broke precedent in setting the names of his six narrators in the table of contents alongside the eighteen stories. In his speculative introduction he

[19] Relevant facts are in John J. O'Meara, "William Larminie, 1849–1900," *Studies* (March, 1947), 90–96.

ventured into a dark area in discussing folk style and distinguished between the style of individual tellers and the style inherent in classes of stories—a new insight. Thus the heroic tales had a fierce quality; tales of domestic incident were quieter. He brought to life his tellers, who ranged from a schoolboy of seventeen to a farmer of eighty.

Other theoretical questions engaged Larminie. Was the Irish tradition one or many? How did it compare with its Gaelic sister, the Scotch Highlands? It seemed curious that the Fenian but not the divine or heroic cycle of Ireland had penetrated to the Highlands. How did the Irish tradition measure against its Aryan cousin in Germany?

Answering himself, Larminie perceived unity in Irish fairy legends but regional diversity between Donegal and Connaught and Munster in the longer fictions. The puzzling relationships between Ireland, Scotland, and the continent he explained with a theory of racial deposits left at different periods by Iberians, Mongolians, and Celts in Ireland. These answers are not fashionable, but the questions are worthy.

Larminie died in 1900, but Hyde lived until 1949 and kept producing. He translated two more of his folktale books. *Legends of Saints and Sinners* focused on a pattern that had already intrigued Irish collectors, the blending of pagan with Christian lore. Saint Patrick and Saint Peter performed wonders not unlike those credited to the ancient Tuatha de Danaan but with a moral purpose and Christian motive. Hyde noted that the grotesque Devil and malignant witch were conspicuously missing from Catholic Ireland. *Mayo Stories Told by Thomas Casey* (1939), published a year after Hyde became the first president of the Republic of Ireland, presented the repertoire of one shanachie who alternated strange wonder tales with circumstantial narratives about his own experiences. The concentration on an individual narrator reflects the modern emphasis on tellers as well as texts. These books tell only part of the service Hyde rendered to folklore studies. Through his standing in the nation and his professorship in Irish language and literature at the National University in Dublin, he elevated folklore from a hobby into a respected field of knowledge. And in James Delargy he had an assistant who would revolutionize collecting methods.

As a young man Delargy had gone into the Gaelic-speaking islands and western counties to collect texts. He was the first to use the Ediphone as a recording instrument, in county Clare in 1929. Two years earlier he had been named editor of *Béaloideas*, the journal founded by The Folklore of Ireland Society. Beginning his academic career as assistant to Hyde in the 1920's at University College, he became lecturer and professor of Folklore and in 1935 Director of the now world-famous Irish Folklore Commission.

Practical organization and a visionary dream created the Commission. Delargy perceived how puny were the efforts of a few random authors to explore all the folklore of a culture, and he devised a new machinery that has amassed the sources for a thousand books. Guiding principle of the Commission was a central archives fed by resident county collectors who would canvass their home areas—an idea implicit in the collecting technique of Campbell of Islay. An initial government grant, supported by President Eamon de Valera, awarded the Commission one hundred pounds for each of thirty-two counties. The appeal to the government lay in preserving cultural traditions of the nation in the dwindling national tongue.

With the founding of the Commission, the old-time shanachie who had kept intact the oral culture finally emerged as a living personality and a gifted wordsmith. In his address of 1945 to the British Academy on "The Gaelic Story-Teller," Delargy sketched some of these spellbinders. Perhaps the most renowned is Peig Sayers (1873–1958), born in the Dingle Peninsula of county Kerry but who lived most of her life with her husband on the Great Blasket Island nearby. From this "queen of the Gaelic storytellers" the Commission's collector recorded three hundred and seventy-five narratives, forty of them long wonder tales. The collector Seósamh Ó Dalaigh has described her conversing and reciting. "Great artist and wise woman that she was, Peig would at once switch from gravity to gaiety, for she was a lighthearted woman, and her changes of mood and face were like the changes of running water. As she talked her hands would be working too; a little clap of the palms to cap a phrase, a flash of the thumb over her shoulder to mark a mystery, a hand hushed to mouth for mischief or whispered secrecy."[20] Noted Celtic scholars like Robin Flower and Kenneth Jackson spoke with her and praised her natural gift of oratory and sense for the lilting rhythm that stamped the pure Irish. She dictated her memories to her son, weaving her faultless oral prose about events tiny and large, from the quarrel of neighbor women over a hen (turned by the village children into verses which she sang), to a terrorizing visit from the Black and Tan. So Peig became an author, and her book was translated into English as *An Old Woman's Reflections* (1962), with a photographic portrait of herself as frontispiece. This was a long road from the faceless peasant tale-teller of the nineteenth century.

The collectors too have assumed a new role. Through the courtesy of the Commission I spent a week in late November, 1951, in county Kerry with one of their indefatigable field collectors, Tadhg Murphy (Ó Murchadha). Tadhg was born and grew up on a farm twelve miles southeast of the little coastal town of Waterville, speaking Irish as his first tongue and hearing folktales from his father. To the ordinary national schooling he added a summer's course for a teaching certificate and from 1925 to 1935 taught night classes. When Professor Delargy came to the Ballinskelligs district in 1927 on field research, he met Tadhg and encouraged him to contribute Gaelic tales to *Béaloideas*. Eight years later the Vocational Educational Committee of Ireland loaned him to the newly formed Irish Folklore Commission and ever since, day and night, winter and summer, Tadhg had cycled through the Iveragh Peninsula, his Ediphone packed in a box over the handlebars. Shortly before my coming he had bought a car, but it was in the repair shop, Tadhg having neglected to release the emergency brake during a trial run. Yet within the radius of his cycle Tadhg had been able to prospect continuously for sixteen years; when I met him he had begun his ninety-first diary—the logbook of the collector's field visits which accom-

[20] Quoted by W. R. Rodgers in his introduction to Peig Sayers, *An Old Woman's Reflections*, trans. from the Irish by Seamus Ennis (London, 1962), p. xiii.

panied the manuscript of texts mailed into Dublin. Yet for all
his years in the field and his own vast knowledge of the Dingle
repertoire, he kept hearing fresh items and was jarred into
astonishment to get a completely new legend the day he took
me to see one of his oldest informants, who lived on a mountainside.

If you want picturesqueness with your folklore, the thatched
stone farmhouses lying among the slopes and peat bogs of county
Kerry provide a watercolor setting. As we drove into the hills
in our hired car, Tadhg casually pointed to a little yellow building set like a flyspeck in the midst of empty stretching bogs and
high ranges. "That's the schoolhouse," he said. Not another sign
of life met the eye as one looked to the horizons, but in the
morning barefooted children trooped from lonely farms for miles
to converge at that spot. Nine miles over a dirt road brought
us to the mountainside dwelling where William (Liam) Stack had
lived every day of his eighty years. Liam stood before a hayrick
cutting plug tobacco for his pipe, with the mountain slope rising
dizzily on one side and a blue lough lying at its foot on the other.
Soon Tadhg was chatting with him across a wooden gate. The
mountain mists curled up the valley as we spoke and dampened
our bones, but still Liam and Tadhg talked on, although my
frozen fingers could scarcely hold the notebook. Old Liam in his
torn clothes, the white stubble of his beard covering the clean
features of the Irish farmer folk, and thickset genial Tadhg with
a felt hat tipped a bit rakishly over one ear, both sucking deep at
their pipes, blended into the rugged scenery. A little less scenery
and a little more warmth would have suited me better, but at
any rate I was seeing a long-time collector in action.

The observer notices curiously how the rural families take for
granted the visits of the folklore collector. He has become an
institution like the priest and the postman, and receives a friendly
welcome and often a high tea when he comes. The old men
respond eagerly to his arrival, both from a glow of social pleasure
and a sense of the value of his work and their contribution. The
bonds of a fading language and a county kinship, the sanction
of the government, and the backlog of many congenial inter-

views, all facilitated Tadhg Murphy's task. One countryman on whose neighbor Tadhg had called even complained because Tadhg had passed him by.

In former days the collectors had come from outside and above, from the educated, aristocratic, and professional class, to peer curiously in to the peasant culture beneath them. Now the collectors came from the ranks and spoke with their own people, not to publish curious books but to record their common legacy and to honor its carriers.

Within his own collecting span Tadhg had seen the shanachies and their night-long *Märchen* and hero-tales fade away. Gradually he had discarded his Ediphone and turned to pad and pencil to write down the shorter conversational anecdotes about overlookers, spirits, fairies, and dunces which still abounded. These were the stories told me in Kerry. Three, concerned with the leprechaun, the pooka, and a dream of treasure, echoed legends first made known by Croker. Others, on overlooking with the evil eye, matched cases set down by Lady Wilde and Lady Gregory. Tadhg himself far eclipsed any storyteller to whom he introduced me, for he had garnered all their stores, adding them to his own, and become the supreme shanachie of Kerry. The day I left he recounted an extraordinary narrative which he had collected from a teller who heard it from a farmer-fisherman, Seán Palmer, who claimed he had voyaged to America with the fairies (Number 39 in this book).[21]

Fieldworkers like Tadhg Murphy have laid pipelines from the streams of folk tradition in the counties to the central reservoir in Dublin. There the labor of processing takes place: processing in the sense of constructing orderly systems to locate items. This task has been acquitted since the creation of the Irish Folklore Commission by its Archivist, Sean O'Sullivan, who is himself a living archive, with phenomenal knowledge of the Commission's holdings. Professor Delargy met him in 1934, when O'Sullivan was a primary schoolteacher in Waterford, county Kerry, already

---

[21] An account of my trip with the tales obtained was printed in R. M. Dorson, "Collecting in County Kerry," *Journal of American Folklore,* LXVI (1953), 19–42.

interested in collecting from two oral poets; he had placed an
advertisement in the local paper asking for variants of their
poems. Delargy saw the ad, and lifelong partnership resulted.
To further his archival work O'Sullivan visited Sweden, master-
ing the comprehensive classification evolved by the Swedish
folklorists, and he adapted their concepts for his *A Handbook of
Irish Folklore* (1942), one of the half dozen key works on folklore
in the English language. To the perennial question, "What is
folklore?," the best short answer is "Consult O'Sullivan's *Handbook.*" Here is no ambiguous attempt at definition, but a practical set of questions on every conceivable aspect of traditional
behaviour, a panorama of folklore in its broadest sense, encom-
passing the full round of economic, social, recreational, seasonal,
and domestic practices. The *Handbook* both grew out of and
contributed to the archives; the questionnaire was framed upon
the kinds of folkstuff already known and collected, and it served
to guide the full-time and occasional field workers in their further
quests. Although intended as a work of reference as much as an
actual tool, collectors have sometimes queried their county sages
point by point throughout the book and taken two years to complete the interrogation.

As a second key to the Irish treasure house, O'Sullivan brought
out in 1963, with Reidar Christansen (editor of the *Folktales of
Norway*, a companion volume to the *Folktales of Ireland*), an
index to the international tales in the Commission's archives,
The Types of the Irish Folktale. A casual peerer into this index
may be frightened at the endless lists of numbers and abbrevia-
tions that meet his eyes, hardly bedtime reading fare, but a
closer acquaintance will lead him to admire the scope and
pertinacity of this catalogue. Some forty-three thousand versions
of popular tales (the Commission's stock as of 1956) are identified according to the international system, and their location
given in the manuscript notebooks of the archives. In addition,
O'Sullivan sleuthed through the labyrinth of printed sources,
sampling five hundred books, one hundred and fifty journals and
serials, twenty-six newspaper files, and twelve manuscript deposi-
tories in his search for already recorded variants. *The Types of*

the Irish Folktale thus points the tale scholar to every known instance of the vast number of folktales recorded in Ireland.[22]

This is the first volume of tales from the plenitude of the Irish Folklore Commission to be selected and translated for English readers. Appropriately Sean O'Sullivan, who knows the archives so intimately, has prepared the selection. The *Folktales of Ireland* now takes its place in the gallant history of Irish achievement in the world of folk story.

RICHARD M. DORSON

[22] It contains a splendid bibliography. A detailed bibliographical essay by Reidar Christiansen will be found in Johannes Bolte and Georg Polívka, *Anmerkungen zu den Kinder- und Hausmärchen der Brüder Grimm*, vol. V (Leipzig, 1932), "Irland," pp. 55–64. Two informative booklets which bring modern folklore to bear on the older tale-cycles have been written by Gerard Murphy: *Saga and Myth in Ancient Ireland* and *The Ossianic Lore and Romantic Tales of Medieval Ireland* (both Dublin, 1961). The first edition of *The Celtic Twilight* (1893) has an essay by Yeats ("The Four Winds of Desire," pp. 199–210), with sharp judgments on the Irish tale collectors from Croker to Hyde.

Introduction

The founding of An Cumann le Béaloideas Éireann (The Folklore of Ireland Society) in 1926 marked the beginning of the first organized effort to collect and to study, not folktales alone, but Irish oral tradition on a much wider scale than envisaged hitherto. .The society's journal, *Béaloideas*, edited by Séamus Ó Duilearga since its first issue (1927), has now reached its thirtieth volume. The funds, like those of most societies, came from members' subscriptions, and it was only in 1930, when the government established Institiúd Béaloideasa Éireann (The Irish Folklore Institute) that a small grant from public funds was made available. With the aid of this and of timely, much appreciated grants from the Rockefeller Foundation (1930) and the Carnegie United Kingdom Trust (1931), some collections were made by part-time field workers and three volumes of tales were published.

In April, 1935, the Irish government created Coimisiún Béaloideasa Éireann (The Irish Folklore Commission) with a small annual grant-in-aid for the purpose of collecting, cataloguing, and eventually publishing the best of what remained of Irish oral tradition. I was appointed archivist by the Commission and was sent for three months' training to Landmåls- och Folkminnesarkivet (The Dialect and Folklore Archive) at the University of Uppsala.

In the autumn of 1935, the first full-time collectors were appointed. These were men who had shown, by the work that they had done as part-time collectors for the society and the institute, interest in rural traditions and a capacity for acting as collectors. None of them was a university graduate; rather were they devoted men who knew their local Irish-Gaelic dialect well, had an intimate knowledge of country life, and a deep respect for the custodians of an ancient, orally preserved culture. Over the years, the number of full-time collectors has varied from seven to ten.

After a course of training at the Commission's headquarters at University College, Dublin, each collector was assigned to a particular district, generally an Irish-speaking one, in which the traditions to be collected were richest. His equipment included an Ediphone recording machine, and he was shown how to use it in the field. He was also trained to transcribe verbatim the material recorded into standard notebooks, which he later sent to the office of the Commission.

Long tales and sustained pieces of narrative (*seanchas*) are best suited for Ediphone recording; shorter items in prose and verse can, as a rule, be more easily written from direct narration. When the transcript of tales had been checked against the recording at the office of the Commission and corrections made (if necessary), the wax cylinders were erased and sent back to the collectors to be used again. Because of lack of funds, all field recordings could not be permanently retained at that time.

Full-time collectors were required to keep a diary describing their daily activities. The Commission now has 150 volumes of these diaries; they are an invaluable source for (*a*) descriptions of field work and (*b*) accounts of individual informants, including storytellers, as well as of their style and repertoire. At intervals of from three to six months, the notebooks were prepared for binding. The notebooks of each collector were bound in chronological order in successive volumes which now (1964) total 1674. This procedure was also followed for notebooks of the part-time collectors who helped the Commission in their areas. These collectors were paid according to their results and devoted to the work only that time they could spare from their normal occupations.

Two guidebooks for collectors, which I wrote, were published by the society. Both were based on the system for folklore classification evolved at Uppsala. The first was *Láimhleabhar Béaloideasa* (A Folklore Handbook), issued in Irish in 1937. A much larger guide, *A Handbook of Irish Folklore*, was published in English in 1942; it has now been reprinted in the United States.

With the permission and co-operation of the Department of Education in Dublin and of the Irish National Teachers' Organization, the services of the senior pupils in primary schools in twenty-six Irish counties were made available to the Commission to further the work of collection. A small guidebook containing some fifty folklore topics was issued by the Department to all primary schools. The children were asked to collect traditional material from their parents and neighbors outside of school hours about each of these topics in turn, and they wrote down in school, in lieu of composition, what they had collected. This procedure was followed from July, 1937, to December, 1938. At the end of that period, 5,000 large, standard-sized notebooks (supplied by the Department of Education to the schools) were completed and returned to the Commission. The total schools' collection, amounting to about a half-million pages, although suffering from certain expected defects, covered every school district in twenty-six counties and gave a good idea of at least some of the available oral material. This collection has been bound in 1,126 volumes and is kept separately from the main MSS collection compiled by the full- and part-time collectors and other correspondents. Encouraged by the interest shown by many primary teachers in this work, the Commission selected approximately 600 of them as local correspondents, and they gave invaluable help by replying to the hundred or more questionnaires which have been issued by the Commission during the past twenty-five years.

The manuscript collections of the Commission now (1964) total more than 1,500,000 pages. The detailed cataloguing of the contents is an enormous and exacting undertaking. About 200,000 reference cards have been made (under the entries outlined in the *Handbook*), and an additional interim catalogue gives general references to the contents of those volumes which have not yet been excerpted in detail. As the Commission has at present six full-time collectors at work, the collections are still growing. Collectors are now equipped with tape recorders, and the tapes are being preserved.

As well as collections from the field, the Commission now has an excellent library of about 20,000 items in many languages. Most of the standard works on folklore and ethnology are available. There is also a large photographic section and thousands of recordings, on tape and disc, of folksongs, folktales, and social-historical narratives.

The Commission has had to make the scope of its collections as wide as possible in order to try, even at this late date, to preserve a picture of conditions in Ireland in recent centuries as reflected in oral tradition. The publication of the *Handbook* enabled the collectors to collect not only folktales but as much as possible of traditional custom, belief, and local history. A large body of information of this kind has now been written, and it remains for future researchers to assess the historical and social value of what has been recorded.

During the course of collection, it was only natural that thousands of versions of the approximately 800 international folktales to be found in Ireland should be recorded. *The Types of the Irish Folktale*, mentioned in the Bibliography, gives references to about 43,000 versions of these tales collected to November, 1956. Hundreds of others have been recorded since. So rich has Ireland, especially the Irish-speaking areas, been in folktales to the present day, that not a week has gone by during the past twenty-nine years without enriching the Commission's collection of tales by dozens of new versions. These include tales of the Ulster heroes (Cúchulainn, Conor mac Neasa, Conall Cearnach, and others), tales of the Fianna, so-called hero tales, religious tales, romantic tales, humorous stories and anecdotes, as well as thousands of legends of all kinds. Some tales are of the international kind listed by Antti Aarne and Stith Thompson. Others are peculiar to the Gaelic-speaking areas of Ireland and Scotland and have their own distinctive pattern, although using motifs that are widely known elsewhere.

As the Irish-speaking areas of Ireland have best preserved traditional lore of all kinds, the Commission concentrated its collectors for several years on counties such as Waterford, Cork, Kerry, Clare, Galway, Mayo, and Donegal. The old man or woman in these districts who had no folktales to tell was the exception. It is generally conceded that the parish of Carna, in West Galway, had more unrecorded folktales in 1935 than did all the rest of western Europe. The Commission's workers, as well as other individual collectors, were fortunate in finding the art of storytelling in full vigor in many districts, with outstanding narrators in possession of large repertoires and eager to co-operate with them to the best of their powers. Wherever our collectors went, however, they were told that it was a pity that they had not come thirty, twenty or even ten years before when certain famous storytellers were still alive. Although this was true and much to be regretted, still it is possible that what has been recorded will give a fairly satisfactory picture of the reper-toires and styles of traditional storytellers through the ages.

An English translation of tales told by such expert storytellers as, for example, Éamonn a Búrc, Peig Sayers, Muiris (Sheáin) Connor, and Jimmy Cheallaigh—to name but a few—gives but a pale shadow of the original Irish narration. The voices, with their many modulations, are silent on the printed page; the audience is absent; only the pattern of narrative and the proces-sion of motifs remain.

Although there are still thousands of people in Ireland who can tell stories of many kinds, the need and the occasions for telling them are quickly passing. The fireside scene of former years, lighted by only the peat fire or an oil lamp, is now illuminated by electricity, while a newspaper, a radio, or a television set is not far away. Tales are now rarely, if ever, told at wakes or in fishing boats. The traveling beggar, who was formerly welcomed in every parish for his tales as well as for the news he brought from other districts, has almost completely disappeared from the roads. The spalpeen no longer travels (except from Connacht and Donegal to England and Scotland) to plant the crops or save the harvest, bringing back with him stories of his adventures as well as newly acquired folktales. Very soon, memories of Irish storytelling on the grand scale will be found only in recordings and in books such as this.[1]

In choosing tales for the present volume, I have tried to avoid,

---

[1] For Irish storytelling and its background, see J. H. Delargy, *The Gaelic Storyteller* (British Academy Rhŷs Memorial Lecture; London, 1945).

for the most part, ordinary versions of tales known in Ireland and elsewhere and have sought to give examples of international or national tales with a peculiarly Irish flavor. All but two (Nos. 38 and 49) I have translated from the original Irish manuscript in the Irish Folklore Commission (IFC). The seven categories of tales which I have selected are, by no means, fully representative of the range of Irish storytelling. It is to be hoped, however, that readers will be given a flavor of certain types of tales told in Ireland.

Ireland is lacking in most of the exotic fauna to be found in other lands, hence the comparative paucity of animal tales. The fine quality of Irish storytelling is most evident in the longer tale-types, such as those which I have selected for Section II, Kings and Warriors. Tales of this kind are to be heard only in the Gaelic-speaking parts of Ireland (and Scotland). They are unique in western Europe and have a long tradition behind them. I have thought it desirable to give eight examples of these tales, despite their length, to illustrate the craftsmanship of their original composers and the consummate skill of generations of storytellers who have preserved them at Irish firesides. The religious tales (Section III) deserve special mention also—blended as they are from pagan and Christian sources. The deep religious feeling of the Irish people is expressed in such stories, and I have seen audiences listen to them with the silence accorded to a sermon in church.[2]

The tales in Section IV illustrate popular belief in aspects of the Otherworld. So strong was the belief in fairies in Ireland to recent decades that it is not surprising that a large corpus of tales has been based on it. These stories show that, to our forefathers, the fairy world was almost as real as the one in which they themselves lived. The origin of the fairies was known, as were the places in which they lived; and there was constant communication between them and mortal men. But there was also the human fear that the fairies might abduct men, women, or children to replenish and renew their own stock, leaving changelings behind. Running through all this mass of folk

[2] I have edited a collection of these tales under the title of "Scéalta Cráibhtheacha," *Béaloideas*, XXI (1952), with summaries in English.

belief was the mingling of the fairies and the dead; both seemed to be part of the same milieu. Section V has a few tales to illustrate the belief in preternatural powers said to be possessed by certain individuals. Several volumes could be devoted to stories about the supposed powers of hags and "wise women," children born after their father's death, poets, smiths, and scores of others.

Richard Dorson has suggested that a few tales be included about historical characters, and this has been done in Section VI. Many individuals such as Dean Swift, who has become a folktale character in the Irish countryside, had to be omitted. Finally in Section VII, a few examples are given of humorous tales about foolish or clever people as well as about individuals of unusual strength.

SEÁN Ó SÚILLEABHÁIN

Irish Folklore Commission, Dublin

Contents

VII   THE WISE, THE FOOLISH, AND THE
STRONG

Part I
Animals and Birds

· 1 · *The Fox and the Heron*

Once upon a time long ago, the birds could talk. There was a wren living in the Glen of the Wrens, and it happened that he ran short of money. He had a large family to rear; so he asked the heron for the loan of twenty pounds at sixpence per pound per year interest. The loan was to be repaid at the end of a year and a day.

The heron lent the twenty pounds, but when the year and the day were over, the wren didn't come to pay the debt. So the heron had to go to the wren's house. When the heron looked in through the door, the two old wrens and their twelve young ones were hard at work threshing oats. The heron couldn't make out which of them was the old wren, for they were all the same size; so she had to return home disappointed.

On her way home, she met the fox, and he sunning himself outside his house. He asked her what business brought her that way, and she told him the whole story.

"Now, my friend," said the fox, "you must go back to the wren's house tomorrow, and when you see them all threshing, you must say, ' 'Tis easy to know the strong blow of the old man!'"

Early next morning, the heron returned to the wren's house. The wrens were all inside threshing, and the heron called out, "'Tis easy to know the strong blow of the old man!"

Out from the threshers jumped the old wren and struck his fistful of oats against a stone, shouting, "I was even better when I was younger."

In rushed the heron and she caught him by the neck. "'Tis to you I gave the twenty pounds," said she, "and pay it back to me now, along with the interest."

The wren had to go to the chest and pay her the money. She went back home satisfied.

On her way home, she met the fox near his door again, and he asked her how she had got on.

"I got on well," said she, "and I'm very thankful to you for the advice you gave me. It was a good trick."

"I have another piece of advice to give you now," said the fox. "There are a lot of men working in the fields, and you must tell them that you lost your purse in that big pool over there. Ask them to dig a trench to drain the pool. It is full of eels, and as quickly as the men throw out the eels, you can be drawing them home, and you'll have enough fish for a year and a day."

"Very well," said the heron. "I'll do as you say."

She saw the men working in the fields and told them that she had lost a big purse of money in the pool beyond, and that it would be worth their while to dig a trench and drain the pool to find the purse. The men set to work until they had let every drop of water out of the pool. Then they started to throw the mud up on the bank. It was full of eels, and the heron dragged them home as quickly as she could. By evening, she had done a fine day's fishing, and she was very grateful to the fox for the advice he had given her.

Now at that time the heron had four milch cows, and she used to sell the butter to customers in the town. She thought to herself that it would be well for her to make a match with the fox and marry him. He was resourceful and keen and would mind the house well when she would be doing her business in town. She married the fox and soon afterward, she had four crocks of butter made up for sale. What did the fox do but turn out the butter from each crock, eat the bottom layer of each, and put the rest back again so that each crock appeared to be full. Then one day, he got worried. How would he explain it to his wife when the loss was discovered the day she sold the butter? Clever and all though he was, he couldn't think of any plan.

A few days later, the heron tackled the ass to the cart, and she and the fox loaded the crocks of butter. When she reached the town, she went to the store and the buyer and herself lifted the crocks onto a table which was covered with a linen cloth. When she saw that some of the butter was missing, she was surprised and ashamed.

"So that's what you have done to me," said she, thinking of the fox. "I'll get my own back on you."

On her way home, she met a shepherd in a field near the road. He had four score of young lambs. One of them was black, and he was more proud of this black one than of all the rest.

She stopped her cart and spoke to the shepherd. "You'll lose your black lamb tonight," said she.

"How is that?" asked the shepherd.

"The fox will take him," said she.

"At what time, do you think?" asked the shepherd.

"Oh, sometime after midnight," said the heron.

She went home, and when the cart reached the door, she pretended to be dying. The fox was in the house, and when he didn't hear her making any sound outside, he looked out. There she was, lying almost dead in the cart, speechless and lifeless.

"What has happened to you at all?" cried the fox. "Or is there anything in the world that will cure you?"

He took her in near the fire and put a warm iron to the soles of her feet. He heated milk for her, but she wouldn't taste even a spoonful of it or anything else. When midnight came, she spoke some word, but he couldn't understand it.

"Is there anything in the world that will cure you?" said he. "If there is, I'll get it for you."

"If I had the shepherd's black lamb, I'd be all right on the spot," said she.

"If that's all, you won't be sick much longer," said the fox.

Out he rushed and ran across the fields. The shepherd and his neighbors were watching the lambs, and they had hounds and dogs with them. They set the hounds after him. Off through the field ran the fox, twisting and turning, to escape them, but he only ran into the dogs, and they started to tear him into pieces. The heron was in the air above him while this was happening, and when he caught sight of her, he screamed for her help.

But her answer was, "'Tisn't eating my butter you are now, you rogue. You have enough to attend to."

·2· *The Fox and the Eagle*

There came a very bad year one time. One day the fox was near the shore of the Lakes of Killarney, and he couldn't find a bird or anything else to eat. Then he spied three ducks a bit out from the shore and thought to himself that if he could catch hold of them, he would have a fine meal. There was some water parsnip with very large leaves growing by the shore, and he swam out to it and cut off two big leaves of it with his teeth. He held one of them at each side of his mouth and swam toward the ducks. They never felt anything until he had taken one of them off with him.

Very satisfied with himself, he brought her ashore, laid her down, and decided to try and catch the other two as well—'tis seldom they would be on offer!

He caught a second duck by the same trick and left her dead near the first. Then out he swam for the third and brought her in. But, if he did, there was no trace of the other two where he had left them.

"May God help me!" said he. "I have only the one by my day's work. What'll I do? I wonder who is playing tricks on me."

He looked all around but couldn't see an enemy anywhere. Then he looked toward the cliff that was nearby, and what did he spy but the nest of an eagle high up on it.

"No one ever took my two ducks but the eagle," said he. "As good as I am at thieving, there's a bigger thief above my head."

He didn't know how to get at the eagle. Then he saw a fire smoldering not far away, where men had been working at a quarry a few days before. They had a fire and it was still burning slowly under the surface of the ground. He dragged the duck to the fire and pulled her hither and thither through the embers. Then he left her down on the grass and hid. The eagle must have been watching out for the third duck too, for down he swooped and snatched her up to his nest. No sooner did the dead duck's body touch the dry nest than the nest caught fire—

there were live embers stuck in the duck's feathers. Down fell the blazing nest with the three dead ducks as well as the eagle's three young ones inside it, so the fox had six birds for his supper. Didn't he get his own back well on the eagle?

·3· The Fox in Inishkea

Long, long ago, this district was pillaged by a fox. One day he would be west at Falmore, the next day below in Ballyglass. On a fine, warm summer's day, a man from this place was going to town with a donkey load of fish. Who should be coming toward him near the strand, but the fox! The fox knew that there was something in the baskets on the donkey's back; so he lay down and pretended to be dead. The poor man thought that he was dead; so he caught him and threw him on top of one of the baskets.

"Your skin is worth a good deal of money," said he. "Wasn't I lucky to find you?"

The man, little thinking that the fox was doing him any harm, and his donkey travelled on. The fox was throwing out a fish now and again, until there wasn't a single one left in the baskets.

When they were near the town, all that the fox did was to jump out of the basket. He upset the straddle and baskets, and it was then the poor man saw what had happened. The fox went back and picked up the fishes and had a fine meal.

The fox went as far as Léim Lake. He saw a fine flock of geese out on the water. He started to whistle at them until he drove them onto dry land. Then he caught one of them by the neck, threw her across his back and went off with her. That's the way he was robbing the people, and they couldn't catch him. He used to steal geese, ducks, hens, and lambs.

Some men from the island of Inishkea came to the mainland one day and left their boat on the strand at Falmore. They went shopping to Blacksod. The fox came to where the boat was. He kept looking toward Inishkea and thinking that if he could go out to the island, it would be easy for him to get plenty to eat. He knew that his skin was valuable, so he made up his mind to stretch himself out on the strand as if he were dead, and when the captain of the boat found him, he would throw him on board and take him to the island. So down he lay, from ear to tail, and when the boatmen found him, they put him into one of their bags that contained a few loaves of bread. It wasn't long before they reached Inishkea. When they took the bags out of the boat and opened the one the fox was in, out he jumped and ran off. When they looked into the bag, not a loaf was left.

He made his den in a high cliff and sallied out whenever he got the chance and caught something to eat. The den was just under the edge of the cliff at the top, and a briar which grew beside it reached up to the top of the cliff. He could get up from the den and back again by catching hold of the briar. The Inishkea men often chased him with their dogs, but it was useless for them. When they hunted him to the top of the cliff, the fox would swing himself down to the den by the briar. But the dogs would be running so fast after him that they would go head over heels over the cliff and break their necks on the rocks below.

Many's a fine dog was killed in that way!

At long last, the people of the island noticed how the fox was saving himself. It was time they did. One day they cut the briar with a knife, leaving it in the same position. If the fox caught it then, down he would go. They chased him over the island, and when he caught hold of the briar to escape, it gave way. Down he fell and he was killed. That was the end of the fox on Inishkea.

·4· *The Magpie and the Fox*

The magpie had a nest in a holly bush. The fox robbed it and killed the young ones, so the magpie had a grudge against him. One day when the fox had nothing to eat, he met the magpie.

"Fine day," said the magpie.

"Fine day," said the fox, "but I'm fasting."

"You won't be so; you'll have enough to eat soon," said the magpie.

Two girls, carrying keelers on their heads, came toward them. They were on their way to the turf bog. One of them carried slices of bread and butter for the turf cutters, and the other had a keelerful of curds.

"You'll soon have plenty of food now," said the magpie to the fox. "I'll throw down some of the food for you."

The magpie flew up into the keeler that contained the bread and butter and started to throw slices down to the fox. After awhile, he flew to the other keeler, took up mouthfuls of the curds, and threw them down also. It wasn't long until the fox had to stretch out on his belly.

"Oh," said he, "I fear I have eaten too much. I'll burst. I'll die. I have eaten too much. What'll I do?"

"I'll tell you what must be done," said the magpie after awhile. "I know where a doctor lives, and I'll go and steal a purgative from him."

"Please do or I'll die," said the fox, "I have eaten too much."

Instead of going to the doctor, the magpie went to a man who kept hounds. "There's a fox in a certain place," said the magpie, "and he has eaten too much. Bring your hounds and kill him."

The magpie returned to the fox. "Did you bring me the purgative?" asked the fox.

"I didn't," said the magpie, "but the doctor himself is coming, and he has made up a purgative for you."

It wasn't long until one of the hounds bayed. The fox cocked his ears.

"There are dogs coming!" he cried.

"Only small dogs running after sheep," said the magpie.

Two hounds rushed up, and the fox shook himself.

"Here's your purgative now, and try it," said the magpie.

The fox shook and stretched himself, but it was no use. The hounds caught him and tore him to pieces. That's the purgative he got.

·5· *Two Women or Twelve Men*

There was a fox that had three young ones, and when the time came to teach them how to fend for themselves, the old fox took them to a house. There was great talk going on inside the house. He asked the first two young ones if they could tell him who was in the house. They couldn't. Then he tried the third.

"Who is inside?" asked the old fox.

"Either two women or twelve men," said the young one.

"You'll do well in the world," said the old fox.

·6· *The Grateful Weasel*

There was a man in this townland long ago, and one morning in the springtime, he set out to drive his cattle to the pasture. It was the time of sowing the potatoes, and the rest of the family had gone to the potato field. The man took off his shoes, as he had a good distance to travel with the cows and calves. He could travel more quickly barefoot, and it would not take him long to put on the shoes again when he returned. He was anxious to join the others at the potatoes, as the season was running late.

When he had driven the cattle to the commonage, he set out for home. While passing a small garden near the house in which potatoes and turnips were stored in "pits," what did he see in the garden but a huge rat fighting a weasel! The rat was winning the fight. He rested his two hands on the fence, watching them.

"I won't let that rat kill the weasel," said he, jumping over the fence.

The two were fighting viciously, screaming, and whining. He went close to them, but they must not have noticed him, for they never looked at him. He drew close to them and tried to put his foot on the rat to give the weasel a chance of killing it. What did the rat do but bite the back of his foot and cut it deeply! When he felt the bite, he aimed a blow at the rat with his stick. The weasel then attacked the rat still more fiercely and never stopped until she had it killed. Then she licked herself clean, got rid of the hairs of the rat that were stuck in her teeth and claws, and went through a hole in the fence. The man saw her no more.

He left the garden and went home with his foot dripping blood. On reaching the house, he washed the wound and bandaged it, and put on his shoes. He went off to the potato field, and his foot was very sore. The others were hard at work, and he didn't tell them anything about what had happened. The pain was so great that he had to return to the house before long. He took off his shoe and saw that his foot was very swollen.

When he didn't return to the field, his son went to the house to see what was wrong and found him stretched in the corner near the fire. His foot was swollen and bleeding. He then told the son what had happened.

"You'll do no more spring work this season, I'm thinking," said the son. "Your foot is very swollen, and it will swell more."

"It can't be helped now," said the father. "Let ye keep on with the potato seed, and I may be all right tomorrow."

When they came home at dinner time, the foot had turned blue and even the toes were swollen. They bathed it with warm water and put on a poultice of *dearg-laoch*, which was said to be good for a swelling. Still, the foot kept on swelling, and he spent the evening and night wide awake, complaining of the pain. They didn't know what to do. Doctors were not as plentiful then as they are now, and people tried cures with herbs and things like that.

Next morning the rest of the family went off to the potato field, and the man of the house remained at home, feeling worse than ever. The door was open. He had just taken off the bandage and poultice to bathe his foot again, when what did he see coming in the door but the weasel! She came toward the fireplace where he was seated on a small stool and laid a small green leaf that she had in her mouth on the flagstone in front of the fire. When she had done that, she went out the door. After a little while, she came back again with another little leaf of a different kind, which she laid beside the first. She did this a third time, bringing a new kind of leaf once more. Then she went out the door for the last time, and the man saw her no more. He knew that she had brought the leaves to him to cure his foot; so he laid them on the wound and bound them up with a bandage. Then he fell asleep and, when he awoke, the swelling had left his foot and it was cured.

·7· *The Man Who Swallowed the Mouse*

There was a man in Rinnard one time. He felt very thirsty one evening after a day's mowing; so he took a bowl of thick milk to drink. The kitchen was half dark, as lamps and lights were scarce at that time. He swallowed the milk, and what was in it but a mouse! He never felt anything until he had swallowed the milk, mouse and all.

Every day from that day on, especially when he would lie down, he could feel the mouse running about and dancing inside of him. At that time, the doctors were not as good as they are now, and no doctor or anybody else could help him. He told all of his friends about the mouse, for he knew that they wouldn't wish anything to be wrong with him.

One woman came to see how he was, and she said that the best thing to do was to put a piece of roasted bacon and a piece of mutton on a plate on both sides of his mouth when he lay down in bed. The cat should be kept in the room too. When the mouse would smell the roasted meat, she would come out to taste it.

The man tried this remedy for three nights. On the third night, didn't the mouse come out and start to eat the meat! She hadn't eaten much before the cat killed her. The man lived to a great age after that happened. That story is as true as any I ever heard!

·8· *The Cat and the Dog*

Long ago the dog used to be out in the wet and the cold, while the cat remained inside near the fire.

One day, when he was "drowned wet," the dog said to the cat, "You have a comfortable place, but you won't have it any longer. I'm going to find out whether I have to be outside every wet day, while you are inside."

The man of the house overheard the argument between the two and thought that it would be right to settle the matter.

"Tomorrow," said he, "I will start a race between ye five miles from the house, and whichever of ye comes into the house first will have the right to stay inside from then on. The other can look after the place outside."

Next day, the two got themselves ready for the race. As they ran toward the house, the dog was a half-mile ahead of the cat. Then he met a beggar man. When the beggar man saw the dog running toward him with his mouth open, he thought he was running to bite him. He had a stick in his hand, and he struck the dog as he ran by. The dog was hurt and started to bark at the beggar man and tried to bite him for satisfaction.

Meanwhile the cat ran toward the house, and she was licking herself near the fire and resting after the race when the dog arrived.

"Now," said the cat when the dog ran in, "the race is won, and I have the inside of the house for ever more."

·9· *The Sow and Her* Banbh

An old sow and her young *banbh* were thieving one day, and a dog was set to chase them. They ran at their best with the dog at their heels.

"I won't go there any more, any more, any more," grunted the old sow.

"That's what you say always, always, always," grunted the *banbh*.

·10· *The Old Crow Teaches the Young Crow*

There was an old crow long ago, and he made a nest. After a time, only one of his brood remained with him.

One day the old crow took the young one out into the field to teach him how to fly.

When the young crow had learned how to fly and was able to go to any part of Ireland, the old crow said, "I think that you are able to fly anywhere now and make your living by yourself. Before you go, I want to give you a little advice that will protect you from danger, as it has protected myself."

"Tell it to me," said the young crow.

"If you are ever in a potato field or cornfield and see a man coming toward you with something under his arm or in his hand, fly off immediately, fearing he may have a gun and may shoot you."

"I understand," said the young crow.

"Another bit of advice to you," said the old crow. "If you see a man bending down as he comes toward you in the field or on the road, fly off as fast as you can, for he will be picking up a stone to throw at you. If he has nothing under his arm and if he doesn't bend down, you're safe."

"That's all very well," said the young crow, "but what if he has a stone in his pocket?"

"Off you go," said the old crow "You know more than myself!"

· 11 · *The Cold May Night*

There never was as cold a night as Old May Night long lon; ago. It was the eleventh of May.

Hundreds of years later, there came a very cold evening. Tl Old Crow of Achill was alive at the time, and he felt the gre. cold. He didn't know how he would survive the night; so he flew off to a wood some distance away. He hovered about, and what should he spy on top of the highest tree in the wood but a bird's nest. He decided to pass the night in it.

When he went to it, he found an eagle's fledgling inside. The mother eagle was away, looking for food; so the Old Crow took hold of the fledgling in his beak and carried it off and killed it somewhere in the wood. He threw the body into some bushes and flew back to the nest.

It wasn't very long until the old eagle returned with a big lump of meat from somewhere. Night had fallen, and she thought that it was her fledgling that was in the nest. She dropped the meat, and the Old Crow began to eat it with joy. Then the old eagle lay down on top of him. She spent the whole night rising up and jumping about and complaining—for it is said that birds and animals could talk at that time—that she had never felt a colder night.

The Old Crow of Achill was covered with sweat during the night, fearing that when day came and the eagle saw him, she would kill him. The eagle kept complaining about the cold, and at last the Old Crow remarked that there had been a colder night.

"How do you know that," asked the eagle, "seeing that you only came out of the shell a month ago?"

"Yes, there was a colder night—Old May Night," said the Old Crow.

"I find it hard to believe you," said the eagle.

"Such a night did come," said the Old Crow. "If you don't believe me, go to an old blackbird in a certain forge. She'll be there before you, and you'll find that she will tell you that a colder night than last night came one time."

The old eagle got angry. She flew off and never stopped until she came to the Blackbird of the Forge. The Blackbird was inside before her, standing on an iron rod. The Blackbird welcomed her.

"This is what brought me here," said the eagle. "A young fledgling of mine came out of the egg a month ago. Last night was the coldest I ever experienced, and I spent it rising up out of the nest with the cold. When dawn was near, my young one said to me that there had been a colder night, but I can't imagine how it could know, and it only a month old. It told me if I didn't believe it to go to the Blackbird of the Forge to find out."

"Well, I'm the Blackbird of the Forge, and last night was the coldest I ever felt. I was put into this forge when I was young. This iron rod on which I am standing was so many inches long and so many inches thick at that time. Once every seven years, I used to rub my beak to it, and if I rub it once more, it will break. I have been here that length of time, and last night was the coldest I ever felt; but," said the Blackbird, "you must go to a certain bull in a certain field. If he can't tell you, I don't know where you'll find out about it."

The eagle flew off and never stopped until she reached the field. The bull was there.

"What brought me here," said the eagle, "is that a month ago a young fledgling of mine came out of the egg. Last night was the coldest night I ever felt, and I spent the whole night rising up out of my nest to try to keep myself warm. Then when the dawn was near, my young one told me that there had been a colder night. I can't imagine how it could know, and it only a month out of the egg. It told me if I didn't believe it to go to you. Have you ever heard of a colder night than last night?"

"No, I haven't," said the bull. "I have been here for thousands of years, and two horns have fallen off me each year. They have been used to make a fence around this one-acre field, and only the two horns on my head now are wanting to complete the fence.

"I am," said the Blind Salmon of Assaroe. "A night colder than last night came without any doubt. I was here on Old May Night, the eleventh of May, long ago. It was freezing. I was jumping up and down in the water. It was freezing so hard that when I jumped up one time, the water had frozen when I came down. I was frozen into the ice and couldn't free myself. About two hours after daybreak, what should be passing but the Old Crow of Achill. He saw me frozen in the ice. Down he flew and started pecking at the ice with his beak. He made a hole in the ice and picked out my eye and ate it. That's why I have had only one eye ever since, and that's why I'm called the Blind Salmon of Assaroe. But look here," said the Blind Salmon, "as sure as I am here, it was the Old Crow of Achill that was in your nest last night and not your young one!"

"Ah, it can't be," said the eagle.

"It was," said the Blind Salmon. "Only he could have told you about Old May Night."

The eagle returned angrily home, but when she reached the nest, neither her fledgling nor the Old Crow was there. The Old Crow had left, and it was well for him. If she caught him, his days would be ended.

That shows how long I have been here. And still, last night was the coldest night I ever experienced. But the Blind Salmon of Assaroe is older than I am, and he might be able to give you some account of it."

"Where is the Blind Salmon of Assaroe?" asked the eagle.

"In a certain river," said the bull, naming it. "That's where he always is."

Anger came over the eagle, but she flew off and never stopped until she reached the river. She watched the part of the river where the bull said the Salmon might be, and what did she see below her but the Salmon swimming in the river. She spoke to him, and he replied.

"Are you the Blind Salmon of Assaroe?"

"I am."

"Did you feel cold last night?" asked the eagle.

"I did," replied the Salmon.

"I never felt a night so cold," said the eagle. "What brought me here to you is that I have a young fledgling, and I spent all of last night, jumping up and down in the nest, trying to keep it and myself warm. Toward morning, the fledgling, which is only a month out of the egg, said to me that there had once been a colder night. I had never heard of it. It told me if I didn't believe it to go to the Blackbird of the Forge at a certain place, and he might know. I went to the Blackbird of the Forge, and he told me that he had been perched on an iron rod so many inches long and so many inches thick since he was young. Once every seven years, he rubbed his beak against the iron rod, he said, and one more rub would cut it through. He said that last night was the coldest he had ever experienced. He advised me to go to a certain bull in a certain field, because he might know. I went to the bull, and he told me that last night was the coldest he had ever felt. He had been in the field for thousands of years; a pair of horns had fallen from him each year; and the fence around the one-acre field was made of these horns; only the two horns on his head were needed to complete the fence. That was his age. But he told me to go to the Blind Salmon of Assaroe, so that he might tell me about it, and you are that Salmon."

"I am," said the Blind Salmon of Assaroe. "A night colder than last night came without any doubt. I was here on Old May Night, the eleventh of May, long ago. It was freezing. I was jumping up and down in the water. It was freezing so hard that when I jumped up one time, the water had frozen when I came down. I was frozen into the ice and couldn't free myself. About two hours after daybreak, what should be passing but the Old Crow of Achill. He saw me frozen in the ice. Down he flew and started pecking at the ice with his beak. He made a hole in the ice and picked out my eye and ate it. That's why I have had only one eye ever since, and that's why I'm called the Blind Salmon of Assaroe. But look here," said the Blind Salmon, "as sure as I am here, it was the Old Crow of Achill that was in your nest last night and not your young one!"

"Ah, it can't be," said the eagle.

"It was," said the Blind Salmon. "Only he could have told you about Old May Night."

The eagle returned angrily home, but when she reached the nest, neither her fledgling nor the Old Crow was there. The Old Crow had left, and it was well for him. If she caught him, his days would be ended.

That shows how long I have been here. And still, last night was the coldest night I ever experienced. But the Blind Salmon of Assaroe is older than I am, and he might be able to give you some account of it."

"Where is the Blind Salmon of Assaroe?" asked the eagle.

"In a certain river," said the bull, naming it. "That's where he always is."

Anger came over the eagle, but she flew off and never stopped until she reached the river. She watched the part of the river where the bull said the Salmon might be, and what did she see below her but the Salmon swimming in the river. She spoke to him, and he replied.

"Are you the Blind Salmon of Assaroe?"

"I am."

"Did you feel cold last night?" asked the eagle.

"I did," replied the Salmon.

"I never felt a night so cold," said the eagle. "What brought me here to you is that I have a young fledgling, and I spent all of last night, jumping up and down in the nest, trying to keep it and myself warm. Toward morning, the fledgling, which is only a month out of the egg, said to me that there had once been a colder night. I had never heard of it. It told me if I didn't believe it to go to the Blackbird of the Forge at a certain place, and he might know. I went to the Blackbird of the Forge, and he told me that he had been perched on an iron rod so many inches long and so many inches thick since he was young. Once every seven years, he rubbed his beak against the iron rod, he said, and one more rub would cut it through. He said that last night was the coldest he had ever experienced. He advised me to go to a certain bull in a certain field, because he might know. I went to the bull, and he told me that last night was the coldest he had ever felt. He had been in the field for thousands of years; a pair of horns had fallen from him each year; and the fence around the one-acre field was made of these horns; only the two horns on his head were needed to complete the fence. That was his age. But he told me to go to the Blind Salmon of Assaroe, so that he might tell me about it, and you are that Salmon."

Part II
Kings and Warriors

Part II
Kings and Warriors

·12· *The King Who Could Not Sleep*

Long ago King Cormac was king of all Ireland. He had palaces in many places, and when the summer would come, the king would travel from one to another, partly for pastime and partly to hear how his kingdom was getting on.

Cormac had one son but he died. He was left with three daughters as beautiful as human eye had ever seen. They had nothing to trouble them night or morning but sport and pleasure —walking along the shore, bathing, and so on. And when Cormac returned home in the evening, they ran out joyfully to meet him with a kiss.

Things went on in that way until a very warm summer came. On the first day of June, King Cormac decided that he and his wife would make a tour through Ireland, spending awhile in each of his palaces. He took many of his servants with him and ordered new servants to be hired in their stead until he returned. He intended to be away for three months: June, July, and August. He was made very welcome at each of his palaces, and the people there would run out to meet him when he arrived.

The three daughters remained at home and were in and out each day as usual, enjoying themselves. You have often heard, however, that when the cat is out the mice may dance—and that was the way with King Cormac's daughters.

There was a big lake below the palace, and nothing would satisfy them but to go swimming there, although they had often been warned not to. Well, a very fine warm day came, and the three went out swimming in the lake. The youngest girl was not as strong as the others. When they were out in the middle of the lake, a big otter raised his head near them. The three made for the shore as fast as they could, but the otter overtook the youngest and swam with her until she was close to the edge. The two eldest ran home crying and told the servants that their sister had been killed by an otter. When the servants reached the edge of the lake, they were met by the girl on her way home, but she was without any clothes. They were delighted that she was alive. (But wait till you hear what happened. This story is as true as gospel.)

Time passed until King Cormac sent a letter to say that he would arrive home on a certain day. All were glad at the news: the neighbors, his daughters, and the servants. It was customary for the daughters to go to meet their father whenever he returned, and this time they went a couple of miles along the road to greet him. When they met him, each of them ran to shake his hand and to kiss him. The two eldest were in front and the youngest behind.

When she put out her hand toward her father, he shouted, "Get out of my sight! Three months ago when I left home, you had a maiden's look in your eye and the bloom of youth in your cheeks; now I see that you are a pregnant woman."

The poor creature ran off in tears. When Cormac reached the palace, he went into the large room and seated himself on a magnificent chair. Cooks were moving about, preparing a meal. Cormac shouted that his youngest daughter should come to him.

"What do you want me for, Father?" she asked.

"Get down on your two knees on the floor," said he, "and tell me what happened to you since I left, or I will put my sword through your body."

She finally told him, crying and moaning, what had happened to her with the otter in the lake.

"I believe what you tell me," said the king; "if you had told me anything else except the truth, I would have cut off your head. I know that you could not have avoided what happened and could not save yourself. It may be all for the best."

Time went by, and a midwife had to be found. A fine son without deformity or blemish was born to King Cormac's daughter. The old king was delighted at the birth of a boy, since his own son had died. Oh, such care was never lavished on any child in the kingdom. They took him out on their shoulders and in on their shoulders. Everything he asked for was given to him, and he grew strong and healthy.

When he was seven years old, he was sent to school, and when he had learned enough he walked in and out and here and there with the king. He called Cormac his father—he didn't know anything better. One day, while they were walking along the shore, Cormac complained that he felt tired.

"I have been noticing, Father," said the boy, "that for the past few years you have been failing in health and getting stiff of limb. Wouldn't it be better for you to hand over the crown and the ruling of the country to me? I'm fine and young and clever enough to look after your affairs, and you won't have to leave the palace at all."

"What put that into your head, my dear boy?" asked Cormac. "Don't you know that you will rule the country soon enough? There is no one else to fill my place but you."

A good while after that, they went out together another day, and when they were returning home, the old man complained that he was tired.

"You had better hand over the throne to me," said the boy. "Then you can rest at home always."

"Whoever put that notion into your head, my treasure," said the king, "were no friends of yours. I don't wish to hand over the throne to you as long as I am able to move about myself. You are sure to take my place, as I have no other son."

At that, the young fellow spoke in an angry voice, "If you don't give it to me willingly, I will take it in spite of you."

When he reached home, the boy asked his mother to get some food ready for him.

"What is wrong with you, my son?" she asked.

"My father won't hand over the ruling of the country to me. Well, if he doesn't do it of his own accord, I'll take it by force."

His mother took no great notice of this until he became unfriendly toward the whole household and they couldn't get any good word from him.

He took food for the road with him and walked all day until the late evening came on him. He saw a light in a big house by the roadside, and he went in. The old hag who was inside had all the welcome of the world for him, King Cormac's son. She well knew who he was, and she asked him to stay until morning. He did and before leaving, he asked her where was Fionn mac Cumhaill living. She told him, as well as she was able, how far off Fionn's castle was and said that he would be sure to get work there.

"You'll get there by nightfall," said she; "just when the soldiers are returning home."

It was true. He walked on all day, and at nightfall he came to Fionn's place. He met the soldiers in the street and asked where their master was. Fionn came out, and the boy told him that he wished to be hired.

"How much pay will you want?" asked Fionn.

"The bargain I want to make with you is this," said the boy. "I will stay with you for a year and a day, and if you find any fault with me, you can pay me whatever you wish. But if you find no fault with me, I will fix my own reward."

"That's a bargain," said Fionn.

Fionn thought that he would surely find some fault with the lad; nobody was perfect; so the boy entered the service of Fionn.

Back at the palace, poor King Cormac was troubled and feeling his age as well. Near the palace was a small house in which Gaibhne Gabha lived; he looked after King Cormac's horses and shod them and did other jobs about the palace. This smith had three daughters, the youngest of whom was sixteen or seventeen years of age. King Cormac went to the smith and suggested that if he sent the youngest daughter to work in the palace he would lose nothing by it. The smith said that, of course, he would and welcome; so the daughter entered the king's service.

She was there only two days when the king's wife died. She was old. He was alone now, having neither wife nor son. After she was buried, the whole household was very sorry for the king and they prayed every day that he might be consoled.

One day the thought struck him, that if he married the smith's young daughter, God might send them an heir for the throne. Although the girl was very young, the king spoke to her, and she agreed to marry him, so they were married according to the custom of the time.

Time passed until the boy's year and day of service with Fionn was coming to an end. Fionn realized that, unless he found some fault with the boy, he could deprive him of the leadership of the Fianna. He went to visit an old wise man who was blind. This old man was a prophet, and Fionn told him about the bargain he had made with the boy.

"You'll catch him out without any delay," said the old man, "if you follow my advice. Leave your sword outside your door tonight when you are going to bed. Don't fall asleep. About two or three o'clock in the morning, call the boy's name and, if he doesn't answer, you'll have found fault with him."

"I'll try it," said Fionn.

Fionn went home and that night when they had all gone to bed, he left his sword outside the door. He stayed awake till between two and three o'clock; then he called the boy by name.

"What do you want me for, master?" asked the boy, pulling on his clothes.

"I forgot my sword outside the door," said Fionn. "If it rains, it will get rusty."

The boy went out and brought in the sword. He then asked Fionn if he wanted anything else; Fionn said he didn't.

Next day Fionn made off the blind old man again and told him what had happened.

"Well, you have only one other night left," said the old man. "If you don't catch him, there's nothing to be done. Call him by name at the same time tonight; if he answers you, you'll have lost your chance."

That night Fionn called the boy by name when all were asleep.

"What do you want me for, master?" asked the boy, jumping out of bed and pulling on his trousers.

When he reached where Fionn was lying, Fionn pretended to be asleep and snoring.

"What do you want me for?" asked the boy.

"Did I call you?" asked Fionn.

"You did, indeed," said the boy.

"If I did, it must have been in my sleep," replied Fionn.

The boy went back to bed. Next day the year and day were up.

"I hope," said Fionn, "that you will not take the leadership of the Fianna from me. You are the best boy I have ever had under my roof."

"I don't want to take any leadership from you," replied the

boy. "I haven't even thought of it. All I want is that you fight King Cormac for a day."

"O my!" cried Fionn. "What am I to do? Isn't he the king that's over me? But that's the bargain, and I must carry it out. What day would you like it to be?"

"Any day that suits yourself," said the boy.

"Well," said Fionn, "we must give King Cormac a chance to get his army together."

"I'll give him a month from today," said the boy. "And I will convey the news to him."

And so he did. He made off to King Cormac and said to him, "Since you wouldn't give me the crown of your own free will, I will make you give it to me by force, unless you defeat Fionn's army and myself a month from today."

He returned to Fionn and carried on as he had done.

A few days before the battle was to take place, King Cormac spoke to his wife, "You had better go home to your father," said he, "because I will be killed in this battle and so would you."

He put his hand into his pocket and took out a belt with a yellow plate on it on which his own name was inscribed.

"Now," said he, "if God sends you any child, which I hope He will, put this belt on him; and when he will be able to read this inscription, he will know his father's name and gain his rights from the thief who is coming to take his place. On the morning of the day of battle, you are to come out on the field to me, and I will give you enough gold and silver to rear the child. In a small basket, which I have hidden at the side of that cliff to the east, you will find a bootful of gold and another of silver."

When the day of battle arrived, the officers and colonels and leaders assembled, and the fight began. There was charging and noise amid the powder smoke and men screaming as they were wounded in the fray. The smith's daughter went out to see King Cormac, but she could not recognize him among the other fighters.

Cormac was killed in the battle. Fionn mac Cumhaill and his men returned home. The country's leading men met to see what was to be done next, and they decided that King Cormac's son, as he was called until then, was the lawful heir to the throne.

The whole country knew differently, however. The new king, therefore, was elected, and the name he was known by was King Conn.

The new king began to make new laws which changed everything that had been done before. Those who could not pay their rent were to go to prison and stay there until they paid. The people came to hate Conn. In Cormac's reign, the weather had been very fine; harvests were plentiful; the island of Ireland was happy and beautiful. When Conn became king, the wind changed to the north; the land refused to yield crops; summer became winter. Even the chimneys of the palace became crooked with hatred for the king, and half of them fell down. The royal seat was a miserable and deadly place.

That's the way things were. But wait until you hear more. When the smith's daughter found that she was bearing a child, she sent secretly for a midwife who lived nearby and asked her to go with her to a lonely place in a wood that was there. The midwife came and the two of them went to the wood, and before long the smith's daughter gave birth to a son.

As soon as the child had been born, the mother said to the midwife, "This is a belt which King Cormac asked me to put on the child, if it should be a boy."

She put on the belt, and no sooner was it fixed around his waist as he lay on some cloth by their side than a she-wolf emerged from the wood. She snarled at the two women, and they fainted. She took the child in her mouth and carried it off to the cave where her own cubs were. Not a tooth touched the child, but the wolf licked him and kept him warm. There in the cave, she suckled her own three cubs and the child.

When the two women recovered their senses, they looked about, but the child had disappeared, and they did not know where to look for him.

"Don't say a word to anyone about this," said the mother to the midwife, giving her two guineas. "Say that I had not been feeling well, and there won't be any more about it."

The child remained with the she-wolf, which looked after him as if he were the apple of her eye and cared for him more than she did for her own cubs. Time went by, from day to day, from week to week, from month to month, until the child was one-and-a-half-years old. On fine days, he would leave the cave with the cubs, and they played together in the wood.

One day there chanced to be some hunters passing through the wood with their hounds and hunting gear of the time, and they caught sight of the child playing with the cubs on a nice grassy slope. The cubs were cleverer than the child, and they ran as fast as they could into the cave, where they hid underground. The child also escaped before the hunters could catch him. They thought it very strange that a child should be in such a place, so they sent word secretly to others who had hounds. Next day they all came and hid themselves around the cave. When the sun shone out after midday, the wolf emerged from the cave with the three cubs and the child trotting after her. They began to play. The old wolf lay on her back on the grass and played with the child with her legs. She paid far more heed to the child than to her own cubs. In rushed the hunters with their guns, and they all scattered. The hounds ran off after the wolves, but all the hunters wanted was to take the child. They caught him before he reached the cave. He was very wild and tried to escape. The belt had sunk into his flesh and could hardly be seen at all. Finally the hunters noticed it and read the inscription on the plate. They all said that it was a belt of King Cormac's, who had been dead long since, but someone had put it on the child.

They held a meeting to decide who should get the child. They all agreed that he should be given to an old nobleman named Cormac mhac Gheolan, who lived a good distance away with his wife and had no children. He was the one who should have the child. Cormac mhac Gheolan, therefore, got him, and when the wife saw him she had as much welcome for him as if he were the King of Glory himself. She got two nurses to mind the child, and you may be sure it was he that was well cared for. Time passed until he was nine or ten years old. He was given everything he asked for.

He was sent to school for some years to be taught in the manner of those times. When the boys were allowed out of school to play at midday, they took their hurleys and ball and played a game. The boy was very good at hurling, and every day he was the best of them all. He was much bigger and stronger than the others. They didn't like to be beaten in the game. Like all people, some of them were unmannerly, and they started to call him by a nickname: Son of the Wolf. He didn't take any great notice of it the first day, but when they all gathered around him the next day after he had won and started shouting "The Son of the Wolf that was found in the wood," he began to wonder what they meant. The next day, when even some of the girls joined in the nickname, he lost his temper and ran home.

"I won't go to school any more," he told his foster father. "The whole lot of them were calling me names today and for the past three days. I beat them all at hurling, and they are calling me 'The Son of the Wolf that was found in the wood.'"

"Don't take any notice of them," said old Cormac mhac Gheolan. "Let them call you what they like. They are jealous of you."

"I'll go one day more, till I see," said the boy.

Next day he went to school again, and he won the game not only from the boys but from the master himself. The whole lot —the boys, the girls, and even the master—started at him until they made a laughingstock of him. He left them there and ran home with their jeering in his ears.

"I know they must have some reason for the name," said he, "when even the master himself started at it. Only for it being true, he wouldn't join in. I won't stay here another day or night with you," said he to old Cormac, "unless you tell me the reason for it."

"Well, I'll tell you the reason," said Cormac. "You were found in the wood along with a she-wolf and her three cubs, and the hunters left you here with me to be the heir to my lands. You can see for yourself that there's no one else to succeed me."

"Had I anything or any clothes on me when I was found?"

"You were as naked as when you came into the world except for a small belt you were wearing."

"Where is the belt now?" he asked.

Old Cormac kept the belt in a trunk. He went down into the room and fetched it. The boy read the inscription on the plate.

"Well, one thing is certain," said he. "I'm no son of a wolf.

I'm the son of a good man, King Cormac himself. If I live till tomorrow morning, I am going to say goodbye to ye for awhile until I see what has happened to the place where my father lived."

Next morning, old Cormac's wife prepared a good meal for him, while she cried at the thought that he was leaving them. Cormac handed him a big purse of gold.

"Put that in your pocket," said he. "You might need it before you return."

He bade goodbye to Cormac and his wife and took to the road early in the morning. He didn't know in what direction to go. He could only ask everybody he met where had King Cormac lived.

The evening came on, very cold and wild. He came to a high fence at the roadside, which hid a small house behind it. There was an old man herding a few sheep by the road, and who was he but the smith, Gaibhne Gabha, his grandfather.

"Have you any idea whereabouts did a king named Cormac live?" asked the youth.

"I'll show you," said the old man with tears streaming from his eyes. "That palace over there on the side of the hill is where he lived. He is dead for almost twenty years. A thief who hasn't given us peace day or night since he took the crown has taken his place. We had fine weather while we had King Cormac; we had a crop of everything we planted; even the trees were bending to the ground with the weight of berries. Since this thief came, the wind has gone north; summer is like winter; the land has refused to bear crops; and the chimneys have turned crooked with hatred of him. And he has made a law; if these three little sheep of mine go into his land, he will keep them for himself."

The boy saw that the old man was talkative; so he asked him if he could keep him until morning.

"Well, I'll do my best," said the old man. "I can see that you know a good deal."

The old man took him up to the house and told his three daughters that the stranger with him was on his travels and would like to have lodgings until morning.

"Of course, he can," said the three together.

"I must run to the shop," said one of them.

The youth put his hand in his pocket and handed her two guineas.

"Spend that in the shop," said he, "and bring a pint of whiskey so that we can drink a glass."

The shop wasn't far away, and when she returned, she got ready a good meal for the stranger. He and the old man were taken into the room where the food was. When they had eaten their fill, the youth gave the old man a glass of whiskey.

"I'm worried about the three little sheep," said the old man. "I must go out to keep an eye on them. If that thief lays hold of them, I'll never see them again; so I'll have to leave you."

The youth sat at the table, talking to the youngest girl and smoking his pipe. He put his two hands to the back of his head, as you have often seen people do, and raised his body up higher on the chair. His belt became visible, and the moment the girl caught sight of it, she recognized it and started to cry.

"If you don't want me to stay until morning, I can go to some other house," said the youth.

"O,'tisn't that at all!" said she. "'Tis the name on that belt you have on."

"How do you know the belt I'm wearing?" said he.

"I married King Cormac a short time before he was killed," said she. "He gave me that belt and told me if I had a child to put it on him, so that he would know who his father was. I went to the wood, and when the child was born, I put the belt on him. A wolf took the child, and I have never got trace or tidings of him since. How did you get the belt?"

"I see! I see!" said the youth. "You are my mother, and I am home."

The girl was delighted and she told the rest the news.

"Where is the old man?" said the youth.

She called him in, and the youth filled two other glasses of whiskey and gave one to the old man. They started to talk, and the old man told him how bad a king Conn was. Someone had to sit up with him every night telling him stories, and anyone whom he disliked or didn't satisfy him was shot or hanged next morning. "I understand," said the youth.

"Run out," said the old man to one of the daughters; "and see where the sheep are."

When she went out, she found that one of King Conn's men had taken away the three sheep which he had found trespassing on the king's land. She ran back with the news.

"May our ill luck go with them," said the old man. "We'll have to do without them now."

"You won't," said the youth. "I haven't finished with this king yet. You must go to him," said he to the old man; "and demand your sheep back. Say that you only went in home to warm your hands and they were missing when you returned."

"I won't go," replied the old man. "He'd kill me."

"If you don't go, I will," said the youth.

"It would be a pity that you'd be killed," said the old man. "I'll go myself."

The old man went to the palace and met the king. He told him that his three sheep had only crossed the boundary fence, and he would like to get them.

"Didn't you know well," said King Conn, "that I wouldn't break for you the law I made? If I did, somebody else would come tomorrow and another the next day, looking for their animals. I'm going to stand by the law I have made."

"I'm willing to leave the rights and wrongs of the case to the first man that comes along the road," said the old man.

"I'll agree to that," said King Conn, thinking that nobody would have the courage to oppose the law he had made.

The old man returned home and told the youth that the king had agreed to leave the matter to the first person who came along the road.

When morning came, the old man and the youth and the daughters got up and ate their breakfast. The old man then got ready to go to the palace and asked the youth not to be far behind him. He met the king, and they walked over and hither along the road, waiting for somebody to come along. At last the king saw a strapping young fellow coming toward them. He saluted them, and they replied in the manner of the time.

"You're a stranger on this road," said the king.

"I am. I have never passed this way until now."

"Well, 'tis somebody like you I want," said the king. "I issued a decree through this island that everybody should keep their animals from trespassing; if they didn't, they would lose them. This man here had three sheep. He knew well about this decree, and now he wants it changed."

The old man then told his own side of the story.

"I had three sheep," he said, "and every day I minded them. I went home yesterday evening to warm my hands; when I came out again the sheep were gone. I hadn't a four-footed animal in the world but them, and it seems unfair that they are taken from me."

"You knew," said the youth, "that you shouldn't have let the sheep over the fence, knowing the king's decree. On the other hand, keeping them altogether is a heavy punishment."

"Well, we have agreed to let the first comer decide," said the king. "What is your decision?"

"This is what I think," said the youth. "You are both the same in my eyes. Get your men to shear the wool off the sheep and keep it in lieu of the grass which they ate. If you catch them trespassing again, keep them altogether, but let them go this time."

The youth walked off along the road by himself. The king's servants shore the sheep and then gave them back to their owner. (That was that, but wait until you hear more.)

Two days later, the king sent one of his servants for the old man to tell him stories all night, hoping to get his own back from him. When evening came, the old man washed his face and tidied himself up to go before the king.

"Where are you going?" asked the youth.

"To keep company with that thief," said the old man. "I know that he is planning my death!"

"You won't stir a foot out of here," said the youth. "I'll go in your stead. I have plenty of stories for him."

"No!" cried the old man. "It would be a shame that you should die. You are young, and my life is nearly over. I haven't much longer to live."

"He won't kill me as easily as you think," said the youth. "So take your ease and stay at home."

The youth thrust his sword into his scabbard, and said, "I want to find out what this king is like."

On entering the palace, he turned toward the kitchen. The servants were all eating their supper around a table, and none of them asked him to join them. He walked boldly to the table after a while and sat down like themselves. They glanced at one another, thinking him unmannerly for sitting without being invited.

"I think that, as I'm staying in the palace tonight, the least I ought to get is a bite to eat," said he.

When the cooks heard that, they sent in food and drink to him; every bite of it tasted like honey; no two bites had the same taste; and no two bites were of the same food. The cook who was getting food ready for the king came down and told him that the king wanted him. He went to the king.

"I don't recognize you," said the king.

"I'm a stranger here," said the youth. "I am staying in a house down there where there is an old man with three daughters. The old man told me that your majesty had sent for him to tell you stories till morning. He was taken ill after dinner, so I took pity on him and told him that I would come in his stead tonight."

"Very well," said the king.

Everything in the room where the king was lying was so polished that you could see your reflection everywhere. There was a fine fire and fine, comfortable seats. The king himself was lying on a bed of birds' down beside the fire.

"Start off now," said he to the youth, "and tell me the best stories you have."

The king turned his own face toward the wall with the bed-clothes drawn up over his head. When dawn was breaking next morning, he turned to face the youth.

"You are the best man at *fiannaíocht* and storytelling that has ever entered my palace or my city," said he.

"I don't believe you heard the half of what I told you," said the youth.

"I heard every word you said since you sat down there last night," said the king.

"You couldn't have," said the youth. "You were asleep half of the time."

"I wasn't asleep," replied the king. "I haven't closed my eyes in sleep for seven years, or maybe for seven more along with that."

"Then," said the youth, "you must be half like an otter."

"Don't say that again," said the king angrily.

"I say again that you couldn't have heard the half of what I told you," said the youth.

"I heard every word," said the king. "And don't say again that I'm half like an otter."

He rose up on his elbow in bed.

"Is your mother alive?" asked the youth.

"She is."

"Well, go to her and ask her where you came from."

The king jumped out on the floor in his shirt and went through the palace until he reached the bed his mother was lying on. He caught hold of her arm and shook her.

"Mother," said he, "where did I come from?"

"From where but from the King Cormac, my son? He was your father."

"Well, what did she tell you?" asked the youth when the king returned.

"She said that I am King Cormac's son," replied Conn.

The king lay down again and covered his head while the youth continued with the stories. After awhile the king praised him again for his storytelling, and the youth said he couldn't have heard half of what he said.

"I heard every word," said the king.

"Then you must be half like an otter," repeated the youth.

"If you say that again, I'll leave your head on the floor," shouted the king, stretching out his hand for his sword which was at the head of his bed.

"Come! Come!" said the youth. "I have a sword too!" He put down his hand and drew it out of the scabbard.

"Take your sword," said he to the king, "and go back to your mother, catch her by the throat, pull her to the edge of the bed, put your knee under her back, and the tip of your sword to her breast, and swear that you will put the sword through her body unless she tells you the truth about your father."

The king rushed back to his mother's room, took her by the throat, pulled her to the side of the bed, and placed the tip of his sword against her breast.

"Now," said he, "tell me the truth about where I came from."

The mother knew that he was in earnest and was terrified of him. She told him about how she and her sisters were bathing and how the otter came to her.

"That's the true story about how you came," said she. "You are no son of King Cormac."

"I understand now," said the king. "I knew there was something strange about me. That youth is the most truthful that has ever come to this palace."

When he returned to his room, he took the youth by the two hands and threw himself on his knees, asking his pardon.

"I was on the point of murdering you," he said. "And now I know that you were telling the truth."

The king dressed himself and sat for a while conversing with the strange youth.

"Before another week is out," said the youth, "I will be able to give you the power of sleeping."

"If you can do that," said the king, "I promise to give you half of my possessions and the crown after my death."

"Put that in writing," said the youth, "and I will quickly do my part."

The king sat down and wrote the promise to give him half of his possessions there and then and the crown after his death, if he helped him to sleep.

"Haven't you good boats in your harbours?" asked the youth.

"I have, plenty," said the king.

"Well, fetch one of them and attach a long chain to it on the shore, so that it can float to the center of that lake in front of the palace. Anchor it in the middle of the lake, and have your bed of birds' down on deck. Have a canopy over the boat to keep off the rain. I promise you that you will sleep."

And so it was done. The king got the boat fitted out with a canopy overhead and his bed of birds' down on deck. Then King

Conn entered the boat and lay down on the bed. The boat drifted out from the shore with the waves until it reached the middle of the lake. The king fell fast asleep as soon as he lay down, and although he spent three days and three nights sleeping and snoring, there was no sign that he had slept enough.

What was in the lake but his father, the otter! He felt the smell of a human being, and up he came the next night and entered the boat. He grabbed the sleeping king, dived to the bottom of the lake with him, and killed him. When the servants thought that he should have slept his fill, they pulled the boat in by its chain. There was no trace of the king on his bed or in the boat. They started to search for him and dragged the lake with hooks. They found his headless body on the bottom. They were very troubled. The body was taken to the palace and waked and buried. The youth went to see Conn's mother and told her that her son had handed over everything to him before he died.

"If you wish," said he, "we will get the leaders to sit in judgment, and I will see that you get whatever they decide for you."

The leaders and lawyers assembled and the youth showed them King Conn's testament, which gave him the crown after his own death. They gave orders that all of King Conn's servants should leave the palace. The youth had the crown placed upon his head, and he became king in succession to Conn. He sent for Cormac mhac Gheolan and his wife to come and end their days with him. He also brought to the palace his grandfather, his mother, and her sisters. Then he sent an invitation to the four quarters of his kingdom. Rich and poor gathered, and such festivities took place as had never been seen in Ireland before. The tenants were overjoyed that a new young king had been elected to rule over them.

And that's the end of my story: King Cormac's son taking the place of King Conn.

That story is as true as that you're alive.

·13· *Céatach*

A long, long time ago—if I were there then, I wouldn't be there now; if I were there now and at that time, I would have a new story or an old story, or I might have no story at all—there was a king and a queen in Ireland, and they were married. They had only one son, and the name that they gave him was Céatach, Son of the King of Cor from Ireland. When the son was fifteen years old, they heard about a magician in Greece and decided to send Céatach to learn athletics and deeds of valor from him. They did.

When Céatach had been a year and a half with the magician, one fine day when the magician and his wife were between heaven and earth, teaching athletics and deeds of valor to Céatach, Son of the King of Cor from Ireland, to the Son of the King of Maol, to the Son of the King of Ul, and to the Son of the King of Olachtaí, there came from the Eastern World a warrior named Steel Skull, and he abducted the magician's daughter. When the magician returned home, he noticed the smell of Steel Skull throughout the house and found that his daughter had been taken off.

"Son of the King of Maol," said the magician, "will you go after Steel Skull and take my daughter from him? If you do, you can have her in marriage."

"I will," said the Son of the King of Maol.

"You have been with me here only five years," said the magician. "If you had another year here, you could follow him. How is your courage, Son of the King of Olachtaí?"

"It is good," he replied.

"You have been here with me only three years," said the magician. "If you had a fourth year here, you could follow him. How is your courage Céatach, Son of the King of Cor from Ireland?"

"Very good," said Céatach. "A mouthful I won't drink and a bite I won't eat, till I go to the Eastern World after your daughter and find where she is—either that or lose my head in the attempt."

"You have been here only a year and a half, Céatach," said the magician. "If you had another year here, you could follow him."

"I'm able to do now what I will be able to do after another year here," replied Céatach.

It was no use talking to him. They spent that night in three ways: a third at storytelling, a third at *fiannaíocht*, and a third in deep restful sleep until the following morning.

Céatach rose, donned his *fubuíneach, fabaíneach* dress, and grasped his thick-backed thin-edged sword. Down he went to the wild billowy sea. He took a gold ring from his finger and made a large capacious ship out of it. He leaped onto the middle of the deck. He hoisted up the bulging, billowing sails from the bottom to the top of the masts. He made the rough gravel sink down to the bottom of the sea and churned up the fine sand. He didn't leave a mooring rope without pulling, a new oar without bursting, or an old oar without breaking. The small eels and the big eels of the eastern sea and the western sea came entwined on deck to him, offering service and sport and music to the Son of the King of Cor in Ireland, on his way to the Eastern World.

When he reached there, he dashed three waves against his ship, a gust of wind going through her, and the sun splitting her. He put the mooring of a year and a day on her, even though she might be there only a minute. Then he turned her into a green stone on the strand with seaweed growing on her.

He walked up through the kingdom with his sword in his right hand until he came to the house of Steel Skull, the giant. When he struck the challenge pole demanding battle, he didn't leave a foal in a mare, a lamb in a sheep, a child in a woman, or a kid in a she-goat that he didn't turn around nine times in their mothers' womb and back again. He didn't leave an old castle without demolishing, a new castle without bending, an old tree without breaking, or a new tree without twisting. On his sword it was inscribed that there wasn't a warrior under the earth or upon it who could defeat him. The giant's herald came out and demanded to know what he wanted.

"Fight with Steel Skull," replied Céatach, "or else the daughter of the magician in Greece."

"Too soon you'll get fight," said the herald. "You won't have long to wait for Steel Skull. He's covering himself with a suit of armour from the top of his head to the soles of his feet. Every blow that he will give you will go from the skin to the flesh, from flesh to bone, from bone to marrow, and from marrow to *smiortán* through your ribs. Each blow that you aim at him will glance from his body as would a drop of rain from a glass bottle."

It wasn't long before Steel Skull came out. They attacked each other like two wild bears, two fiery dragons, two hawks, or two eagles for seven days and seven nights. They then fought as two noble warriors with their swords on the ground in front of the palace. Suddenly the daughter of the Greek magician appeared at the uppermost window and she saw the fight going on below.

"Bad cess to you, Son of the King in Ireland," she cried. " 'Tis a bad place you came to meet your death, where nobody save myself will cry over your body. Why don't you remember all the athletics and feats of valor my father and mother ever taught you?"

When Céatach heard that, the blood that was in the soles of his feet mounted to the top of his head. He rushed backward a little and then struck Steel Skull a blow near the apple of his throat, cutting off his head. The head went up into the air whistling and came down humming, in the hope of joining the body again. But Céatach was ready for it. He kicked the head with his huge right boot and sent it a ridge and seven acres away.

"Lucky for you that you did that," said the head. "Had I joined the body again, it would have taken more than half of the Fianna to prise me loose."

"It wasn't to let you rejoin the body that I cut you off, you good-for-nothing," replied Céatach.

He ran into the palace. The daughter of the Greek magician was coming down the stairs and, as ill luck should have it, in her way was an old man who had been in the palace for twelve hundred years. Céatach took hold of him by the two legs, swung him over his shoulders, and dashed him against the wall, whitewashing it with his brains. The Greek magician's daughter smothered him with kisses, drowned him with tears, and dried him with fine silken cloths and her own hair. They divided the night into three parts: a third at storytelling, a third at *fiannaíocht*, and a third in deep and restful sleep until morning.

No sooner did day break than the warrior arose. He said his prayers, combed his hair, and asked God to direct him. He and the Greek magician's daughter decided to get married and they did. They then thought that they should return to Greece. So they put what they needed aboard the best vessel that Steel Skull had and sailed forth, making for Greece. When they were about half way, Céatach, Son of the King of Cor in Ireland, suddenly thought of the Fianna.

"I heard about the Fianna when I was young," said he. "I have never seen them, and as I happen to be on my travels now, I will sail home to see what kind of men they are."

"You won't," said his wife.

"I will," said he.

"You won't!"

"I will!"

What with the dint of arguing and talking, they didn't feel anything until the vessel was high and dry on the strand below the house of the Fianna of Ireland. Céatach took his wife by the hand and led her to the city of the Fianna. The Fianna of Ireland had twenty-one houses; there were twenty-one rooms in each house, and twenty-one fires in each room. Around each fire sat twenty-one of the Fianna. The moment that Céatach and his wife entered, Conán caught sight of the woman and fell in love with her. Out he ran, as fast as he could, and went to an old wise man.

"Céatach, Son of the King of Cor in Ireland, has just arrived below," said Conán, "and he has the most beautiful wife that wind or sun ever shone on. I'll die if I don't get her for myself after I put Céatach to death."

"Bad cess to you," cried the old man. "Don't you well know that nobody has a beautiful wife in these times except the man who is able to fight for her."

"Stop your gab," said Conán. "My forefathers and myself have been feeding you so that you could tell us our fortunes. You'll

quickly lose that feeding, and even your head, unless you tell me
how Céatach can be killed, so that I can get his wife."

"Rather than lose my feeding or my head," said the old wise
man; "I advise you to put Céatach under a year's *geasa* to go to
the Magician of the Mountain and get from him the loan of his
Rough Hound. Our Fianna soldiers, as you know, have their
hands full every day fighting himself and the hound."

When Conán got back to the house, he was no sooner inside
the door than he said, "Céatach, Son of the King of Cor in
Ireland, I put as a judgment and *geasa* on you to go to the
Magician of the Mountain and get the Rough Hound on loan
from him."

All that Céatach did was to leap out onto the floor.

"Fionn," said he, "I hope that you will take good care of my
wife until I come back."

"I give you my hand and word," said Fionn mac Cumhaill.
"Even if you are absent for a year and a day, your wife will be
all right until you return."

Céatach struck his two palms together, and the wind that
issued from between them lifted Conán and stuck him to the
rafters.

"That's where you'll stay, Conán," said he, "be it short or long
that I am away."

He rushed out of the house. He went over a hill at each jump
and across twelve glens at each step until the darkness and the
end of the day was coming and until the white garron was seeking the shelter of the dockleaf, although the dockleaf would not
be the better for waiting for him. When black night had fallen,
he was close to the house of the Magician of the Mountain. The
Magician was sitting in the doorway, combing his hair. Céatach
jumped in through the door over his head.

"*Fú fá féasóg.*" said the Magician. "I can smell a lying,
thieving Irishman. To eat you in one bite would be too little for
me, and to eat you in two bites would be too much. I don't know
what I'll do with you, except I blow you up into the air or put
you under my feet in the mud or put you under the top thong of
my old shoe."

"May you be a thousand times worse off a year from tonight," said Céatach. "You know that I haven't come here that you might get justice and satisfaction from me. I came to get them in full from you."

"What is your mission?" asked the Magician.

"Conán sent me to get the Rough Hound on loan from you."

"Neither you nor the Rough Hound will go home alive to tell the tale," said the Magician. "Which do you prefer: to wrestle on red flagstones or to stab with gray knives against each other's bulging ribs?"

"I prefer to wrestle on red flagstones, where my fine-drawn noble feet will be rising, while your big unshapely ugly paws will be falling," said Céatach.

Out they went. They attacked each other as would two wild bears or two fierce bulls for the length of seven nights and days. They made hard places soft and soft places hard. They drew wells of spring water up through the center of the green stones with the dint of choking, killing, striking, and testing each other. At last, Céatach gave him a twist which buried him to the knees in the ground. A second twist buried him to his waist; and a third to the upper part of his chest.

"Clay over you, churl," shouted Céatach.

"Yes," said the Magician; "you are the best warrior born of man and woman that I have ever met. If you release me from here, I will give you half my kingdom during my life and the whole of it after my death. I'll give you my slender black steed, which can catch the March wind ahead of her, although the March wind behind her cannot overtake her. I'll give you my sword of light, which will brighten the world from east to west, and myself and the Rough Hound will be your servants all the days of your life!"

"May you be a thousand times worse off a year from tonight," replied Céatach. "Many's the place where I would get a bite of food to put in my own mouth, but it would be hard to fill your big stomach. Still, 'twill do me no good to kill you."

He took the Magician by the two ears, pulled them until they were seven yards long, and dragged him out of the hole. He then made a yoke, as you would for a young ram when taking him to the fair, and attached it to the Rough Hound and the Magician of the Mountain. He cut a switch, and all three started on the journey back to the Fianna.

Next morning, as day broke, the twenty-one maidservants that the Fianna had went out for water for the breakfast, and they saw Céatach approaching with the Rough Hound and the Magician of the Mountain tied with a yoke. The girls almost broke their necks as they ran in with the news, crying that not one of the Fianna would survive till next morning, since Céatach was coming with the Rough Hound to desolate the world.

"What's this?" cried Fionn mac Cumhaill. "I knew that no matter how long Céatach would be away, it is he who would put an end to the Fianna."

No sooner had he said this than in rushed Céatach, dragging the Rough Hound and the Magician of the Mountain on the yoke behind him. Conán fell down from the rafters. As soon as his two feet touched the floor, he ran out to the old wise man and asked him how he could put Céatach to death.

"Haven't I already told you," said the old man, "that no man has a beautiful wife these days but the man who is able to fight for her? What the devil is tempting and vexing you? If you anger Céatach, he won't leave one of the Fianna alive; they'll all be dead by morning."

"Stop your gab," cried Conán. "My forefathers before me and I have been feeding you to tell us our fortune or any other prophecy we needed. If you don't help me now, your head will be off."

"Well, rather than lose my feeding and my head," said the old man; "You must put Céatach under a year's *geasa* to go to the house of the King of the Western World and get the loan of the Honey Dish. No prince or king's son or giant who has ever gone for it before has ever returned alive."

Conán returned to the house. No sooner had he stepped inside the threshold than he said to Céatach, "Céatach, Son of the King of Cor in Ireland, I put as a judgment and *geasa* on you to go to the house of the King of the Western World and bring me the loan of the Honey Dish, which is being guarded by the Poisonous Ram. No prince or king's son or giant who ever went to get it has returned alive."

"That's easily done," said Céatach.

Down he rushed to the seashore and threw his golden ring out into the water. He made a large, capacious ship out of it, and jumped onto the middle of the deck, followed by the Rough Hound and the Magician of the Mountain. He hoisted his sails, and they never stopped until they reached the Western World. Céatach moored his ship to last for a day and a year, even though he might be there only for a minute. He then turned it into a green stone with seaweed growing on it.

He walked through the island. It happened that the son of the King of the Eastern World was marrying the daughter of the King of the Western World that night, and a feast to last seven nights and seven days was in progress. Three musicians were playing when Céatach reached the outside door. As soon as he heard them, he snatched three wisps of straw from the lintel of the door and made three sets of bagpipes out of them: one for himself, one for the Magician of the Mountain, and a set for the Rough Hound. The three of them started to play outside in the yard, and when all who were attending the feast in the palace heard the fine pipe music outside, they caught hold of the pipers within and threw them out of the palace. They brought in Céatach, the Magician of the Mountain, and the Rough Hound, and the three sat down to play. There was no better entertainment under the sun than the fine music they played with the dint of magic mist and conjuring.

When a good part of the night had been spent with their playing, Céatach asked for a drink. So well was his music liked that the Honey Dish was brought to him to drink from. He drank, and recognized the vessel he was seeking. He had kept an eye out for it, as any thief would, so that he would know where it was and be able to snatch it later. The night wore on. The Honey Dish had been placed on a table, and above it was the head of the Poisonous Ram that was watching it. After a time, Céatach started to play again, and his music put everybody in the palace asleep with the dint of magic mist and conjuring. He made one leap toward the dish, and a second leap outside the door with the Magician of the Mountain and the Rough Hound at his heels. A third leap brought him down to the seashore.

Céatach had his overcoat under one arm and the Honey Dish under the other. At his heels was the Poisonous Ram. All that Céatach could do was to throw his coat over the side of a rock that was near him and hide at the other side. So anxious was the ram to attack Céatach that he thought he was hiding under the coat. He gave it a powerful butt with his head, and drove it as far as his two shoulders in through the rock. All Céatach did was to jump up and draw a blow with his sword across the ram's neck. The head remained fast in the rock, and the body fell to the ground with not a sign of life in it.

They sailed away full of joy. In the meantime, the mother of Céatach's wife had heard that her daughter had reached Ireland and she thought that the Fianna had killed Céatach and kept her daughter. So she declared war on the Fianna and named the day for battle. When Céatach arrived back one night, it wasn't women were troubling Conán but the war that was to break out next day. On the following morning, the Fianna were ready with twenty-one ships to sail to Greece.

When Céatach and his wife were in bed the previous night, Céatach said, "I'll go along with the Fianna tomorrow to help them in the fight against your father and mother."

"You won't go to fight against my father and mother," said she.

"I will," replied Céatach.

"You won't," said his wife.

"I will."

"You won't. Why should you go?"

"I'd feel ashamed if my people, my own kingdom, were defeated by any kingdom on earth," said he.

So he got ready next morning.

Just as he was going on board the same ship as Fionn mac Cumhaill, Céatach's wife said to Fionn, "Fionn, if Céatach is coming home dead, you must have black sails hoisted. If he's alive, have white sails."

"I'll do that," answered Fionn.

"That's all I'm asking of you," said she.

They sailed away for Greece, and when they reached that country, the king had twenty-one ships ready to oppose them.

In addition, the Son of the King of Maol and the Son of the King of Olachtaí were in battle array on the strand. As day dawned, when they were about to start fighting, Céatach asked Fionn mac Cumhaill would he and his men prefer to fight the twenty-one ships or the two warriors on the strand. Fionn said he and his hosts would prefer to fight the two noble warriors.

"If so," said Céatach, "then I will fight the twenty-one ships by myself."

The Fianna landed on the strand to fight the Son of the King of Maol and the Son of the King of Olachtaí. Céatach sailed out to do battle with the twenty-one ships, and by noon every man on the twenty-one ships had been slain by Céatach, Son of the King of Cor in Ireland. He then came ashore. By that time, nine of the Fianna had fallen at the hands of the two noble warriors.

"I heard great praise of you and your men, Fionn," said Céatach, "but I fear that they are not half as good as they are made out to be. Let you and them sit down now, while I see what I can do by myself."

The Fianna sat down. At that moment, the Son of the King of Maol was high up in the sky in the form of a poisonous lion.

"Son of the King of Maol, come down and fight me here on land in the guise of a warrior," shouted Céatach.

"No!" said the Son of the King of Maol. "Let you come up as a poisonous lion to meet me."

Céatach rose on the toes of his two feet, and by the strength of his two hands, he rose in the sky as a poisonous lion. He wasn't there a minute and a half when he had the head cut off the Son of the King of Maol. Down he came to earth as a handsome, fine warrior and called on the Son of the King of Olachtaí to do likewise. The Son of the King of Olachtaí refused but invited Céatach to rise to meet him as a poisonous lion. For the second time, Céatach rose up on the toes of his two feet, and by the strength of his two hands, he rose up in the sky as a poisonous lion. They attacked each other and continued for seven nights and seven days in the guise of two fiery dragons, two hawks, and two eagles, until there was never a bird ever created that they didn't make of themselves. No one could say that either was better or worse than the other. Into the sea they went then, and there

wasn't a kind of fish ever created that they didn't make of themselves for seven nights and seven days more. Then they came on
land as two warriors and fought each other with swords for a
further seven nights and days, until they both had to lie down on
the strand with the dint of cold, weariness, thirst, and hunger,
although neither of them had succeeded in getting in a blow on
the other during the twenty-one days. Then they suddenly rushed
at each other, and each drove his sword through the heart of his
opponent. Both fell down dead. When Fionn saw Céatach falling, he rushed over to draw the sword out of his heart.

"Don't pull the sword from my heart for a while yet, Fionn,"
said Céatach. "I have a few words to say to you before I die."

"I won't pull it so," answered Fionn. "But I thought that the
sooner the sword was withdrawn, the shorter would you be in
pain."

"If you drew out the sword, Fionn, my blood would come out
in one spurt. I have something to say to you."

"What is it?" asked Fionn.

"Didn't my wife ask you, when you were leaving home, to
hoist black sails if I were brought home dead?"

"Yes, she did," replied Fionn.

"And what are you going to do?" asked Céatach.

"I'll hoist the black sails," said Fionn.

"That's the worst thing you could do, Fionn," said Céatach.
"My wife has magic power, and if she blows her breath against
your ships, she won't leave a person or animal, sheep or lamb
or horse, alive within a distance of a hundred miles of any lake
or sea. She'll drown them all with the blast, for she doesn't mind
what happens to anybody, once I am dead."

"Is that all you wish to tell me?" asked Fionn.

"That's all," said Céatach.

Fionn then pulled the sword from Céatach's heart, and
Céatach died. Twenty-five men of the Fianna took the body
aboard the ship and placed it below deck. There it was kept while
they sailed home with white sails up.

Since the day they had set out for the war, Céatach's wife had
not slept a wink. She just walked the strand. At last she saw
the ships coming with white sails up. There wasn't a woman

ever under the sun who was more delighted and more proud than she, thinking that her husband was alive. When his ship was within a league of the land, Fionn leaped from her deck and came down on dry land.

"True enough it is, you deceitful thieving little Fionn," she cried. "I am without a husband, since you are ashore ahead of him, for no man ever took precedence over him since he reached manhood."

"Your husband isn't dead at all," said Fionn. "The weariness and slumber of a warrior have been on him now for three nights and days below deck, and we can't rouse him. Go aboard yourself and try to wake him."

With one jump she was on deck, and with a second one she was below deck. When she saw Céatach dead, she fell in a faint. No sooner had she reached the ship than Fionn cut the mooring rope with an axe and let it drift with the currents and waves of the great sea.

For seven nights and seven days, she swooned over the body of her husband. On the eighth day, she went on deck but could see nothing of God's creation except the sky and the sea. She gave the ship two-thirds of its full power of motion and sailing and sailed on for a day and a year. At the end of that time, she was running out of food. She saw land far away and she sailed towards it. When she reached it, she moored the ship as firmly as if it were to be there for seven years.

You never saw an island or a kingdom more wild with heather, furze, and sedge than the place she had reached. She walked along, but there wasn't a sign of a human being or animal of any kind—sheep or lamb, cow or horse—to be seen. It was a bare mountain. She decided that she would lose nothing by climbing to the top to see what was at the other side. She hadn't long to live, in any case, she thought. She made her way slowly along, almost dead from hunger and fainting very often. When she reached the top, she saw, some distance away, a ruined castle with only one room remaining. Smoke was rising from it; so she made for it and went in. There was nobody inside, although there was a nice fire burning. A table was laid in the middle of the floor and on it were three cups of tea, three prints of butter, and three loaves of bread. Being overcome with thirst, cold, and hunger, she took a bit out of each of the loaves, some butter from each of the prints, and a sup from each of the cups.

She had barely swallowed the last bite and sup when she heard somebody approaching outside the castle. Three men entered; one had lost an arm, the second had lost both arms, and the third had lost his left cheek. All three were losing blood as they came in. They went into a room that was there and returned as the three finest men on whom wind or sun had ever shone! The poor woman hid herself between the legs of the table with fear. When they sat down at the table, the eldest of the three spoke, "There's a bite taken out of my loaf, a sup out of my cup, and a piece out of my butter print."

"The same has happened to mine," said the second man.

"And the same to mine," said the third.

"Well," said the eldest man, "whether it was a man or a woman did it, he acted fairly toward the three of us. He didn't take more from one than from the others."

They started to eat their meal, and whatever glance the youngest gave toward the wall, he saw the shadow of a beautiful woman upon it. He rose from the table.

"The most beautiful woman that wind or sun has ever shone upon is here under the table," said he.

The second man took a look under the table.

"You won't have her! She's mine!" said he.

"Neither of ye will have her," said the eldest. "I'll take her!"

The three brothers started to kill one another around the floor, fighting for the beautiful woman. She stood up in an endeavor to make peace and told them that she could marry only one man.

"So, if ye leave the choice to me," said she, "I will decide the matter between ye."

"I'm agreed to that," said the eldest.

"And I," said the second.

"I too," said the third.

Each of them was hoping to win her.

"Here's what I'll do now, according to my promise," said she. "I'll marry the eldest one of ye if ye bring back to life my brother, who is lying dead in that ship below there. I saw ye getting rid of your own wounds in the room over there awhile ago."

"I'm agreed to that," said the eldest.

"And I," said the second.

"I too," said the third.

They were delighted with what she had arranged. They fetched their little pot of healing balm and their magic wand and went down to the ship. They went into the hold where Céatach was lying.

When the eldest saw the great size and huge limbs of Céatach, he said, "Upon my soul. I won't bring this fellow to life. We could do with his help, but if he opposed us, devil a bite we'd ever eat."

"I won't revive him, either," said the second.

"Nor will I," said the third.

"May God help me!" said the woman. "What cowards ye are. I am his sister, and I'm going to marry the eldest of ye. Don't ye know very well that my brother will help ye at anything ye want to do in this kingdom?"

She kept on coaxing them until they agreed to revive him. They rubbed the healing balm to him and struck him with the magic wand. Up rose Céatach, Son of the King of Cor in Ireland, as well as he had ever been. His wife knew that she need worry no longer now that her husband was alive again.

"This man is not my brother at all," said she. "He is my husband. And I give ye my hand and word that it is ye he will help as long as he stays in this kingdom."

They had seven times as great an opinion of her as they had before when they heard that—on account of the plan she had carried out to get her husband revived. They returned to the house, and you may be sure, they ate a good supper (although the devil a bite of it did they give me). Afterward they spent awhile doing feats of valor. Then when it was getting late at night, they told Céatach and his wife to go upstairs to bed. They would sleep downstairs themselves. Céatach and his wife slept upstairs until near daybreak. Then they could hear the three brothers moving about and getting ready downstairs. Céatach jumped up, ran downstairs, and put his arms around the three of them. He asked them where they were going.

"That's none of your business," they said. "You and your wife can sleep here until we come back in the evening. But we must be off. We were left here without sister or brother, father or mother, cousin or relative of any kind under God—just we three orphans. Each day, three waves of giants descend on us, trying to kill us and take possession of this place. Each day we kill them all—a wave per man. But they are all alive to attack us again next morning. So we return home badly wounded each evening."

"I'll go along with ye," said Céatach.

"Upon my soul, you won't," cried his wife.

"Indeed, I will," said Céatach.

"No, you won't," said she.

"Yes, I will."

"He can come with us to watch the fighting," said the three brothers; "but we won't ask him to take any part himself. He can just look on."

"Well, ye have no business coming home tonight if Céatach isn't with ye," said his wife.

Céatach went off with them, and they reached the battlefield just as the sun rose. Then they saw the three waves of giants coming toward them.

"We had better get to work," said the eldest brother.

"Sit down there," said Céatach. "I want to see how good a man I am still."

He forced the three brothers to sit down. Then he took his sword and attacked the three waves of giants. By noon, he had them all lying dead in one single heap.

"Come home with us now," said the brothers when the giants were killed.

"There's little use in my going home with ye today, if these giants will be all alive tomorrow," said Céatach. "Isn't it better for me to remain here and see how they come to life each night?"

"We won't face home at all," said they. "Your wife will murder us if you don't return with us."

All the same, he made them go home. When they left him, Céatach lay himself down among the bodies. Meanwhile, his wife was scolding the brothers for coming back without him. They told her that they had asked him to come home and that he had refused.

The night was foggy and raining. Just as Céatach was falling asleep before dawn, he heard a noise and jumped up. Then he saw a small hag of a woman over near the cliff. She was pushing a churn in front of her and in her hand was a little brush with which she sprinkled what was in the churn on the dead bodies of the giants. As the drops from the brush touched them, up they rose like a plague of flies in autumn.

"Little hag," shouted Céatach, "if you're on my side, I'll be all right. But if you're going to be against me, I'd better stop you now."

He rushed toward the hag and cut off the heads of those whom she had brought to life. But in all the wars he had been through from the start of his life and of all the warriors he had fought, the hag gave him a tougher battle than any.

Finally, when he was cutting off her head, the hag said, "Céatach, Son of the King of Cor in Ireland, I put it as a judgment and *geasa* upon you that you must go to the King of the Bridge and tell him that you have killed the Sow and her Litter."

"That won't be any great trouble to me," said Céatach.

Well, he made off to the King of the Bridge.

"King of the Bridge," said Céatach, "I have killed the Sow and her Litter, and here I am."

"That's the last killing you'll do forever more," said the king.

They attacked each other, but the King of the Bridge lasted only half as long as the hag.

When he was dying, he said, "Céatach, Son of the King of Cor in Ireland, I place as a judgment and *geasa* upon you to go to the King of the Church and to tell him that you have killed the King of the Bridge and the Sow and her Litter, and that you yourself have come to him."

Céatach made off the King of the Church and said to him, "King of the Church, I have killed the King of the Bridge and the Sow and her Litter, and here I am."

"That's the last killing you'll do forever more," said the king.

They fought for a long part of the day and, when the King of the Church was dying, he said, "Céatach, Son of the King of Cor from Ireland, I place as a judgment and *geasa* upon you to go to the Great Hag of the Hills and tell her that you have killed the King of the Church, the King of the Bridge, and the Sow and her Litter, and that you yourself have come to her."

"That won't be too hard to do," said Céatach.

He set off and early enough in the day he saw the hag within a hundred miles of him. He could see the whole world between her two legs, and he couldn't see anything between her and the top of the sky. The hindmost tooth in her head would do as a mast for a ship to cross to America.

He stood in terror before her, but he said to himself, "I may as well die a warrior as a coward, for you old hag can take one stride to equal three hundred of mine. Your big legs are long, and you will catch me by the back of the neck and kill me."

He went close to her and said, "Great Hag of the Hills, I have killed the King of the Church, the King of the Bridge, and the Sow and her Litter, and here I am."

"You'll never again kill anybody," said she.

Céatach and the hag fought each other for seven nights and seven days, and nobody could tell which was the better or which was the worse. On the eighth day, Céatach swung his sword and struck her near the apple of her throat and cut off her head. The head was whistling as it rose into the air, and it was humming as it fell, hoping to join the body again. But Céatach was ready. He kicked the head with his big boot and sent it across a ridge and seven acres of ground.

"'Twas well for you that you did that," said the head. "If I joined the body again, it would take more than half of the Fianna to prise me loose."

"It wasn't to let you join it again that I cut you off," said Céatach.

"I place *geasa* upon you," said the head, "to go to the Great Cat of the Cave and tell her that you have killed the Great Hag of the Hills, the King of the Church, the King of the Bridge, and the Sow and her Litter, and that you yourself have come to her. There are three hundred miles of cave at the end of the kingdom."

When Céatach reached the mouth of the cave, he went three hundred miles under the earth. The cat had not left the cave for three hundred years. On the day that Céatach entered the place, the weather was rough with storm and gale and raging seas. The cat was sitting on the middle of the hearth with its back to the fire. She had three huge humps on her back, and each of them was three times as large as the Twelve Bens. Fear and terror of the cat came over Céatach.

"I'm finished now or never," said he. "My time has come. But if I try to escape through cowardice, you will catch me and tear me to pieces. 'Tis better for me to die as a warrior than as a coward. Great Cat of the Cave," said he, "I have killed the Great Hag of the Hills, the King of the Church, the King of the Bridge, and the Sow and her Litter, and here I am!"

"Devil a person you'll ever kill again," said the cat.

She gave a jump from the hearth, attacked Céatach, tore his liver and lungs from his body, and hung them on the side rafters of the Cave. Céatach was still alive, watching the cat, sword in hand. As she attacked a second time, he noticed a skin mole on her left underside; so he lunged at it with his sword. The cat fell dead. So did Céatach. They had killed each other. Céatach happened to fall under the cat's groin between her two hind legs, and the leg under which he lay completely covered him.

A week passed. The three brothers had been searching for Céatach. Everything they came upon was dead. Nothing was alive. They found the Great Hag of the Hills dead, and finally reached the cave of the cat. They went in and traveled through it until they came upon the dead body of the cat. There was no trace of Céatach to be seen. They decided that Céatach had killed all their enemies and that they were free from trouble for the future. Their worries were over for ever they thought. But where was Céatach?

They then made up a plan that the eldest would marry Céatach's wife. If she struck him six times in every second of the day for the rest of time, it would be wrong for her, and disrespectful to her husband who had freed the kingdom for them. She refused to marry him.

As they were leaving the place, she was tearing her hair from her head and dashing her head against the walls in her sorrow. Just as they were about to mount the stairs of the cave, she fell in a faint. The three brothers returned to revive her by giving her a drink. She opened her eyes and caught sight of Céatach's boot sticking out from under the cat's groin.

"Ah! He's still there. I have found him," she cried.

"Where?" they asked.

She pointed out the tip of Céatach's boot to them. Strong though they were, they had to get a roller to lift the cat's leg off Céatach. At the end of eight days, they succeeded. They rubbed their healing balm to him and struck him with the magic wand, and up he rose as well as he had ever been.

The mistake they made, however, was to put the liver and lungs of the cat instead of his own back into Céatach's body. They made their way home. Céatach was as well as he had ever been, but he had a wild look in his eyes that he never had before. When they were half-way home, didn't a big rat run across the road from an old ruined house that was at the roadside. Céatach sprang after the rat and tried to get in through the old walls to catch it. They then remembered that it was the liver and lungs of the cat they had put back into him. So the brothers returned to the cave and took down from the side rafters the liver and lungs of Céatach. They returned to Céatach and his wife. Over to Céatach they went, opened him up, pulled out the liver and lungs of the cat, and put in his own. Then they rubbed the healing balm to him, struck him with the magic wand, and up he stood as well as he had ever been.

They returned home and held a feast which lasted for seven nights and seven days. I was there with them but, if I was, the devil a taste of the feast did they give me. All that I got from them them was paper shoes and stockings of thick milk. I threw them back at them. They were drowned, and I came safe. Not a word or news have I got from them for the past year and day.

May this company and the storyteller be seven thousand times better off a year from today. And the dear blessing of God and of the Church on the souls of the dead.

One fine day, Fionn mac Cumhaill and fourteen of his men were hunting on the top of Muisire Mountain. They had spent the whole day since sunrise there but met no game.

Late in the evening, Fionn spoke, "'Tis as well for us to face for home, men. We're catching nothing, and it will be late when we, hungry and thirsty, reach home."

"Upon my soul. We're hungry and thirsty as it is," said Conán.

They turned on their heels and went down the mountainside, but if they did, they weren't far down when a dark black fog fell on them. They lost their way and didn't know whether to go east or west. Finally they had to sit down where they were.

"I'm afraid, men, that we're astray for the evening," said Fionn. "I never yet liked a fog of this kind."

After they had sat for a while talking and arguing, whatever look Diarmaid gave around, he saw a beautiful nice lime-white house behind them.

"Come along, men, to this house over there," said he. "Maybe we'll get something to eat and drink there."

They all agreed and made their way to the house. When they entered, there was nobody before them but a wizened old man who was lying in a bent position at the edge of the hearth and a sheep which was tied along by the wall. They sat down. The old man raised his head and welcomed Fionn and his men heartily.

"By my soul," said Diarmaid to himself. "'Tisn't very likely that our thirst or hunger will be eased in this hovel."

After awhile, the old man called loudly to a young woman who was below in a room telling her to come up and get food ready for Fionn and his men. Then there walked up the floor from below, a fine strapping handsome young woman, and it didn't take her long to get food and drink ready for them. She pulled a long ample table out into the middle of the floor, spread a tablecloth on it, and laid out the dinner for the Fianna. She seated Fionn at the head of the table and set every man's meal in front of him. No sooner had each of them put the first bite of food into his mouth than the sheep which was tied along the wall stretched and broke the hard hempen tying that was holding her and rushed towards the table. She upset it by lifting one end of it and not a scrap of food was left that wasn't thrown to the floor in front of the Fianna.

"The devil take you," cried Conán. "Look at the mess you have made of our dinner, and we badly in need of it."

"Get up, Conán, and tie the sheep," said Fionn.

Conán, looking very angry at the loss of his dinner, got up against his will and walked to the sheep. He caught her by the top of the head and tried to drag her toward the wall. But if he broke his heart in the attempt, he couldn't tie her up. He stood there looking at her.

"By heavens," said he. "As great a warrior and hero as I am, here's this sheep today, and I can't tie her. Maybe someone else can?"

"Get up, Diarmaid, and tie the sheep," said Fionn.

Diarmaid stood up and tried, but if he did, he failed to tie her. Each of the fourteen men made an attempt, but it was no use.

"My shame on ye," said the old man. "To say that as great as your valor has ever been, ye can't tie an animal as small as a sheep to the side of the wall with a bit of rope."

He got up from the edge of the hearth and hobbled down the floor. As he went, six pintsful of ashes fell from the backside of his trousers, because he had been so long lying on the hearth. He took hold of the sheep by the scruff of the head, pulled her easily in to the wall, and tied her up. When the Fianna saw him tie the sheep, they were seized with fear and trembling, seeing that he could do it after themselves had failed, brave and all though they were. The old man returned to his place by the fire.

"Come up here and get some food ready for Fionn and his men," he called to the young woman.

She came up from the room again, and whatever knack or magic she had, she wasn't long preparing new food to set before them.

"Start eating now, men; ye'll have no more trouble," said the old man. "This dinner will quench your thirst and hunger."

When they had eaten and were feeling happy with their stomachs full, they drew their chairs back from the table. Whatever peering around Fionn had—he was always restless—he looked toward the room and saw the young woman sitting on a chair there. He got a great desire to talk to her for a while. He went down to the room to her.

"Fionn mac Cumhaill," said she; "you had me once and you won't have me again."

He had to turn on his heel and go back to his chair. Diarmaid then went down to her, but he got the same answer; so did each of the rest of the Fianna. Oisín was the last to try, but she said the same thing to him. She took him by the hand and led him up the floor till she stood in front of the Fianna.

"Fionn mac Cumhaill," said she; "ye were ever famous for strength and agility and prowess, and still each of you failed to tie the sheep. This sheep is not of the usual kind. She is Strength. And that old man over there is Death. As strong as the sheep was, the old man was able to overcome her. Death will overcome ye in the same way, strong and all as ye are. I myself am a planet sent by God, and it is God who has placed this hovel here for ye. I am Youth. Each of you had me once but never will again. And now, I will give each of you whatever gift he asks me for."

Fionn was the first to speak, and he asked that he might lose the smell of clay, which he had had ever since he sinned with a woman who was dead.

Diarmaid said that what he wanted was a love spot on his body, so that every young woman who saw it would fall in love with him.

Oscar asked for a thong which would never break for his flail.

Conán asked for the power of killing hundreds in battle, while he himself would be invulnerable.

On hearing this, Diarmaid spoke.

"Alas!" said he. "If Conán is given the power of killing hundreds, for heaven's sake, don't let him know how to use it. He's a very strong, but a very vicious, man, and if he loses his temper, he won't leave one of the Fianna alive."

And that left Conán as he was ever afterward. He never knew how to use this power that he had, except once at the Battle of Ventry, when he looked at the enemy through his fingers and slew every one of them.

Each of the Fianna in turn asked for what he wanted. I don't know what some of them asked for, but Oisín asked for the grace of God. They say that he went to the Land of Youth and remained there until Saint Patrick came to Ireland, so that he would get the proper faith and knowledge of God and extreme unction when he died. He got them too, for when he returned to Ireland, Saint Patrick himself baptized him and anointed him before he died.

· *15* · *The Coming of Oscar*

One day Fionn and the great hosts of the Fianna went out hunting. They went along and happened to be near the house of Crónán mac Imlit. Crónán was an old man who had spent about twenty years in bed. At any rate, he did not like the Fianna for coming so close to his house when hunting. He had three daughters.

When they heard the noise, Crónán said, "Run out and see who is coming."

The daughters ran out, and when they came back, they told the old man in the bed that it was the Fianna of Ireland, hunting.

"Take those three sticks of dog briar and the three magic hanks outside the door," said Crónán, "and start winding them anti-sunwise. As soon as the Fianna see the work ye are engaged in, each one of them will fall under a magic spell."

They did so, and when the Fianna stood to watch the work, one by one they came under the spell. The daughters went in and told the old man in the bed what they had done.

"Ye have done well, my daughters," said he. "Drag them in now into the Room of the Everlasting Drop and leave them there until ye have time to cut off their heads tomorrow."

They dragged in the Fianna and left them lying under the

poisonous drops, which fell on them constantly. They were in a bad way with nobody to help them.

Goll mac Mórna was not with the Fianna that day; he had remained behind to mind the house where they lived.

"Fionn," said Conán, "if we could bring the *barra bua* close to you, do you think you could play it?"

"I might," said Fionn.

They brought the *barra bua* close to him, and he played it. It resounded seven miles through the hills and seven miles through the lowlands; it was heard by the Beggarman of Kilcorney, the Farmer of Kilkenny, and by Goll mac Mórna on the green field at Howth.

"Heavens!" said Goll. "That is the *barra bua* of Fionn mac Cumhaill. If he is at a banquet or great feast, he wishes me to be there to get my share. But if he is in any difficulty or strait, what more fitting than that I should go to rescue him?"

He put on his suit of armor and off he rushed at great speed. He was swifter than a stream rushing into a river or the wind in a glen; he used to catch up with the wind that was ahead of him, but the wind at his back could not overtake him. He finally reached the place where the Fianna were tied by magic. Crónán's daughters were out watching, and they ran in to their father.

"Oh! There's a very big man coming. You could see the whole world between his two legs and nothing at all between his head and the sky."

"Off out with ye," cried the old man. "Maybe ye can put him under the spell too."

They ran out and started the same magic trick, but if they did, it was no use. Goll ran toward them, and the two youngest attacked him with swords. The fight didn't last long for Goll cut the pair of them in two with the same blow of his sword.

"I have a notion that I'd beat you if you wrestled me," said the eldest daughter.

"I'd like nothing better," said Goll; "for I was used to wrestling with the sons of noblemen on the greensward."

They both took firm unbreakable holds: a hand below, a hand above, and a hand at the top of the wrestling. Anyone who would travel from the south of Ireland to the north of Ireland to watch a battle or hard fight should come to see these two. They used to make the hard place soft and the soft place hard. They used to draw wells of spring water up through the rocks. They used to squeeze the marrow from the thick ends of each other's bones. And ducks could swim in their blood. After a while, Goll lifted the woman off the ground and held her legs upward. He then struck the ground with her and buried her waist deep in the rock.

"Your head off **you**, old hag," he shouted.

"Don't!" she cried. "Don't cut off my head or limbs. If you do, there's nobody alive to free the Fianna for you. I have them under a magic spell. Let me go free, and I'll free them."

"I'd spare your head for even the worst of the Fianna, Caol an Iarainn," said Goll.

He pulled her out of the rock, and she went into the room and released all of the Fianna from the spell. They went away sore and bruised and wounded. The woman, sighing heavily, went in to the old man.

"What ails you, daughter?" he asked.

"I'll tell you," said she.

She said that of all the blows which had ever been struck in any battle, the blow with which Goll had severed her sisters in two could never be delivered by another warrior.

"I wrestled with him then," said she; "but if I did, he got the upper hand of me and I had to let all the Fianna go. That's what makes me sigh."

"And what would satisfy you now?" asked her father.

"Nothing but revenge on the Fianna," said she.

"Bend down there under the bed and see would you get an old sword there."

She bent down and pulled an old rusty sword from under the bed.

"Knock it against the flagstone outside," said Crónán.

When she struck it against the stone, a shower of rust fell from it, and the scream that it gave could be heard in the eastern world. She knocked it against the stone again, and the same thing happened.

"Do it a third time," shouted the old man.

She did so, and the same shower of rust and the same scream that could be heard in the eastern world came.

"Follow the Fianna now," said Crónán, "and take every short-cut until you catch up on them. Place the big toe of your foot against the big toe of Fionn's foot and challenge him to single combat. You'll be able to kill every one of the Fianna who was under your spell. But don't fight Goll mac Mórna, the man who wasn't under your spell before."

She set out and overtook them as her father had directed. She placed the big toe of her foot against the big toe of Fionn's foot and challenged him to single combat.

"I don't feel well enough to fight you," said Fionn. "Oisín," said he to his son, "will you fight this hag on my behalf?"

"I'm not able to," said Oisín. "I'm badly wounded."

"Will you fight her, Lúgh of the Long Hand?" asked Fionn.

"Upon my word," said Lúgh. "I've had my fill of the hag's bonds. Your own flesh and blood has refused you. To say I wouldn't."

At that, Conán spoke.

"Offer a reward to Goll, Fionn," said he. "He'll fight the hag."

"I will, and welcome," said Fionn. "What rewards do you want, Goll? I'll give you anything you ask for."

"I'll take you at your word," said Goll. "Here's what I want: your eldest daughter in marriage, my shield to hang above yours, and the marrow of the bones."

"You'll have them all," said Fionn, "except my eldest daughter in marriage against her will. If she's willing to marry you, you'll get her from me."

"How will we know whether she is or not?" asked Goll.

"Let us send for her," said Conán.

They asked Barefoot Céirín, the swiftest among them, to go for Fionn's eldest daughter. He did, and it wasn't very long until he came back with her.

Fionn asked her the question, "Which man of the seven battalions of the Fianna would you prefer to marry?"

"Goll mac Mórna," said she; "If my father is willing."

"That settles the matter," said Goll.

He and the woman attacked each other with their swords. With each blow of his sword that Goll struck her, sparks flew from her as they would from a quartz stone and a piece broke from his sword. Each blow the woman struck at Goll went into the bone.

The Fianna saw how things were going and shouted to Goll. "What a disgrace after all your brave deeds and fine actions that you should die at the hands of a hag like her."

This rebuke gave Goll new energy. The noble blood rose to the uppermost part of his breast. He drew a mighty blow with his sword at the woman and sent her head in splinters around the field. The Fianna raised joyful shouts and made their way home proudly. Goll's marriage to Fionn's daughter did not take place for a week after their return home. They got married when they had all recovered, and it was the greatest marriage ever to take place in Ireland they said. It lasted almost until a child was born and baptized.

One of the Fianna used to stay up each night to guard the house. It was Oisín's turn this night when in to him came an old half-blind red-haired woman.

"Will you play a game with me?" she asked.

"I don't mind," said Oisín.

They began to play, and if they did, the woman won the game. She was the daughter of the King of Greece and had been sent to the Fianna in the guise of an old woman to have a son by one of them. The King of Greece was very anxious always to have some of the stock of the Fianna in his own country. Oisín and the old woman spent the night together, and she left him before the day dawned.

After some time, she gave birth to a son in Greece. What he didn't grow by day, he grew by night, and soon he was ready to go to school. He and the other boys were always playing tricks on one another, but he was too strong and active for them all. One day, when he was about thirteen or fourteen years of age, in the course of some rough play between himself and another boy, he struck a blow and broke the other boy's jaw. The boy called him names.

"I have only myself to blame," said he. "I should have kept

away from you. We all know your mother, but nobody knows who your father is."

This hurt the other boy, and he refused to go to school that day. He returned home to his mother.

"I want you to tell me, Mother. Who is my father?" he said.

"Oh, run off to school," said she. "What does it matter to you? Someone has made you angry, I see. Go off to school."

"I won't go to school till you tell me who my father is," he answered.

"You should have more sense," said she. "You have a father of whom you need have no shame."

"I'm giving you a third chance to tell me who my father is," said he. "If you don't, I'll cut off your head."

"Oisín, son of Fionn in Ireland, is your father."

"Well," said he, "I won't eat three meals at the same table or sleep three nights in the same bed, until I see him. Goodbye now, Mother."

"May bad luck go with you," said his mother. "I lost my shame through you, and now I haven't even you."

He turned his back on her, got on board an old boat, and set his course for Ireland. When he reached Ireland, he wandered here and there not knowing which direction to follow. He met a girl and started to make enquiries of her.

"Can you tell me what is fear?" he asked.

"Don't be bothering me," she replied. "How do I know what it is?"

He struck her a blow with his palm and turned her face backward.

"That's fear for you," said he.

He left her there. Soon he met an old man.

"Can you tell me, my honest man, what fear is?" he asked.

"I can't tell you, for fear was never put on me," said the old man. "But I want to tell you this; do you see that big house on the hill?"

"I do," said the boy.

"There's a man in that house who knows what fear is. If you care to go up to him, he'll tell you the whole story."

"Who is he?" asked the boy. "What's his name?"

"We call him the Knight without Hair or Laugh ever since he learned what fear is."

"If that girl a while ago had the sense to tell me something like that, her head wouldn't be twisted the way it is," said the boy.

The boy left the old man there and went off to the house on the hill. He walked in boldly. The knight was eating his dinner, and his sword lay on the table beside him. The boy took up the sword.

"Tell me, knight," said he; "What is fear?"

"Have patience, boy," said the knight. "Lay down that sword. Food becomes before storytelling. Eat first, and then I'll tell you, as well as I can, what fear it."

The boy laid down the sword and sat down to eat with the knight. As soon as they had finished, the boy took up the sword again.

"Tell me now what fear is," said he.

"Put away the sword and sit down. Then I'll tell you," said the knight.

The boy laid down the sword once more and sat near the knight to hear his story.

"I was living here with my three sons," said the knight; "three men as fine as you'd get anywhere. One Christmas Day, we were eating our dinner here at this table when we saw a hare out there on the lawn. We left the dinner, and out went the four of us after the hare. He ran off east over the field with me and my three sons after him, and he never stopped till he went into a *lios* to the east of us. We ran in after him, but if we did, we couldn't see any sign of him. All that we found there was an old man sitting on a stool near the fire. We weren't long there when in came twelve *gruagaigh*, each carrying a boar on his shoulder.

"'What brought you here, knight?' they asked.

"I got afraid and started to make excuses, as best I could.

"'Oh, there's no harm done!' they said. 'But you'll have to fall in with the custom in these parts.'

"'What custom?' I asked.

"'You'll have to shave the bristles off one of these boars.

We'll all take a hand in the work. And then we'll boil the twelve of them. And when they're boiled, you'll get a boar to eat, and what you can't eat of it will be forced down your throat with a thick stick.'

"The shaving of the bristles started, and the boars were soon prepared by the *gruagaigh*. They were put down to boil, but when they were cooked, neither myself nor my sons could eat a bite of our boar. The *gruagaigh* caught hold of the boar, tore it in three, and rammed it down the throats of my three sons till they were choked to death.

"'Don't do anything to the old knight himself,' said the old man in the corner. 'Let him go if he promises never to come here again.'

"They kept the bodies of my three dead sons and let me go. I came home here. My hair fell out, and I haven't laughed ever since—that's why they call me the Knight without Hair or Laugh. And to make matters worse, each Christmas Day since that time, the same hare comes out there on the lawn to torment me and remind me of what happened."

"Upon my word," said the boy. "Only for the *geasa* that are on me, I'd stay till Christmas to see the hare."

"What *geasa* are on you?" asked the knight.

"I can't eat three meals on the same table or sleep three nights in the same bed until I see a certain man that's in Ireland," said the boy.

"Don't let that worry you," said the knight. "Christmas is only a couple of months away, and if you wish to stay here, I'll give you different tables and beds during that time."

"I'll stay so," said the boy.

He stayed with the knight from then to Christmas, and he thought that Christmas Day would never come. When it came, he and the knight were sitting at the table eating their dinner; the boy kept looking out the window to see if he would see the hare.

"Great heavens! Do you see him out there?" cried the knight.

The boy looked out, and there was the hare.

"He's there all right," said he, catching up the sword.

"Come on! We'll follow him!" said he to the knight.

"Is it me?" cried the knight. "If you gave me all Ireland, I wouldn't follow that hare."

"I won't or give you half of Ireland either," said the boy. "Nor will I give you much time. If you don't hurry, I'll cut the head off you. "

There was no help for it. The knight got up, crying like a child, and followed the boy, who ran swiftly out. The hare ran off toward the *lios* and barely escaped into it as the boy cut off his tail. The boy glanced around to see was the knight coming; he was, at a very slow pace.

"Hurry up, knight," said the boy. "Now, you go in first."

"I won't! I got enough of it already."

"If you don't, I'll take the head off you," said the boy.

The knight had to enter first. The boy followed and started to search for the hare inside. An old man was sitting on a stool.

After searching everywhere, the boy said, "Tell me, old man, did you see a hare coming in here?"

"I didn't," said the old man.

"Stand up!" said the boy, taking him by the arm and lifting him off the stool. "Maybe 'tis under you somewhere he is."

There was a pool of blood on the stool under the old man. The boy looked at it.

"There's no doubt, you old rascal, but you had active legs under you," said he.

Before the old man could say anything, in trooped twelve *gruagaigh*, each bearing a boar on his shoulder. They welcomed the knight.

"We thought you had enough fright not to come here again," they said.

"I wouldn't have come, either, only for the boy," said the knight. "He made me come."

"Well, you know our custom here?"

"I do, well," said the knight.

They threw down the boars to shave off the bristles. The knight started to shave his own.

The boy said, "Sit down! You're too noble to go shaving boars for the boors of this house."

The knight took a seat. The boy went to work so quickly that he would have twenty boars shaved before one of the *gruagaigh* would have one. The twelve boars were put down to boil, and when they were cooked, one was given to the knight and the boy. They ate hardly any of it, while the *gruagaigh* devoured theirs ravenously.

"I can't eat any more of mine," said one of the *gruagaigh* after a while.

"Can't you, now?" said the boy, taking up a piece of the boar and stuffing it down the *gruagach's* throat with a thick stick.

None of the *gruagaigh* could finish his boar, and the boy rammed what they had left down their throats.

"Now, old man," said he, "I suppose you got plenty of meat from these while you are here; still, you'll get more from me, as fine as you ever got."

He took hold of him to stuff a piece of boar down his throat.

"Oh, shame! Don't!" cried the old man. "For if you choke me, the knight will never see his sons again."

"I'd like to see them too," said the boy. "The knight has great praise of them, but I haven't, although I've never seen them, seeing that the boors of this house were too strong for them. Get the three young fellows for me, at any rate, till I take a look at them."

The old man got a small magic wand and with it touched each of three little stools that were beside the fire. The knight's three sons rose up as well as they had ever been save that their shins were rather speckled from being too near the fire. The boy looked at them.

"They're not bad at all," said he to the knight, "if the ashes were rubbed off them. Now, I won't be with you always; so I'll finish off this old man, fearing he'd play any tricks on you when I'm gone."

He took the old man by the two legs and hit his head against the wall.

"I wouldn't waste the day killing him any other way," said he.

They all returned to the knight's house. The knight was over-joyed.

"What a pity!" cried the boy. "I forgot to ask that old man to put your hair back on you."

"I'm not worrying about that," said the knight. "I may be a knight without hair, but I'm not a knight without a laugh."

The knight and his three sons wouldn't let the boy go away for a couple of months. No fear that he broke his *geasa* either! There was ample accommodation for him.

He finally left them and set out to find where Oisín was. It was summer when he came close to where the Fianna were. He reached their dwelling one fine day when the Fianna were out hunting on the hills. Only the women were at home. He went in and was looking around at all the fine things when he noticed that Goll's shield was hanging above that of Fionn. Oisín's shield was below them.

"Who's the chief man here?" he asked the women.

"Fionn mac Cumhaill," they replied.

"And why isn't his shield on top?"

"Oh, that's some arrangement between himself and Goll; some reward that Goll won."

"It won't be any longer so," said the boy.

He put Fionn's shield on top, Oisín's under it, and Goll's lowest of all. When evening came, he walked outside. The gardens were full of all kinds of fruit, and he spent the evening picking and eating it. As night fell, he lay down under the shade of the trees and fell asleep. When the Fianna returned from the chase, whatever glance Goll gave, he noticed that the shields were changed.

"Which of ye was fiddling about with the shields?" he asked the women.

"'Twasn't any of us," they told him. "'Twas a boy who came in here today."

"A good job for him that I wasn't here," said Goll.

They went off hunting again next morning. Late in the day, the boy woke up from his sleep. He picked more of the fruit and went into the house. He looked at the shields.

"Which of ye changed these shields since I fixed them?" he asked the women.

"Hold your tongue, boy. 'Twasn't we but Goll that changed

them last night when he came home, and 'twas a good job for you that you weren't here before him."

He rearranged the shields. Then he went out for a walk around the gardens, and when evening came, he fell asleep under the trees. When the Fianna returned at night, the first thing Goll did was to look at the shields. His own was at the bottom.

"Why did ye arrange the shields this way?" he asked the women.

"'Twasn't we did it but the boy," they replied. "We told him he was lucky not to be here before you when you came home, but he said that he wasn't a bit afraid of you."

"'Twas well for him that I didn't see him," said Goll. "If it happens again, someone will suffer."

Next morning, the Fianna went off hunting again, and whatever time the boy awoke, he went into the house. He saw that his arrangement of the shields had been upset. He again set Fionn's shield on top, Oisín's under it, and Goll's lowest of all.

"If Goll catches sight of you, he'll kill you," the women told him.

"He'll see me all right, for I'm going to wait for him," said the boy.

And so he did. He didn't go out at all that night, but stayed within until they came home. The first thing Goll did when they came in was to look at his shield. It was down below.

"Who did that?" he asked.

"I did," said the boy, jumping up.

"Why did you do it?"

"Who is the chief of the Fianna?" asked the boy.

"Fionn mac Cumhaill," answered Goll.

"Then Fionn's shield must be on top."

"No," said Goll.

The argument started between them, and soon they got stuck in each other. The Fianna had to separate them. When peace was made, Oisín walked up to the corner and sat down.

"Is there any man here named Oisín?" asked the boy.

"There is," he was told.

"Where is he?"

"That's he above there in the corner."

The boy went up to him.

"I want to ask you had you ever a son?" he asked.

"Ah, leave me alone. I hadn't," said Oisín.

"I'm asking you again had you ever a son?" said the boy.

"I never had a son anywhere as far as I can remember," said Oisín.

"If you hide the truth from me the third time, the whole lot of the Fianna won't protect you from me," said the boy.

"I never had a son," said Oisín. "And still, maybe I had."

He started to tell about his meeting with the old woman.

"That's all I know about it," said Oisín.

"Well, I'm your son, then," said the boy.

At that, Fionn grasped the boy's hand.

"I name you Oscar, son of Oisín, son of Fionn," he said. "For there's no doubt that you are an *oscartha* youth."

Every honor and attention was paid to the boy, and they were all very proud of him. The boy told them that his mother was the daughter of the King of Greece.

"When I found out who my father was," said he, "I couldn't rest until I saw him. Now that I am here with ye, I suppose it is here I must stay."

"And 'tis welcome you are!" shouted the Fianna with one voice.

He remained with them and improved day by day. He was very eager for sports and deeds of valor. He took down Goll's shield and put it at the bottom with Fionn's on top and Oisín's next.

The only matter of contention remaining was the marrow of the bones. Whenever any one of the Fianna had picked the meat off a bone at table, he had to throw the bone to Goll, wherever he happened to be seated. Young Oscar wasn't too pleased at this.

"Why are ye playing at throwing the bones about? Ye'll take the eyes out of one another," he said.

"Maybe you don't know," said they, "that Goll must get the marrow of the bones as a reward for killing the daughter of Crónán mac Imlit?"

"I don't care whom he killed," said Oscar. "He won't get the marrow of my bones. Even if I gave it to him, he wouldn't thank me. Nor will he get the marrow of any other bones that I see being thrown about."

He took hold of the next bone he saw being thrown to Goll and grasped it by the middle. Goll took hold of the bone by both ends. They started to pull and the bone broke. Goll took the two ends, and Oscar kept the middle—it was in it that all the marrow was.

Things went on fairly well between them; yet Goll had no great liking for Oscar. They were always trying to gain an advantage over each other.

"Why don't ye wrestle each other?" asked Fionn. "Whoever loses must yield place to the other."

"I'm satisfied," said Goll.

"Now," said Fionn one morning soon afterward, "ye had better have that bout of wrestling."

They went down some distance from the house.

"Ye must go by yourselves, and let the best man win," said Fionn.

Fionn didn't want the Fianna to be present, because they were divided into two camps: the Sons of Baoiscin and the Sons of Mórna; and he feared that trouble might start between them over the wrestling. Just after the two had left, Fionn had second thoughts.

"I have done wrong," said he. "Goll is angry, and Oscar is too young. Goll will harm the boy when none of us is there to protect him. I'll go down to them myself, but the rest of ye must stay here."

As he was on his way down toward the wrestling, Fionn met Goll coming back.

"Well, did ye wrestle?" asked Fionn.

"We did," said Goll.

"How did the boy do?"

"The boy will be good," said Goll.

"How long could you stand his grasp?" asked Fionn.

"Only as long as it would take me to run around the house, and run quickly at that," said Goll.

"I see," said Fionn.

He parted with Goll and went on down to where Oscar was.

Fionn found him looking up at the trees and picking fruit from them.

"Well, boy, you and Goll have been wrestling, I suppose?" said Fionn.

"We have," said the boy.

"How did Goll do, or do you think is he any good?"

"Goll is good and strong," said the boy.

"How long could you stand his grasp?"

"That's a foolish question," said the boy. "I could stand it as long as it would take you to go around the world, or until sleep or hunger would come over me."

"I see," said Fionn.

From that day on, Goll was always a bit afraid of the boy Oscar, although he was not allowed to carry any fighting weapons. Goll didn't trust him. Still, he saw that the boy was well intentioned. Oscar soon became the best man among the Fianna, but his father, Oisín, and his grandfather, Fionn, were afraid to let him catch hold of a sword or go into battle or any place where he would be in danger of being killed. They knew that a better man than Oscar had never before joined their ranks.

That's how Oscar came to the Fianna. And that's how Goll fought the great fight with Crónán's daughters and won Fionn's daughter by killing the eldest.

·16· *Cúchulainn and the Smith's Wife*

There was a king's son one time, and his name was Cúchulainn. He spent a lot of his time hunting on the mountain. One day while hunting, he broke his sword. He took it home with him and brought it to a blacksmith to mend it.

"You must have it mended by tomorrow," he said. "I can't do without it."

"I can't do it as quickly as that," said the smith. "You must wait for your turn. I have a lot of other work to do before yours. I will fix the sword for you when your turn comes."

"Well, I must have my sword. I can't do without it," said Cúchulainn.

"I'll tell you what I'll do," said the smith. "I'll fix your sword for you tomorrow, if you tell me a story while I'm doing it."

"I'll tell you a story," said Cúchulainn; "but there mustn't be any woman listening to me."

Next morning, the smith and his helper were at the forge when Cúchulainn arrived. The smith lived only a short distance away.

"Run up to my house," said the smith to the helper; "and bring me a handful of straw. When I am mending this sword, I must make it red-hot; so I need a handful of straw to sprinkle some water on it to cool it."

"I'll go," said the boy; "but he mustn't start the story until I come back."

"Never fear. I won't tell a word of it till you return," said Cúchulainn.

When the boy went up to the house, the smith's wife asked him what he wanted.

"The master sent me for a handful of straw to sprinkle water on a sword with," said he. "He's just starting to work on it, and I must hurry. Cúchulainn is going to tell us a story, and a fine one, I'm thinking."

"Everlasting Virgin! What a pity I'm not with ye to hear it," said the woman.

"You have no chance of being there," said the boy. "Cúchulainn said that if any woman was present, he wouldn't tell the story at all."

"Do you know what you'll do?" said she. "Take the band off that sheaf of straw over there, and I'll go into the middle of it. You can take down the whole sheaf with me inside in it and put it in the corner of the forge. He won't know then that there's any woman there while he's telling the story. And I'll be good to you for ever more, if you do that," said she.

"If they happen to notice you, I don't know what'll happen," said the boy. "But I'll do it for you."

He opened the band that was on the sheaf and loosened out the straw. The smith's wife lay down in the middle of it. The boy took the sheaf on his shoulder and carried it back to the forge.

"Why did you bring all that straw?" asked the smith. "All I asked you to bring was a small handful; that would do."

"I'll bring the rest of it back later on," said the boy. "I was in a hurry not to miss any of the story."

"All right," said the smith.

He shut the door of the forge then and started to work on the sword. Cúchulainn then began his story.

"I am a king's son," said he, "and wanted nothing better every day than to be hunting with my dog and gun and sword. There was a harbor of the sea below my father's castle, and I used to go down to the shore every day, looking about me. There was a fine strand there, and one day when I was there, I noticed the tracks of some animal. They were the biggest I had ever seen. I was looking at the marks and wondering what had made them; I followed them along the strand, and I couldn't make out what kind of an animal had made them. I stood for a while, looking towards the east, and what should I see coming in my direction but the biggest man I had ever laid eyes on, driving a bullock in front of him. I knew that he would come past where I was; so I ran up the strand and hid myself behind a large rock. I was afraid of him, for I didn't know what kind of giant he was. He kept on driving the bullock toward me, until he was abreast of where I was.

"'You small fellow up there,' he shouted. 'Come down here a while. I want you.'

"I knew that he had seen me, but I was afraid to move. He gave two other shouts, and then I had to go down to him.

"'Stand back there for awhile,' said he. 'I'm going to kill this bullock.'

"He pulled a mallet out of his pocket and struck the bullock a blow between the two eyes, and it fell on the strand.

"He drew its blood, and when it was dead he said, 'Go up to the top of the strand and collect some firewood. I have a pot here, and we'll boil this bullock in it and eat our fill. 'Tis hard I have earned my share. Before you go, tell me did you ever see any man as big as I am?'

"'I didn't, or any two men together,' I said. 'You're the biggest man I ever saw.'

"'Well, I want you to know,' said he, 'that the man I stole this bullock from is twice my size. I have spent the last week trying to steal the bullock, and 'twas only last night I succeeded. If he follows me and comes on me before I sleep awhile—I haven't closed an eye for a week—I'm certain that he'll kill me with one blow. But don't you worry. Run up and collect some firewood, so that we can eat our fill.'

"I started to collect the firewood and got together all I could, while the big man was skinning the bullock down below me. You never saw anything like the job he made of it. He shouted to me to bring down the wood I had collected, and I did.

"'You miserable wretch,' he cried. 'Is that all you have got? I must go up myself to help you.'

"He ran up with me to the top of the strand, and in one sweep he took all the wood that was there between bushes and everything else. The two of us went down again to where the bullock was. He made a big fire with wood, put the whole carcass into the pot, and placed it on the fire. When the meat was boiled, he gave me a quarter of it and he himself started to devour the other three. I ate as much as I could, and the quarter was so big you'd hardly notice the bit I took off at all. I looked over at him, and he had the three quarters eaten.

"'What's wrong with you, or why aren't you eating?' said he.

"I said I had eaten my fill; I didn't want any more.

"'You miserable wretch!' said he. 'Give me what you have left, and I'll eat it myself!'

"I gave it to him—you wouldn't miss what I had taken out of it—and he ate the whole lot. He lay back on the strand then and asked me to bring the pot and pour the soup into his mouth. I told him I couldn't lift the pot, it was so big. So he stretched out his hand and helped me to lift it toward his mouth, and he swallowed every single drop that was in it!

"'What would that remind you of?' he asked.

"'I never saw anything like it before!' I replied. 'When the soup was going down your gullet, it made noise like a big river on a day of heavy flood!'

" 'Well, I'm full now,' said he; 'but I'm afraid that I'll pay dearly for it.'

" 'Now,' said he, 'the man that I stole the bullock from will come after me to try to catch me. He'll succeed too, I'm thinking, and if he comes on me before I have a snatch of sleep, he'll kill me with the first blow. I have eaten my fill, and if I could sleep a little now, I might be able for him. You must stay here and keep a watch out for him, while I sleep; and if you see any man coming as big as I am, or bigger, you must wake me.'

" 'Everlasting Virgin!' I said. 'How can I wake you from the sleep that'll be on you?'

" ' 'Twill be heavy, all right,' said he. 'If you can't wake me in any other way, put that iron bar over there into the fire and have it red-hot. When you see him coming close along the strand, shove the red-hot iron up my nostril, and I'll wake up.'

"With that, he went fast asleep. I put the iron in the fire and stood near it, keeping an eye along the strand. It wasn't long till I saw something in the distance; at first it looked like a big cloud low in the sky; it kept on moving toward me, and then I saw that it was a person of some kind. I ran to the big man to wake him, but 'twas no use. So I shoved the hot iron up his nostril, and he woke up.

" 'Where is he?' he shouted.

" 'Over there to the east!' said I. 'He'll be here any minute!'

"The giant came up near us.

" 'You dirty thief!!' he roared. 'You thought you'd escape! 'Twas daring of you to steal my bullock. But I'll make small bits of you for it!'

"They made for each other, and you may call it a fight! If anyone was getting the worst of it, I'd say 'twas my own man; I could see that he was weakening. If I was to help anybody, I knew I should give a hand to my own man; so I caught up a good axe that I had with me, and started to hack at the legs of the other below the knees. I kept on at it until he felt me.

" 'You miserable wretch,' he cried; 'you are scratching me!'

"With that, he wiped me off with his hand and knocked me on the strand. When I recovered, I started to hack his legs again.

" 'If you don't stop that,' roared the giant, 'you'll pay dearly for it.'

"I hacked away. At last, the giant put his hand down, caught hold of my head, and dragged me up under his belt. There I was, hanging at his hip, and my feet couldn't reach the ground at all. My little dog had been with me, and when he saw me hanging under the belt unable to free myself, he started to jump up and bite at it. After a time, he succeeded in cutting it with his teeth, and I fell to the ground. When I came to myself, I started to hack at his legs again. As soon as he felt me, he put his hand down again, caught me by the head, and threw me as far as he could. Where should I land but right inside the horn of the bullock."

"Ah! So that's why they call you the Hound of the Horn," cried the woman who was in the middle of the sheaf.

"May the devil take you!" roared Cúchulainn rising from his seat and making for the sheaf. "Didn't I tell you," said he to the smith, "that no woman was to hear my story?"

He would have killed the woman, only for the boy protecting her.

"If you had kept silent, you would have heard the finest story that was ever told!" said Cúchulainn. "Now I have done with ye. That's the end."

They went by the ford, and I went by the stepping-stones. They were drowned, and I came safe.

· 17 · Young Conall of Howth

There were four provinces in Ireland long ago, and they were called Munster, Leinster, Connacht, and Ulster. There was a high king over each province, and other kings under him. Each high king had counselors, and every year they all came together at a meeting house to make laws. Then the high kings signed them.

On one of those days when they were all seated together, a young fellow walked in the door and handed a letter to the man who was nearest to him. He read it and passed it on to the man next to him, and so the letter passed from one person to another until it came back to the same place. Then the high king of Leinster spoke, "I think that it is high time that ye should all have read the letter, and if ye are to give any answer to the messenger, ye had better do so and not keep him standing here."

The messenger had come from a distant country which was being attacked by invaders to ask for help against them.

"I'll go," said the king of Howth, "and take a band of men with me. If any others of ye are going to give help, tell the messenger so."

None of the others spoke, or if they did, the story doesn't say so. The king of Howth had three fine warriors of sons.

"You are to put my crown on your head now and lay down the laws as I have done," said he to his eldest son. "Be just to everybody, and the whole province will be thankful to you. Especially see that the poor get their full rights."

"I won't take the crown," said the eldest son. "I'm active and brave, and I'll go with you."

"You take it then," said the king to the second son.

"I won't," said he. "I'll go wherever ye go, and we'll be together, for I'm active and brave."

"Will you take it, Conall?" said the king to his youngest son.

"I will," replied Conall.

"Now, Conall," said the king, "don't change any of the laws I have made. Leave them just as I have laid them down. And don't have the misfortune of ever even thinking of being unjust to a poor man."

Conall was listening, but if he was, he didn't say, "That's good!" or "That's bad!"

"And, if you get the notion to marry, Conall, before I return," continued his father, "you have my permission. Then the whole kingdom will be yours. On the day that you make up your mind to marry, I want you to go out to the fence of the courtyard and look around you as far as your eye can reach. You will find a wife to suit you within that range of territory. And I want you to take the advice of your counselors."

Conall didn't say "Good!" or "Bad!" but let his father talk on.

The king set out with his two sons and a band of men and reached the country where the fighting was taking place. From the day they arrived, the enemy did not advance a foot; neither did they yield a foot, although up to that time nothing could stop them.

After a time, Conall decided to marry, and if he did, it wasn't to his counselors that he went for any advice about it. He went off to his father's wise man and asked him could he find out where the most beautiful young woman in the whole country lived.

"I'll search my books," said the wise man.

A few days later, he went to Conall.

"I can't find any young woman in the country who is more beautiful than the daughter of the king of Ulster," said he.

Conall got ready, and I'm thinking, he took a good lot of food with him in his pocket for the journey. He mounted his horse and never stopped until he reached Ulster. As he was going toward the king's castle, he came upon a house some distance from it, and as he didn't want to be burdened with his horse at the castle, he approached the house. He went to the door and saluted the man of the house. The man replied, and Conall asked him if he could make room for his horse for awhile, and he would be well rewarded.

"I can make room for your horse and welcome," said the man. "And you'll get a place yourself also, if you wish to stay."

The horse was stabled, and Conall spent the night at the farmer's house, if he was a farmer—he was something like that, in any case.

He talked with the farmer for he wanted to find out about the young woman. The farmer gave a very good account of her. She was there all right, the daughter of the king, a fine beautiful girl who was as friendly to the poor as she was to the highest in the land.

"That's a good character you have given her," said Conall.

"I couldn't say anything different about the girl," said the farmer.

They ate their breakfast next morning, and Conall set out for the castle of the high king of Ulster. The daughter was upstairs in

the *grianán*, the highest story of the castle, with twelve women
minding her. There shouldn't be any thirst or hunger or dirt
on her! Conall walked around the lawn in front of the castle,
as he didn't wish to announce himself until somebody would
come to speak to him. It wasn't long until one of the women
happened to look out the window, and she saw the young man
walking on the lawn. She went and told the princess that the
finest young man she had ever laid eyes on was outside on the
lawn.

"But he's very small," added the woman.

"That's no great fault," said the princess.

She went to the window and spent a while looking at Conall,
and the more she looked at him, the better he appeared in her
eyes. She knocked sharply on the window. Conall looked up to
see what made the noise. She spoke to him, and he replied.

"Wait there a while, young man," she shouted. "We won't
delay you long. We have plenty of quilts and blankets here to tie
together, and we'll pull you up."

"Is it how you want me to go up to you?" asked Conall.

"I'd like to talk to you for a while," said she, "if we can pull
you up."

" 'Tis a cold outlook I have in the world if I must have blankets
and quilts to reach your room," said Conall. "Open the window,
please."

When she opened it, Conall stepped back a few feet, not many,
and rose up by the activity of his limbs and the pressure of his
toes; he put the tip of his sword under him, and the first thing
the princess knew he was standing in the room in front of her!
She took him into the fine quarters she had there and seated him
on a chair. She sat on another chair near him, and they started
to talk. Conall got plenty of care and attention from the women.

"Well, I must leave ye for the night," said Conall when it was
growing dark.

"Will you come again tomorrow?"

"I will, indeed, to keep ye company," said Conall.

He went back to the house where his horse was kept and spent
the night there. Next morning, he didn't ask for a quilt or
blanket to reach the princess's room. The king didn't know that

he was in the castle at all, although he spent two or three days there.

"Do you know the best way to fix things, Conall?" said the princess.

"No, I don't," said Conall.

"Tonight, when you think everybody in the castle is asleep, bring your horse with you, and before day dawns tomorrow, we'll be a long distance away. My father won't know where I'll be when he gets up tomorrow and he can't find me."

"Not a bad plan at all," said Conall.

He went to the castle when all were asleep—as he thought— and she came downstairs and got on the horse behind him. They rode away, but they hadn't gone far when a thought struck Conall. He pulled up the horse.

"Why are you delaying, Conall?" asked the princess.

"A thought has struck me, and I'm going to put it into effect."

"What is it?"

"I'll tell you, and it won't be any lie," said Conall. "I won't let it be said of me in the province of Ulster that I came to steal you from your father and mother. If I can't get you in fair fight, I'll let you stay with them."

He turned his horse about and put the princess back into her room again. He took the horse to the farmer's house for the night and stayed there himself also. Next morning after breakfast, he made off for the king's castle and struck the challenge pole. The king made out that it had never before received such a blow. Outside, Conall beat his shield and called for combat, saying that he was a man who always got what was his due but never gave his due to another—a man who earned his pay hard in bitter fighting. The king sent out a messenger to ask what he wanted. Conall said he wanted the princess or a fight. The messenger was sent out again to find out how many men he wanted against him. Conall named the number, and if he did, he had the last man of them killed before it was very late in the day and no more were sent against him.

Next day he went to the castle again. It seemed that the king hadn't very many soldiers, because the messenger was sent out to ask him to wait a while, as the king himself was getting ready to fight him that day. The king came out when he was ready; he was wearing a special suit of armor which kings and knights wore in those times. No sword had any effect on it. They started to fight. Conall didn't want to harm the king, if he could avoid it by any means. The king was attacking him as hard as he could, but the blows all went wide of the mark. Early in the day Conall saw his chance to grapple with the king, and he knocked him under him on the ground.

"Will I get her now?" he asked.

"You will, and welcome. You well deserve her," said the king.

All the castle folk gathered around them. The king gave a great feast, which lasted for seven days and nights before the marriage. When the seven days and nights were up, those invited all returned to their own homes and castles, and Conall was married. Soon afterward, he told the king that he would have to return home as there was nobody there except the wise man to look after things.

" 'Tis your duty to return," said the king. "A house without a head is no house."

Conall and his wife set out with good provisions for the journey, and had reached the border of the province when Conall suggested that they would take a little rest.

"We have been in the saddle a long time now," said he.

"Do you know what you'll do now, Conall?" said his wife. "Stay on the saddle until you reach your own castle. If you dismount, you will fall into a warrior's sleep for seven days and seven nights; and before the seventh day is up, I may find myself in the eastern world. That would cause you more trouble than to remain in the saddle now."

"I never heard any tune by a woman but to hurry home," said Conall.

It was useless for her to be talking to him. He got off the horse and had barely sat on the ground when he started to fall asleep.

"Get up, Conall!" said the princess. "You're nodding to sleep and you'll be off in a minute."

"What I said to you already, I say again," said Conall. "If anybody comes after you, all you need do is pull me by the ear."

"Little good that will do," said his wife.

He was sound asleep in a moment, and it wasn't long before she saw, wading in through the sea, a huge warrior with a basket on his back. Whenever he spied a fish that he liked, he flicked it over his shoulder into the basket with his toes. She tried to hide herself from him as well as she could, but it was no use. He was so tall that even a bird on the ground couldn't escape his eye. He saw her easily and never stopped or stayed till he stood in front of her.

"There you are," said he.

"Here I am."

" 'Tis funny that I should leave home this morning to seize the daughter of the king of Ulster. If she were behind my back now, I wouldn't take my eyes off you to look at her."

"That shows that you have never seen her. If you did, you'd turn your back on me. 'Tisn't me you'd have eyes for!"

"Stop your chatter! Get into the basket," said the warrior.

"How can I go into your basket, and I married to this young fellow?" she asked.

"That makes no difference to me, whether you're married or not," said he. "Get into the basket."

"If this fellow were awake, I'd say you'd have to fight hard before I'd go into it," said she.

"Is it that child you're talking about?"

"Whatever way he looks in your eyes," said she, "if he were awake, I don't think I'd go into your basket."

"Give over your arguing, and hop in," said he.

"Well, if you're going to force me to," said she, "make a mark on the ground to tell who you are, where you came from, and where you are bound for."

He did as she asked. When Conall awoke at the end of the seventh day, he thought that he had slept only an hour or two at the most. He also thought that as a joke his wife had gone somewhere so that he would have to search for her. He looked around and searched but failed to find her. There were seven or eight boys herding cows and dry cattle nearby, and he went to talk to them. Some of them were small, others taller.

"Have ye seen any woman around here since morning?" he asked one of the big lads.

"We haven't seen any woman since seven days ago," he replied.

"Seven days ago!"

"Yes."

"Where did she go?" asked Conall.

The boy described the warrior who had taken her away.

"Have ye seen my horse anywhere?" asked Conall.

"Your horse is at the other side of that hillock over there, and each day she comes and stands over you, licking and washing you from the top of your head to the soles of your feet. When she has that done, she goes back to graze again."

Conall went back to where he had been asleep and saw the marks the warrior had left on the ground.

"You were quite right in what you told me, boy," said Conall. "Do you know if there is any old boat or ship around here?"

"I know of only one old vessel that's below there on the shore. The cows are rubbing themselves against it every day."

They went down to it.

"Run off, two of ye, now and bring me two spades and shovels to see whether we can put her afloat," said Conall.

When they came back, they all set to work to cut two trenches from the vessel to the water's edge.

When the tide came in, Conall said, "Ye take one side of her now, and I'll take the other."

She must have been·stuck there for years, and the poor boys couldn't knock a stir out of their side. Conall moved his own side of the vessel with his knee. Then he went to the other side and he soon had the vessel on the water. She was leaking badly.

"Is there any place around here where they sell nails?" asked Conall.

"There is; 'tisn't far away."

Conall put his hand into his pocket and gave them a large fistful of money, enough for the nails and something for sweets as well.

"Bring me back a bag of nails and a hammer and knife, if ye can get it," he said.

They weren't long away.

"Now, boys, I'll have to kill your cattle," said Conall.

The boys started to cry.

"Don't be crying at all. Laughing ye should be, for I'll pay ye double the value of every animal I'll kill. Wait till ye see how glad your father and mother will be when they see all the money. I'll start on the cows."

He killed some of the animals and skinned them and nailed the skins to the old vessel until he had fixed her for the sea journey.

"Now, boys," said he, "keep an eye to my horse until I return. I don't know whether I will return or not. If I don't, ye can sell her and divide the money between ye. Take good care of her."

He set out. He hoisted his soft bulging sails on his delightful, beautiful, one-legged vessel, which was smooth and slippery from stem to stern; there wasn't a top feather sticking out or in, except one brown, white-backed, red feather at the topmost mast, which made music, sport and mischief for the hero on board. And the hero that was on board was young Conall from Howth. He sailed over the sea swiftly, and as he did he thought that he saw a harbor some distance off.

"I'll go in here," he said to himself, "to see can I find out what kind of country it is."

He turned the prow of the vessel toward the harbor and sailed in as far as left him suitably deep water for his return when the tide ebbed. He moored her for a year and a day, even though he might be gone from her only for an hour: one rope landward and two ropes toward the sea—where wind would not toss her about or sun split her or birds of the air befoul her. When he had satisfied himself that all was well, he stood at her prow, stepped back swiftly to her stern, and jumped clean over the water on to the dry strand. He turned inward from the shore to see what kind of country it was and whether he could get any information about his wife. He soon met an old man who was poorly dressed. They started to chat, and Conall offered him some money; the story doesn't tell whether it was large or small, but Conall told him to buy some clothes for himself.

"May God reward you!" said the old man. "I have been here for many years, and you are the first to give me anything."

They weren't long chatting when a great crowd of people began to gather on the strand.

"Could you tell me why are all those people collecting?" asked Conall.

"I'm well able to tell you that," said the old man. "Every year the king's three sons play a game of hurling against the men of the rest of the country; if the countrymen score three goals against them, the king must send a pig or a beef as a forfeit to each house in the country; but if the king's sons win, every house in the country has to send a pig or a beef to the king."

"I wonder if they would allow me to play?" said Conall. "I can never get enough hurling."

"I couldn't say," said the old man, who had a very nice hurley in his hand.

"Give me that hurley till I see will they let me play," said Conall.

"I would give it to you and welcome," said the old man, "only that the king's eldest son asked me for it for today's game. That's why I brought it with me."

"Well, if the king's eldest son blames you for giving it to me," said Conall, "you can tell him that I asked to have a look at it and wouldn't give it back. He'll forgive you then."

Conall got the hurley, and when they had all gathered on the strand, he strolled through the crowd, taking no notice of anyone. He spoke to nobody until he stood in front of the king's eldest son. They saluted.

"You're going to have a game?" said Conall.

"We are."

"Why don't just the two of us play against each other?" asked Conall. "I'll go into one of the goals, and you into the other. We'll have great fun."

"If I win, what will you give me?" asked the king's eldest son.

"That island out there," said Conall.

"But that's mine already."

"That island to the north of it then," said Conall.

"That's mine too."

"Well, I'll give you the one to the south of it," said Conall.

"That's mine also."

"Isn't it a funny thing," said Conall, "that I never set foot anywhere up to now without thinking it was mine—unless I was forced out of it. I'll make another bargain with you, then."

"What's that?"

"I'll play a game against your two brothers and yourself. If ye win, ye will have the right to strike an undefended blow with a hurley on me. If I win, I'll have the same right against ye."

"I'm agreeable to that," said the king's eldest son.

They went and stood at the line which divided the strand into two parts for the game. When the ball was thrown in, Conall struck it with his hurley, struck it again as it came down, and without letting it touch the ground, carried it along and scored a goal. The king's three sons ran after him but they had no chance of catching up on him or beating him.

"That's one goal," said Conall.

"It isn't!" said the king's eldest son. "You should have let the ball touch the ground."

"We'll go to the line again," said Conall.

When the ball was thrown in, the king's son tried to lift it with his hurley, but Conall hit it to one side, took the ball along with his hurley, and never stopped till he scored a goal. He kept on playing like that till he scored four goals, and the king's sons couldn't stop him.

"That's four goals now," said Conall. "If it was you who got three, you wouldn't have bothered with the fourth."

"Yes. You won honestly," said the king's eldest son. "I have one request to make of you, if you will grant it."

"What is it?" asked Conall.

"Give us time to go home to say goodbye to our father and mother. We will come back to you then and you can have the forfeit."

"I allow ye to go," said Conall.

Conall walked hither and over on the strand until he came to the old man. He gave him back the hurley and told him what had happened.

"You mustn't have had any desire for satisfaction from them, seeing that you let them go home," said the old man.

"I'm not looking for any satisfaction," said Conall, "I came to this country to fulfil my own quest."

Now there happened to be in the king's castle an old man from Ireland who had been carried off by a griffin in her talons and had been dropped by the bird on the king's land. He had arrived at the king's castle, and the king, the queen, the sons, and the women of the house had been very kind to him. They all loved one another very much. When the king's sons came home after the hurling game, they went into a room by themselves without looking at mother or sister or anybody else. They sat down in the room and not a word out of them. After a while, the king came home and asked had the sons returned yet.

"They have," said the queen.

"How did the game go today?" asked the king.

"That we can't tell you," said the queen. "They never spoke to us when they returned, and we didn't ask them. They're stitting in there in the room with not a word out of them."

"They must have been beaten today," said the king, "to say that they're taking it so badly. 'Tis no great loss to me to send a pig or a beef to every house in the country. They are well used to winning themselves. Why shouldn't they lose now and again?"

"I know nothing about their affairs," said the queen. "I can't give you any information."

The king went to the door of the room and called out the eldest son to the fireplace. "Were ye beaten today?" he asked.

"We were."

"Why are ye taking it so badly that ye wouldn't even speak when ye came home? 'Tis no trouble to me to send a pig or a beef to every house in the country."

"'Tisn't a pig or a beef we lost," said the son. "We're going to lose our heads."

"Is that the way it is?" said the king.

"That's the way. And I wouldn't mind if it was a man that beat us."

"And who beat ye, if it wasn't a man?"

"Well it was a man, but he wasn't the height of my chest."

(Conall must have been on the small side, I'd say.)

"As sure as I'm alive this day," said the old Irishman, "it must

be young Conall. He could never get enough hurling. He doesn't
want your heads. If he did, would he have let ye come home?
'Tis a great shame for ye that ye didn't invite him to the castle.
Maybe he's in need of a bite to eat or a drink. Let someone go
and ask him in. 'Tis nobody but young Conall. Small and all as
he is, no one ever got the upper hand of him."

The queen and her daughter went down to the strand to invite
Conall to the castle. When he saw the two women, he went
toward them. The two women were about to go on their knees
before him, but he told them to stand up—that he wasn't as
important as all that. He asked them if they were troubled about
something to see if he could help them.

"We only wanted to invite you to the castle, noble warrior,"
said the old queen. "You can have the heads of my three sons
at the castle rather than in front of a big crowd of people on the
strand."

"I'll go with you and welcome," said Conall. "But, if I do, it
isn't to get the heads of your sons. I don't want their heads at
all. If I did, I wouldn't have allowed them to go home."

They walked back to the castle, and the king and his sons had
the greatest welcome and handshakes in the world for Conall.
The old Irishman jumped up when he saw him, threw his arms
around him, and asked him would he take his bones back to
Ireland.

"How sure you are that I'll take even my own bones back!"
said Conall.

"That's true enough, Conall," said the old man. "But, if you
do go back there, will you take me with you?"

"I will and welcome," said Conall.

A feast was got ready. Only the first of the food had been laid
on the table when a man strode in the door, snatched up the dish
of meat, or whatever it was, and went off out the door with it.

"Is this some kind of tribute ye have to give him?" asked
Conall.

"No," said the king. "That man is the greatest warrior in this
country, and everybody is afraid to stop him."

"Well, if I knew that," said Conall, "he'd have left the food
on the table."

He stood up. The warrior had gone only a short distance from the door when Conall overtook him. He caught him by the collar and turned him about.

"Put that back where you got it," said Conall.

The warrior obeyed.

"Get up," said Conall to the old Irishman, "and tie up this fellow tightly."

The old man got up and bound every limb of the warrior with hard hempen rope, and left him, lying on his back outside the door under the dripping of the royal candle.

"Were you ever in a worse plight than you are now?" he asked.

"Indeed I was," said the warrior. "Give me a bite of food first, and I'll tell you about it."

The old man loosened his bonds, and he was taken indoors and seated at the table. Nobody interfered with him while he was eating, although he ate almost everything they had for the feast. While the table was being got ready for the others, Conall asked the warrior to tell his story.

" 'Tis I that will tell it," said he.

There wasn't a day that I didn't go out a bit into the sea in a small pleasure boat that I had. One day when I was out, I saw a man coming toward me and his head seemed to be touching the sky. In a basket on his back was the most beautiful woman I had ever seen. Well, the notion struck me that if I could give her one kiss, it would ease my mind greatly; so I brought the little boat in close to him. What did the fellow do but let myself and the little boat pass back between his two legs. I brought the boat close again, raised the mast, and climbed to the top. I put my two arms around the woman's neck and kissed her. The man put back his hand and caught me and bound every bone in my body with hard hempen rope. Then he threw me into the sea. Now, I had the gift that no water could ever drown me; so I drifted on the water in and out as the tide flowed and ebbed. I had no food except any small fish I could catch in my mouth and swallow. I was like that for several days. At last one of the knots in the rope became loose, and they all softened, one after another, till the last knot came free. I was ashore then and decided to go up to a grassy patch at the foot of a cliff to rest myself. I was exhausted. When I got there, I found a griffin's nest with three young fledglings in it. I went into the nest. No sooner did I close my eyes to sleep than they started to pick at me, until at last I got up, twisted the neck of each of them, and threw them out into the sea.

When the mother griffin came home and saw her young ones floating on the water with their necks twisted, she flew to the nest, took me in her talons and flew so high with me that I thought there couldn't be any more sky or clouds above us. Then she let me go. I fell down on to the strand and thought that every bone in my body was in bits. She came at me again and did the same thing to me. I let on to be dead, as she stood over me planning how to kill me. I suddenly pulled out my sword and, with one blow, swept off her head. I decided then that the one house where I could get food was the king's castle. That's what brought me here.

"What's your name?" asked Conall.

"Short Grey Warrior."

"Well, you're not hungry now," said Conall.

"No," said the warrior. "Wasn't I in a worse plight with the griffin than tied up out there by you?"

"You were," said Conall. "And now you'll make a good guide for us."

"I won't be any guide for you. I don't ever again want to see that big man from the sea."

"Give up your arguing. You must come with us," said Conall.

"I'll go, if you promise to hide me under the ballast of your ship when we land," said the warrior. "He might catch sight of me again."

"We'll hide you all right," said Conall.

Next morning when they had eaten, Conall set out in the ship with the king's three sons, the queen, her daughter, Short Grey Warrior, and the old Irishman, and they never stopped till they reached the eastern world. Conall moored his ship for a full year and a day where wind would not toss her or sun split her or birds of the air befoul her even though he might be away from her only for an hour. They went ashore and made for the big man's castle.

Conall's wife was in a room upstairs. She had placed *geasa* and judgment on the big man not to interefere with her for a year and a day; she would marry him at the end of that time. So he had confined her to an upstairs room, and when he went off each day, she got her own meals ready. Conall walked around the castle, looking about him, but he could see nobody. At last, whatever look he gave, he spied her at the window.

"You have fine fresh air up there," he shouted.

"I have," said she. "If you take my advice, Conall, you'll go back home again. It would be a pity that you'd leave your bones here when the big man killed you."

"Here my bones will stay or else you'll come home with me," said Conall. "Come down quickly, or I'll go up for you."

She came down, and he put her on board his ship.

"Sail away as quickly as ye can now," said she.

"No," said Conall.

He gave orders to the king's three sons to go ashore with him, after they had hidden away Short Grey Warrior on board. The big man came down from the castle toward them.

"Now," said Conall, to the king's three sons, "see if I can beat him in fair fight. But, if ye see that I'm getting the worst of it, ye can help me."

"We will and welcome," said they. "We'll give any help we can."

"I suppose it is you who has taken my wife from me, you blackguard," said the big man.

"Not to make you a short answer," said Conall, "you had no wife that I could take. You took *my* wife from *me*. You call me a blackguard. 'Tis you the name fits and not me. I'm not going home until I get satisfaction from you for all the trouble you have caused me."

They attacked each other. For two days and nights they fought, and Conall's fury was increasing all the time. No matter how he tried, the big man could not strike any blow on Conall, who was too expert and swift for him. On the evening of the third day, Conall delivered a warrior's blow so weighty and fierce that it twisted the big man around, and he fell on his back.

"I have you now," said Conall.

"You have. If you spare my head now, you will never need for anything."

"I never wanted for anything before I ever met you," said Conall. "And I won't want for anything after meeting you either."

He sent the king's three sons for the old Irishman to tie up the big man. When this was done, Short Grey Warrior was sent for to get satisfaction for all he had suffered from him. He had to be stopped at last, for, not being satisfied with cutting the big man into pieces, he wanted to mince him altogether.

They sailed away finally and, as they were passing by a harbor, Conall said, "We'll go in here now, to see what kind of country it is."

They hadn't gone very far toward the shore when they saw three castles all facing one another.

"'Tis very strange that these castles should be built that way," said Conall.

They moored their ship.

"I'll go ashore now and bring back an account to ye about them," said the king's eldest son.

He went ashore and met a man at the top of the strand.

"Could you tell me, my good man," he asked, "why these three castles are built facing one another?"

"Take hold of the tips of my fingers, and I'll tell you," said the man.

No sooner had the king's eldest son done so than the other had lifted him off the ground, thrown him over his shoulder, and made a green stone of him. The second son went ashore and asked the man about the castles.

"Take hold of the tips of my fingers, and I'll tell you," said he.

The king's second son was lifted off the ground the next moment, thrown over the man's shoulder, and turned into a green stone. The king's third son went ashore, and the same thing happened to him.

"I must go ashore myself," said Short Grey Warrior.

He went ashore and asked the man why the three castles were built facing one another.

"Take hold of the tips of my fingers, and I'll tell you," said the man.

Short Grey Warrior had barely taken hold of the man's fingers when he was lifted clear off the ground, thrown over the man's shoulder, and turned into a green stone.

"They must be having great fun inside," said Conall. "I must go and see for myself. And now," said he to the old Irishman for fun, "if any of the women make a complaint about you to me when I come back to the ship again, I'll give you more than the griffin gave you."

"There's no stopping you, Conall," said the old Irishman. "You were ever a great joker."

Conall went ashore and made off to the man at the top of the strand.

"Tell me, my good man, why those three castles are built facing one another?" said he.

"Take hold of the tips of my fingers, and I'll tell you," said the man.

"I will and of your whole palm," said Conall. "And maybe, of other parts of you too before we part company."

Conall took hold of the tips of his fingers, but the other man couldn't shift him off the ground. They gripped hold of each other and spent the whole day wrestling until the tide mark was dug up by them. At last the man got Conall down. The next moment, Conall was on top of him.

"I never yet met a man I couldn't keep down," said the other, "except my young brother, Conall. We often wrestled each other, and although I always knocked him down, I was never able to keep him under. He would always come out on top."

"That's he on top of you now," said Conall. "Are you my eldest brother?"

"That's who I am, indeed!"

"How is my father?" asked Conall.

"Getting heavy and old. Many's the blow he has warded off since he came here, and many's the blow he has struck."

"How are ye getting on?" asked Conall.

"The enemies of this country were advancing all the time until we arrived, and the soldiers, making no fight, were being driven before them like animals. But since we came, they haven't advanced a foot; neither have we driven them back."

"Revive my men," said Conall.

"You'll get them, gladly," said his brother.

When they were revived, the six of them set off for the battle-field, traveling by day and resting, like any workmen, by night. Conall's father got a great surprise when he saw him.

"How are you, Father?" asked Conall.

"I'm getting plenty to do. Still, I'm not doing too badly."

"Take a rest for yourself now," said Conall next morning after breakfast. "I'll take your place today."

Conall and his two brothers, the king's three sons, the Short Grey Warrior, and any other who joined them went into battle that day. They killed so many of the enemy that the rest fled in terror, and those they couldn't overtake drowned themselves. There wasn't a single one of the enemy to be found that evening except the dead ones.

They came home that evening and had a great night together. Next day, Conall took his father, his two brothers, the king's three sons, and the Short Grey Warrior on board his ship. He took the king's wife and her sons and daughter back home, and returned to Howth with his own relatives. I hear that he is alive and strong there still.

· 18 · Art, King of Leinster

There was a king long ago, and if there ever was, there often was and will be again. The place where he was living was Leinster. He was a very good king, especially to the poor. Whether he was told good news or bad news, he always tried to make things better than they were. He was getting fairly old and began to worry a lot that he had no heir for the kingdom after himself. One day he went to a wise man that he had and asked him did he know any way by which he could have an heir for the kingdom after his death.

"I'll search my books," said the wise man. When the wise man had searched his books, he came to the king. "I have no answer to your question, honorable king," he said, "either from the start or the middle or the end of my books. However, a thought struck me—I'm not asking you to follow it except you wish, for I don't know whether it will do any good or not."

"What have you in mind?" asked the king.

"I have been thinking," said the wise man, "that since I have failed in other ways, you might give a great feast for the whole kingdom from end to end; invite every poor man or woman who is walking the roads as well as every king or knight, high or low. And when both rich and poor, noble and lowly, have feasted to their fill, you must stand before them yourself—don't depend on anybody else—and ask them to pray that God may give you an heir for the kingdom. They will all do as you ask."

The king got ready the great feast. He invited the whole province and even people outside it, and they all came. When each had eaten and drunk his fill, the king walked about among them and asked them, if they pleased, to pray to God for an heir to the kingdom after his death.

Within a year (or let us call it a year), a young son was born to the king's wife. The child had a fillet of silver on the back of his head and a fillet of gold on his forehead. Any man or woman who saw the child would have to admit that he was the son of a king or a knight. What he did not grow by day, he grew by night, so that the clothes which suited him one month were too small for him the following month, and new ones had to be got for him. When he grew up, he was sent to school and later on to a school for princes. The king and his advisers wished him to marry, young though he was, before he would set out for any foreign country, fearing that some harm would befall him.

But whenever marriage was mentioned to Art, King of Leinster, as he was called, he would say, "O, we're young yet. We'll wait another year." (That saying is still common in this country. Any young girl or fellow for whom you'd be arranging a marriage would say, if they didn't like the match, "We'll wait another year.")

After some time, although he was still young, Art himself decided to marry; so he went to the wise man and asked him did he know in which land in the world did the most beautiful princess live who would suit him as a wife.

"I'll search my books," said the wise man.

He did so and came back to Art.

"I can't find any princess who is more beautiful and suitable for you to marry," he said, "than the daughter of the king of the kingdom of dark men."

He got ready for the journey with food and whatever else he needed and set out in his ship the next morning. He hoisted his soft bulging sails; there wasn't a top feather turning in or out in his delightful beautiful one-legged, slender, smooth vessel, from stem to stern, except one brown, white-backed, red feather on top of the highest mast, where it made music, sport, and mischief for the hero on board. And the hero on board was Art, king of Leinster, from Ireland. He never stopped or lessened his pace, and fast though the ship was sailing, he used to stand in the stern and at each step which he took he would press his foot firmly on the deck and thus make her go faster still.

He sailed into the harbor of the king of the dark men and anchored his ship where the water was suitably deep. He moored her for a year and a day where the wind would not rock her or sun split her or birds of the air befoul her, one rope seaward and two toward land. He stood at her prow and ran backward till he stood at her stern. Then he rose up by the strength of his legs and the muscles of his toes, placed the top of his sword under him, and made a clear jump over the water onto the dry strand. When he placed his feet on earth, he looked about him and thanked God that things had gone well so far. He walked inland, but there was no sign of habitation to be seen. Late in the evening, he met an old man. Art spoke to him, and the old man returned the greeting.

"What kind of country is this, good man?" asked Art. "I have walked a long way since I came ashore, but I haven't met a single house."

"It is a good country," said the old man. "And you're not far now from the biggest house in it, a castle belonging to the high king."

"Is it far from us?" asked Art.

"It isn't far from you at all. But the best advice I can give you is to stay here with me tonight. You'll have tomorrow morning for what you want to do."

"It mightn't be bad advice," said Art.

They went to the old man's house, and if they did, the low-sized wife that the old man had—she was fairly old—was inside before them. She welcomed the stranger and got busy preparing a meal for the three of them. When they had eaten, they sat by the two sides of the fire, talking to each other. Art started to question the old man about whether the king had any daughters.

"He has a daughter, all right, but she's very queer," said the old man.

"What way is she queer?" asked Art.

"This way," said the old man. "Her father has built a wall this height all round the castle for her, and there are iron spikes two or two and a half feet long stuck in the wall. There is only a single one of these spikes that hasn't the head of a prince or a knight stuck on it. I hope I'll never see your head on that."

"And why are all these heads there?" asked Art.

"I don't know. 'Tis a question I can't answer for you," said the old man. "I'd say 'tis how she doesn't want to leave a prince or a knight alive in the country. She won't marry anyone except he brings to her the head of a warrior in the eastern world, and they are all failing in the attempt. She's putting *geasa* on them all to come back and have their heads cut off if they fail in their task."

"And why do they come back to have their heads cut off?" asked Art.

"They come," said the old man. "Now you're a strong man, and a warrior, but these heads will make you shiver."

When he had eaten his breakfast, Art went toward the king's castle. He walked around, looking at the wall and the heads and the castle. His blood was rising at what the old man had told him. At last he went up to the challenge pole and put all the strength he had and he hadn't into the blow he gave it with the palm of his hand. The king felt the castle shake as well as the chair he was sitting on.

"Heavens! That's the heaviest blow that has been struck on

that challenge pole since it was erected," said he. "Whoever struck it must be a terrible strong man, the blow he gave it. I thought I felt the chair shaking under me."

He sent out a messenger to see what the man outside wanted. The messenger asked Art what was troubling him.

"I want the king's daughter or fight," said Art.

The messenger returned to the king.

"What does he want?" asked the king.

"He wants your daughter or fight."

"What kind of a fellow is he?" said the king.

"As long as I have been in this castle, I have never seen such a fine man," said the servant.

"'Twas easily known by the blow that he is strong," said the king. "Go out to him and tell him he'll get his answer before long."

The messenger went out, and Art waited. It wasn't long until the king and queen and their daughter went out to him, and if they did, none of them invited him in for a bite or a sup or worried whether it was long or short since he had eaten. The daughter told him that it wasn't fighting or quarreling she wanted but the head of the warrior from the eastern world, that she would marry only the man who could do that and that the man who failed to bring it would have his head cut off.

"And do you imagine that I'm so foolish as to come back to you to have my head cut off, if I don't have the warrior's head for you?" asked Art. "If I return at all without the head, I'll come, not to have my head cut off, but to challenge you to fight."

Faith, that answer from Art took the edge off her grandeur and haughtiness.

Art returned to the old man and spent the night with him again. Next morning after breakfast, he made off his ship, hoisted his soft bulging sails on his delightful, beautiful, one-legged vessel, which hadn't a top feather turning in or out, except one brown, white-backed, red feather that was making music, sport, and mischief for the hero on board. And the hero on board was Art, king of Leinster, from Ireland. He never stopped or lessened his pace until he reached the eastern world. From far out in the bay, he noticed a harbor inside. He faced his vessel toward the harbor until he saw that she would require that depth of water, if he weren't to have the trouble of putting her afloat again. He moored her for a year and a day, even though he might be gone from her for only an hour where the wind would not rock her or the sun split her or the birds of the air befoul her: one rope seaward and two toward land. When he had tied her up to his satisfaction, he stood at her prow and ran backward till he stood at her stern. He rose up from her stern and leaped clean in over the water on to the dry strand.

When he placed his feet on the earth, he looked about him and thanked God that things had gone so well so far. He walked inland, but if he did, there was no sign of habitation to be seen. He had walked a good part of the day when he thought he could see a house some distance away from him. He made up his mind to go toward it to see would he get lodgings for the night, as it was very hard on a stranger to be traveling by night in a strange country where he didn't know east from west. He went up to the house. Inside was an old man busy at something with his back toward the door. Art stood outside and put in his head. He took a great start out of the old man when he spoke, as he didn't expect anybody. He turned around and saluted Art.

"Would you be able to give me lodgings for the night, my good man?" asked Art. "I'm a stranger here and don't like to be out at night."

"You'll get lodgings and welcome," said the old man. "My trouble is that they won't be good enough for you."

"Nobody can be blamed for being able to give only what he has for himself," said Art.

"Draw up near the fire," said the old man.

Art did so.

The old man could not take his eyes off him, and after a while Art said, "You have some reason for looking at me so hard."

"I have, except I'm making a great mistake. From the minute I laid eyes on you, I've been thinking in my mind that you must have some strain of relationship with the king of Leinster."

"Where did you meet the king of Leinster or how do you know him?" asked Art.

"I spent a good while in his company," said the old man, "and if I did, 'tis he was the good and upright man. May I ask if you are any relation of his?"

"Did you ever hear that he had any children?" asked Art.

"I didn't, except that he had one son."

"That's the son that's talking to you now," said Art. "Did you ever hear tell of Art, son of the king of Leinster?"

The old man went off and washed his hands and face, fearing that he would not be clean enough to get some food ready for Art. Soon the meal was ready on the table.

"Other people's cooks could feel very proud," said Art, "if they could prepare a better meal, or even one as good."

"I have plenty of practice at it," said the old man. "Still I'm thinking it isn't good enough for you."

"It suits me fine. I wouldn't find any fault with it, even if it were far worse."

When they had eaten the meal, the old man couldn't talk about anything but about the king of Leinster: how good he was to the whole province, especially to the poor and even to people ouside the province; how he had always tried to help everybody.

"And now that you have told me your name, would you mind telling me what brought you to this country?" he asked.

"I don't mind at all," said Art. "The *geasa* of a young woman have brought me here. She wants the head of a certain warrior. Do you know anything about him? Is he far from here or will it take me long to reach him?"

"I'll be telling you all about him. You'll be staying here for the night."

When morning came, he got his breakfast for Art, and then the two of them went out for a walk. Art was taking in everything, and he liked the country around.

"How far away is this warrior?" he asked.

"Not far at all," replied the old man. "Do you see that tall tree over there, in the field above the house?"

"I do," said Art.

"You will find the warrior you are looking for asleep near it. If you happen by any chance to get his head, for sun or wind or any reason in the world, don't fail to bring it here to me. You won't cut of his head while he's asleep, will you?" asked the old man."

"You needn't fear," said Art, "that I will cut it off unknown to him, if I can't do so in fair fight."

"I knew well you wouldn't do a cowardly act," said the old man.

Art went toward the tree and stabbed the warrior in the leg with his sword. He rose up and asked Art what he wanted.

"I want your head in fair fight," said Art.

"'Tis the devil's own work that ye are all coming for my head," said the warrior. "Here I am, interfering with nobody or going to make trouble for ye. Why are ye all after my head?"

"We have nothing at all against you," said Art. "A young woman's *geasa* are the cause of it all."

"I'll be ready for you in a minute," said the warrior.

He rose up and got ready for the fight. Any man who wished to see a hard struggle should have watched Art and the warrior fighting. The frightening thing was that, so well trained were they both, neither of them could get in a blow at the other. Fiery sparks flew from their swords. Late in the day, when both were tiring a little, Art struck a powerful blow with all his might and turned the warrior about so that he fell on his back on the ground.

"I'll have your head now," shouted Art.

"Take it and welcome," said the warrior. "Only for being able to take it, you wouldn't get it. Neither would I get yours, if I weren't able. Take it now."

Art drew a great blow at the warrior and struck him on the neck, cutting off his head. He took the head in his hand and was going toward the tree, when three grey crows flew over him, as if they were trying to snatch the head from him. Art became afraid that they would pick out his eyes, so he threw the head on the fence, in order to pick up a stone to throw at them. When he raised his head again with the stone in his hand both the warrior's head and the crows had vanished. Art was so cool-headed and hearty that the loss of the head did not worry him. He returned to the old man as happy as he had left him.

"You didn't get the head?" said the old man.

"I did," said Art.

"And where is it now?"

Art told him what had happened.

"Didn't I tell you not to leave it out of your hand if you got it?" said the old man.

"Well, I thought my eyes were more important to me," said Art. "If they picked out my eyes, I'd be wandering around this country, blind for the rest of my life."

"They wouldn't have picked out your eyes at all," said the old man. "Once you had got the head, you should have held onto it. You have made a lot of trouble for yourself by losing it."

The old man had a fine vat of water ready.

"Take off your clothes now and throw yourself into that and wash yourself," said the old man.

When Art had washed himself, the old man told him to get into another vat of water which was near him. This made him as fresh as he had been early in the morning.

When night fell, the old man said to him, "You had better go to bed now. You know the old saying that a man can rid himself of his weariness best while lying down." Next morning, after breakfast, the old man said, "Try to get the head again today, and on no account let go of it until you bring it here to me."

Art found the warrior asleep before him. He pricked him with his sword, and he stood up.

"Yesterday wasn't enough for you," said the warrior.

"Nothing will satisfy me, until your head or my own will fall," said Art.

They attacked each other, and late in the evening, Art struck a powerful blow which turned the warrior about and he fell on his back on the ground.

"Your head is mine," shouted Art.

"It is, small thanks to me," said the warrior.

With a strong blow, Art cut off his head and took it up in his hand. He was going toward the tree when he met four men, who were carrying a coffin.

"Where are ye making for, good men?" asked Art.

"We're burying a headless body," said one of them.

"A headless body," cried Art. "Show it to me."

"We will and welcome," said the men, laying down the coffin.

When Art saw the headless body, "That's as fine a warrior as my eyes have ever seen," said he. "If this head which I have here fits him, he won't have to be buried without a head."

He put the head on the headless body and it fitted exactly. The next moment, the coffin, the body, and the four men had vanished from sight. Art took it all calmly and returned to the old man as happy as he had set out.

"Did you get the head?"

"I did," said Art.

"And where is it?"

Art told him.

"I don't know what to say to you," said the old man. "You'll ever be a little fool by them in this country."

"Whether I will or not," said Art, "I couldn't let such a fine warrior go headless to the graveyard, while I had a head for him in my hand."

"You are a good man, Art. You couldn't be anything else."

Art washed and cleaned himself in the vats again until he was as fresh as he had been before.

They spent a long part of the night talking, and next morning, when they had eaten their breakfast, the old man said, "I knew well, Art, that you were like your father. I have tested you for the past two days, and you have even a greater heart than your father. It was I who took the warrior's head from you during past two days to see what kind of man you were. I have the head here in my room, and I will give it to you now. That warrior has been my only protection here, and only a brave man like you could have taken his head. Don't give it to the woman who put *geasa* on you at all. All you need to do is show it to her, throw it up into the air, and it will come back here to me. Don't have anything at all to do with that woman. She is the greatest villain that ever wore a shoe, and she is only laughing at the heads of all the princes and knights that she has on spikes. Go home to your father, and you will find a woman of your own choice who will make a good wife for you."

"Whether I do or not," said Art. "I won't take her home with me. I'll fight her instead."

"Don't fight her at all or bother your head with her," said the old man. "Do as I told you."

When Art reached the castle of the king of the dark men, the king's daughter was watching out for him, I'm thinking. He walked about on the field outside the castle, and it wasn't long before she put her head out through a window.

"Have you brought it with you?" she asked.

"Would you know it, if you saw it?" asked Art.

"I would well," said she.

"Is this it?"

"That's it, indeed," said she. "Hand it up to me."

"I am under no compulsion to give it to you, only to bring it to you," said Art.

When he said that, he threw the head up into the air, and even if it had no power of its own, the force behind it would have sent it a long distance away.

"You can stay where you are now," said he. "Maybe some other princes or knights will be foolish enough to come back to you to have their heads put on spikes."

He turned from her on one foot and left her there. He returned to the old man and stayed with him until morning. After breakfast, the old man accompanied him to the shore, and they bade goodbye to each other. Art went on board his ship, hoisted his soft bulging sails again on his delightful, beautiful, one-legged vessel, which hadn't a top feather turning in or out, save one brown, white-backed, red feather on top of the highest mast, where it made music, sport, and mischief for the hero on board. And the hero on board was Art, king of Leinster, from Ireland. He never stopped or lessened his pace until he reached the part of Leinster where his father was—I suppose it was somewhere near Dublin. When his parents saw him coming, and they having no expectation of ever seeing him again, they were overcome with joy. Art's father felt as young again as he had been on the day of his marriage. He felt very proud of his son.

They passed some time together, and nobody asked him, needless to say, why he hadn't brought home a wife with him. One day when Art was walking on the shore, he saw a delightful, beautiful one-legged vessel coming into the harbor.

"I'll wait and see what this good man wants, be it fight or something else," said Art.

The man on board steered the vessel into suitably deep water and moored her, one rope seaward and two ropes toward the land. He tied her up for a year and a day, although he might be away from her only for an hour. Then he jumped ashore and stood in front of Art. They saluted each other, and it wasn't long until the stranger asked Art would he play a game.

"I'm tired of these games," said Art. "There's not much to be gained by them."

"Never mind that. It will pass the time for us."

The stranger was the magician of the eastern world. They played, and didn't Art win the first game.

"Name your forfeit," said the magician.

"Too soon you'll hear it," said Art.

"The sooner the better."

"I place as *geasa* and judgment upon you," said Art, "not to sleep two nights in the same bed or eat two meals at the same table until you bring me the most beautiful princess under the sky of Araíocht together with her twelve handmaids and her horse."

"The devil mend me, Art," said the magician. "Only for my ardor, I'd be at home now. I have spent seven years on the lookout for that princess, and it was only this morning that I came upon her, bathing with her twelve handmaids. I have herself and the handmaids and the horse on board my vessel."

"Bring them here to me quickly," said Art, "or I'll follow your vessel, and where you'll stop, I'll stop too."

"Oh, don't have any worry. They'll come in to you without fail."

The magician went out to his vessel and brought ashore the princess, her twelve handmaids, and her horse. He bade goodbye to Art and sailed away, sad and sorrowful, and was it any wonder?

When his father and mother and the rest of the household saw Art coming with the princess and the crowd of women, they were filled with joy. The king welcomed them and asked Art where they had come from. Art told him all and said that he was going to marry the princess. The king gave a great feast for the whole country, and it lasted seven days and seven nights. When the seven days and seven nights were up, all the people returned home, and Art got married to the princess.

About a year later, Art's wife gave birth to a son. The child had a fillet of silver on the back of his head and a fillet of gold on his forehead. Neither man nor woman could see the child without saying that he was the son of a king or a knight. While she was in bed with the child, Art's wife gave orders to his father to follow Art wherever he went. She well knew that the magician was watching him.

So his father went everywhere with Art, until one day when they were walking together Art said, "You can walk on now, and I'll be home before you. I'll wait here a little while."

The father walked on by himself. He was too polite to look back, so he looked ahead. No sooner had he turned his back on Art than the magician stood before him.

"Will you play a game today, Art?" he asked.

Art didn't like to refuse, since they had played a game already. He said that he would, so they started to play. Just then, Art's wife saw his father coming in alone and asked him quickly where Art was.

"Didn't he return yet?" said the king.

"No," said Art's wife.

"Well, he told me that he'd be home before me."

She threw herself out of the bed, pulled on some clothes, and ran to where Art and the magician were playing. The magician had won the game just when she reached them.

"You did that very nicely," said she to the magician.

"I did," said he.

"Well, as sure as I'm talking to you now," said she, "the forfeit you name may be the cause of your own death yet."

She and Art returned home. The magician had placed a judgment on Art not to sleep two nights in the same bed or eat two meals at the same table until he would bring him the Truth of the One Story and the Sword of Light. Art remained at home for a while, eating at different tables each morning, noon and night, and sleeping in a different bed each night. One morning when he was getting up, he told his wife that he would not be from bed to bed and from table to table any longer but would set out on his quest.

"You have a stiff task ahead of you," said his wife. "The Sword of Light is in the possession of a brother-in-law of mine. His name is Balor Béimeannach. He was as fine and as noble a man as ever entered a house—as fine and noble as you are—until a few years ago when that scoundrel of a magician caused trouble between himself and his wife that's my sister. Up to that time my brother-in-law used often to visit my father's house, but since the magician caused the trouble, none of us has ever gone to my sister's house nor has she or her husband left their castle. Only their servants go in and out. You'll have your work cut out for you to get the sword."

When Art was ready to leave the following day, his wife gave him her own horse.

"Give water and wheat to the little horse now," said she. "Get on her back when she has finished, and she will take you to the door of my youngest brother's house this evening. They will all recognize that she is my horse, and you will have to tell them all about how we met and got married. My father and mother have been heartbroken since the morning the magician took me away. They don't know where I am or whether I am alive or dead."

The little horse stayed not for hill or mountain or glen or fence or sea until she landed him at the young brother's door that evening. The servant that was minding the house caught sight of the little horse through the window and ran to tell the master, wherever he was, writing or reading. The servant almost took the frame off the door with the dint of excitement.

"Good heavens, woman! What fright are you in?" asked the master.

"No fright at all, master," said she; "only your sister's horse is outside in the field, and no one can remember ever having seen a finer warrior than the man that's riding her."

The master ran out, and his first salute to Art was to ask him where he got the horse. Art told him the whole story and said that his lost sister was as well as he would want her to be, at home after him, with her young son.

"That's great news!" said the master. "We had no account of her."

He told Art to get off the horse, and a servant was ordered to stable and dry and feed her and make her comfortable for the night. After a meal, Art and his wife's brother sat talking, and most of the brother's talk was about how bad the magician was and the harm he had done. Next morning, after himself and the horse had been fed, Art mounted the saddle and bade goodbye to them. He was off with the little horse, and by evening she landed Art at the door of the house of another brother of his wife. The servant that was minding the house caught sight of the little horse through the window and made off where her master was, in great excitement.

"What's wrong with you?" asked the master.

"Such a thing," said she. "Your sister's horse is outside in the field and no man or woman ever saw a finer warrior than the man that's riding her."

The master went out.

"Where did you get that horse, my good man?" he asked.

Art told him, from the first word to the last, how he had got the horse and how his sister was married to him and was at home, as well as he would want her to be, with her young son.

"Your account is a great gift. We had no news of where she was," said the master.

He told Art to get off the horse, and a servant was ordered to stable and dry and feed her and make her comfortable for the night. Art and the second brother spent most of the night talking, and almost all of the talk was about the magician. Next morning, after himself and the horse had been fed, Art mounted the saddle and bade goodbye to them. That evening, he was at the house of the third brother. The servant that was minding the house caught sight of the horse through the window and made off to her master with the news that his sister's horse was outside in the field. The master went out, and his first salute to Art was where did he get the horse he had. Art told him from the first word to the last how he had got her, and that his sister was married to him at home, and that she was as well as he would want her to be, with her young son.

"Your account is a great gift. We didn't know whether our sister was alive or dead."

He told Art to get off the horse, and a servant was ordered to stable and dry and feed her and make her comfortable for the night. After eating, they spent a part of the night talking to each other. But 'twas the same story with this brother—all he could talk about was the magician. They got up next morning and ate their breakfast.

"Now," said his brother-in-law to Art, "tonight you will be at the house of your wife's father. There's no doubt but the little horse will knock a start out of them."

Art mounted the saddle and bade goodbye to them. He went off with the little horse like the wind, and he never stopped till he landed at the father-in-law's house fairly early in the evening. Whatever servant was minding the house caught sight of the horse through the window and made off to her master in great excitement.

"What fright is on you now?" asked the king.

"No fright at all, your majesty," said the servant, "only that your daughter's little horse is outside in the field."

The king went out. The queen went out. All that were in the castle went out. And the first salute the king gave Art was to ask him where he got the horse. Art told them from the first word to the last, and that he was married to his daughter, and that she was as well as he would want her to be, at home after him, with their young son.

"The account you have for us is a wonderful gift," said the king and queen. "We didn't know whether our daughter was alive or dead."

The king ordered a servant to stable and dry and feed the horse and make her comfortable for the night. The king and his son-in-law spent a part of the night talking, and the king asked Art what had brought him that way. Art told him, and the king started to tell him again all the harm and trouble the magician of the eastern world had caused between his son-in-law, Balor Béimeannach, and himself.

"'Tis Balor Béimeannach that has the Sword of Light," said

the king. "He's as good as two men, and as long as he has the sword in his hand, 'twill be hard to beat him."

"All I can do is try," said Art.

"Now," said the king, "you won't take my daughter's little horse with you at all tomorrow. I'll give you one of my own. You'll find Balor sitting on a chair inside the window of his castle, and the Sword of Light will be hanging on a hook over his head. You must back your horse to the window and ask Balor is he there. He'll say that he is, and he'll ask what you want. The minute you tell him that you want the Truth of the One Story and the Sword of Light, you must dig the spurs into your horse and make for the gate."

Art rode to the castle and told Balor inside the window what he wanted.

"You'll get them right away," said Balor.

Art didn't wait to hear what he said but drove the spurs into his horse and galloped for the gate. Just as the horse was rising to jump the gate, Balor caught up with her and cut her in two with his sword. The front half, with the saddle and bridle and Art, fell out over the gate. Art went home to the king and told him his fine horse was dead.

"Don't mind that," said the king. "'Tisn't shortage of horses is troubling me, but shortage of stables for them."

Art took another horse with him to Balor's castle the following day, and the same thing happened. Balor cut the horse in two again, just behind the saddle, and Art came home walking. He refused to take any horse with him the next day.

"All right," said the king. "Now Balor hasn't eaten a bite or slept a wink since the first day you went to the window to him. When you steal up to the gate, take off all your clothes except your shirt and trousers. Climb over the gate, if you can, and go on tiptoe up to the window. Balor will be half-asleep inside, and he'll have all the doors and windows open in order to run after you easily. The Sword of Light will be hanging over his head, and you must get a hold of it. The minute the sword will feel the strange hand touching it, it will give a scream that will be heard all over the country. But you must hold on to it. If you loosen your hold, you're finished."

Art did as the king told him. When Balor heard the mighty
scream that the sword gave, he fell backwards onto the floor in
his sleep.

"I have it now," said Art.

"You have, and no thanks to me," said Balor. "Would you
mind my asking why you came for it?"

"I wouldn't," said Art, telling him the whole story from the
first word to the last.

"Well, 'tis many a year and a day since the magician of the
eastern world started making trouble between myself and my
wife and her father. I'm here since, with no one coming near me.
You can take the sword away with you now or leave it until
tomorrow, and I'll give you my hand and word that I'll help
you to carry it tomorrow."

"I'll take your word and welcome," said Art.

"I'll be very glad to go with you to my father-in-law's castle
tomorrow," said Balor. "We haven't seen each other for years, on
account of the magician. When we get there, I'll tell you the
Truth of the One Story."

The following day, Art went back to Balor and the two of
them brought the sword to the king's castle. You may be sure
there was a great welcome for Balor and his wife, and there
was no hunger left on them. They had kinds of food and drink
that we don't know at all.

When the feast was over, Balor said to Art, "Now I'll tell you
the Truth of the One Story. When the magician came between
myself and my wife, she turned me into a white horse. Any day
that she didn't need me herself, the neighbors would use me.
I got neither food nor drink, and everybody whipping me all
they could. All the time, I could think like a man, but what was
the use? The only way I could become a man again was if the
bridle was taken off my head. One day, as I was drinking water,
I used to lift up my head after wetting my lips and champ the bit
with my teeth, and the boy who was holding the reins thought
that I was unable to drink. He took off the winkers, and as soon
as it slipped off my head, I was a man. When the boy saw who
I was, he fell in a faint, and I had to spend two hours trying to
revive him. I don't know how my wife found out what had

happened, but no sooner did the boy and myself go in the gate than she struck me again with her magic wand and turned me into a fine big bull. Am I telling any word of a lie?" said Balor to his wife.

"Indeed, you're not," said she. "Your last word is as truthful as your first."

"Well, I was going around as a bull then, but I had the mind of a man all the time. I started to do all the damage I could to the land and the crops and everything. One evening, when I was coming in through the gate with the cows, my wife struck me again and turned me into a wild dog. Am I telling any word of a lie?" said Balor to his wife.

"Indeed, you're not," said she. "Your last word is as truthful as your first."

"I went off to the hill then as a wild dog," said Balor, "but I had the mind of a man all the time. I and other wild dogs killed every hen and duck and goose and turkey that she had. And when we had them all killed and eaten, we started to destroy the wheat and oats and all the other crops on the land. She guessed well enough that it was I that was doing the bad work so she appointed a day for the hounds to hunt us. The hunters knew well where our den was, and all the kings and knights came with their dogs for a day's hunting after us. They set fire to the den, and we were blinded by the smoke inside. Outside the den, they had a lot of good fighting dogs, and no sooner would one of us rush out than he would be torn to pieces by them. I stayed inside the last of all, keeping an eye out to see could I escape in any way. My father-in-law was on the horse nearest the mouth of the den. I gave a leap out over the dogs and landed beside the horse, and before the dogs could collect their wits, I had jumped onto the back of the horse. My father-in-law ordered all the hunters and dogs to stand back. I had claimed his protection, he said, and he would take me home with him.

"So he did, and I don't think that, since the world was created, there ever was so faithful a dog as I was. I went everywhere with my father-in-law. Now, at that time no house of a king or a knight was without a magic wand, which used to be taken out only once every seven years. My father-in-law dressed himself

in a special suit of clothes—it would gladden your heart to see it
—when he took out the wand, and the two of us went for a walk.
We hadn't gone far when he came to a muddy hole of water.
I threw myself into it and started to roll about in it. You couldn't
make out what kind of animal I was when I came out. I had a
suspicion that if I rubbed my dirty coat to his suit, he would get
cross with me and strike me with the wand. And when I was
getting too close to him, he struck me with it, and I became a
man once more just as I'm talking to you now. When my father-
in-law saw who I was, he fell in a heap, and I had to spend an
hour trying to bring the life back into him. It was all I could do,
so great was the fright he got. The two of us returned home then,
and he ordered a big fire to be made of timber and tar and oil
and everything. Then he sent for his daughter—that's my wife
here. Am I telling any word of a lie?"

"Indeed, you're not," said his wife. "Your last word is as true
as your first word."

"When the fire was blazing strong," said Balor, "he gave
orders to throw his daughter into it. But I took hold of my wife
and said that I wouldn't allow her to suffer a death like that, no
matter what kind of a life we'd lead together afterward. I got her
pardon from him. I took her home, and ever since, we have been
living as happily as we were the first day ever. But I was so
ashamed that I didn't go outside the door of the castle since, until
I left it today. Am I telling any word of a lie?"

"Indeed, you're not. Your last word is as true as your first,"
said she.

They all got ready then to go to see Art's own wife. The king
and his wife, Balor Béimeannach and his wife, and Art and the
little horse never stopped until they reached Dublin Bay. Their
ship was full of presents for Art's son. (If the two of us had it all,
we wouldn't want for anything.)

"Now," said Balor Béimeannach, "the magician will surely
meet us where ye played the game, and he will want to get the
Sword of Light. Tell him that you were not under any *geasa* to
give him the sword, only to show it to him. Ask him is that it,
and he will have to admit that it is. Then give it into my hand
and start to tell him the Truth of the One Story."

The magician of the eastern world was waiting for them at the place where they played the game, and when he saw the crowd, he got a surprise.

"Did you bring it, Art?" he asked.

"I did," said Art. "Is this it?"

"It is," said the magician. "Give it to me!"

"I don't have to give it to you at all," said Art. "All I had to do was to get it."

He handed the sword to Balor Béimeannach. Art started to tell the magician the Truth of the One Story, but so impatient was Balor to attack the magician, that he didn't let him hear much of it. He cut the magician into small pieces. So the prophecy of Art's wife came true that that was the forfeit that would cause his death.

They went then to the castle of the king of Leinster, and if ever anybody saw a feast of pride and rejoicing, it was there he saw it. The feast lasted for seven days and seven nights in honor of Art and his people, and when it was over, everybody made off to his own home.

That's the end of the story.

•19• *The Speckled Bull*

Once upon a time, and a long time ago it was, there was a king and a queen in Ireland. That wasn't in your time or in my time but in the time of people who are long since dead and gone.

They had one son, the finest man that ever walked on green grass. Every woman in the country was after him, each thinking that she would get him. The daughters of the gentry came to see him, but he didn't give them a second look. There were two sisters living near the palace, one of them about seven years older than the other, and whenever the prince went out walking or hunting, he used to call upon these girls on his way home. The upshot of it was that they became friendly. The eldest girl took a great "notion" for him and thought that he might marry her, but he paid no attention at all to her. Needless to say, he preferred the young sister, and the end of it was that he married her. Sisters and all though they were, the marriage made the eldest very jealous, and she wouldn't mind if she saw her sister drowned in a pool of water.

At the end of a year or so, the prince's wife gave birth to a son. Her husband happened to be out hunting at the time, and the only one with her was the jealous sister. She made up her mind to get rid of the child and to tell the prince, when he came home, that his wife had given birth to a kitten. That might cause trouble between them. So what did she do but wrap the child up in a dirty piece of *báinín* and throw him into the river. The prince returned home at twilight, went to his wife's room, and saw her lying in bed.

"What's wrong with her?" he asked the sister, who was minding her.

"I don't know," said she. "That's a nice wife you married. I thought she was going to have a child, and what had she but a kitten."

"And what did you do with it?" said the prince.

"What would I do but throw it in the river?" said she.

The prince was very sad at what he heard, but he said nothing and kept his troubles to himself. He remained as friendly as before with his wife, and when she got well again, they lived happily. A year later, while the prince was hunting one day, didn't his wife give birth to another son. And the sister tried the same trick again. She placed the child in a small box and threw the little creature, alive and all, out into the river.

"Now," said she, "when he comes home this evening, I'll tell him 'twas a strange wife he married, who could only give birth to animals, like the pup today."

When the prince returned in the evening, he didn't see his wife about the house, so he went to her room and found her lying asleep in bed. Her sister was with her, and he asked her what was wrong.

"Well," said the sister, "if you wanted to marry, you had all the women in the world to choose from. And look whom you married. Your wife has just given birth to a pup."

"And what did you do with it?"

"What would I do but throw it in the river. I saw that it wouldn't be a thing to have about the house, and that you wouldn't want to see it."

"If that's the way things were," said the prince, "you did well to get rid of it."

"If you had married me the day you married, things wouldn't be this way," said she. "I'd have borne proper children."

The prince had his own opinion about the whole affair, but he said little. (There's a proverb that 'tis hard to outwit the women, and it looks like being true.) The sister kept on at the prince till she came between himself and his wife, and one day he said that he would banish her.

"Don't do that," said the sister. "Leave her to me, and I'll fix her so that she won't trouble you ever again."

"Very well," said the prince.

At that time, some people had a thing called magic, and when they struck somebody with a magic wand, they could turn him into a green stone. That's what the eldest sister did. She struck the prince's wife a blow and made a green stone out of her and left her outside the door where every drop of dirty water from the house would be thrown on top of her. Then she and the prince got married.

It happened that there was a man fishing at the mouth of the river the day the second child was thrown into it, and he saw the box caught in a bush that was growing on the bank. He threw out a hook and hauled in the box to his feet. No sooner did he lift it up than he heard the cry of the poor child. He pulled off the cover, and inside was the nicest little boy that he had ever laid eyes on. He had no children of his own, although he was married, and he thanked God for sending a child to him like this. He took him out carefully and never stopped till he brought him home to his wife. She was seven times as delighted as her husband. She took him in her arms and was as fond of him, or maybe more so, as she would have been if he were her own child.

The boy grew strong, and the news about the fine child the fisherman's wife had went around. Everybody was wondering about it, because she had no children before. The news went from mouth to mouth, and the end of it was that the prince's new wife heard it. She had a suspicion immediately about how the child had been got, and she couldn't close an eye, day or night, until she'd see the child and find out where he had come from. One day while the prince was out hunting, she set out and never stopped till she found out the fisherman's house. She greeted the wife in the manner of those times, and the wife welcomed her in the same way. The child was lying in a cradle near the fire. She hadn't much to say before going over to the cradle, and she immediately saw that he was her sister's son.

"Isn't he a fine child, God bless him?" said she.

"He's a good boy, thank you," said the fisherman's wife.

"What a pity it is that he isn't your own," said the other.

"Of course, he's my own. 'Tis unmannerly of you to come into my house and say a thing like that. I don't know who you are or where you're from."

"I'm not telling any lie," said the prince's wife. "And to prove it, you will have to kill that child. You think that he is a normal child of this world, but he isn't. He's a changeling that the hill-folk have left with you, and unless you take my advice, you'll regret it for many a long day."

The fisherman's poor wife became terrified.

"Well, if that's the way," said she, "I won't have any more to do with him. Take him away and do whatever you like with him. I couldn't find it in my heart to lay a finger on him."

"Yes, 'tis better to give him to me, and he won't give you any more trouble for the rest of your life."

The prince's wife took away the child and cut his throat immediately. It troubled her no more than if it were a chicken she were killing. Then she took the body out into the garden and buried it in a lonely corner. Her heart was satisfied as she made her way back to the palace.

When the fisherman returned home that evening, he missed the child, and no wonder, and asked his wife where he was. She told him the whole story, and he almost went out of his mind. But what was the use when the harm was done?

A tall tree grew up from the child's grave in the corner of the garden, up and up to the sky in the space of a couple of nights, and it bent down to the ground with all the different fruits that ever grew on a tree.

Now, the prince had some cattle grazing on the fisherman's land, and one day they were driven into the garden where this tree was growing. There was a big speckled cow among the herd, and instead of starting to eat the grass like the others, she started to eat the fruits on the tree. She began to give so much milk that they hadn't enough vessels to hold it. And then, although there was no bull, when her time was up she gave birth to a male speckled calf. Everybody was surprised at this—the prince as well as the rest. He made up his mind to go to see what kind of grazing the cow had, and when he entered the garden he saw the tree of the fruits. He asked the fisherman about it, and he told him the whole story about the child as I have told it to you.

He took his cattle away from the garden and returned home. He said nothing about what he had seen and heard; he wouldn't give his wife that much satisfaction. As soon as he changed the cattle, the speckled cow was just like all the others, not differing in any way. Her speckled calf ran about after her, and in no time at all he was as fine a bull as there was in Ireland. They intended to castrate him, but there weren't enough men in Ireland to catch and hold him. They had to leave him as he was.

The prince's wife heard about the bull, and she had a suspicion that unless he was killed, he would be the cause of her own death some day. She didn't know under God how to put an end to him. She remained awake at night, trying to think of some plan to get rid of him, and at last she hit upon one. She would pretend to be dying and would whisper to a doctor who was in the district that nothing would cure her but the heart and liver of the speckled bull to eat. She was sure that, rather than let her die, the prince would agree to that, and welcome.

One day the prince went out hunting as usual. When she found him gone, she made off to the doctor and told him her plan. She gave him a big fistful of money, and he promised to do what she asked. Then she returned home. She spent the rest of the day working and when she thought it was time for her husband to be returning in the evening, she went out and brought in a cock and drew its blood. She put the blood into a vessel.

Then she went to bed, pretending to be very ill. She put the vessel of blood under the head of the bed. She heard him coming in and took a mouthful of the blood and as soon as he darkened the doorway, she bent out over the edge of the bed and spouted the blood from her mouth into the vessel on the floor. He got a terrible start.

"What in God's name is wrong with you?" he cried.

"I don't know what it is," said she, "but I have been spouting blood since dinnertime. Get the doctor!"

The doctor was sent for and came immediately. He had been waiting for the call and had even been paid by the woman who was pretending to be sick. He went to her room and examined her pulse.

"She's very ill," he said. "I'm afraid she won't last long."

"Is there anything in the world to cure her?" asked the prince.

"Only one thing to my knowledge," said the doctor. "You have a speckled bull. You must kill him and give your wife his heart and liver to eat. If you don't, she will die."

" 'Twould be very hard for me to do that," said the prince. "If 'twere anything else, I'd do it gladly. But how can I kill that bull? We tried before to catch him and found that there weren't enough men in Ireland to tie or hold him, let alone kill him."

"Well, you have two choices," replied the doctor, "let your wife die or kill the bull."

"I can't let her die, and I can't avoid it unless I collect all the men in the country," said the prince.

He sent word through the kingdom, asking every man who could to come immediately to help him in his great trouble. The men began to assemble, and when he thought there were enough to hold the bull, they all entered the field and tried to catch him. One of them threw a rope on top of him. At that, the bull gave a roar and rose up into the sky, dragging along with him the man who held the rope, and he didn't touch the ground again until he was seven miles away. Off went the bull through the air, like the March wind, and never touched earth until he reached a field in the eastern world, where the cattle of the king of the eastern world were grazing.

Next morning, when the milkers went out to milk the king's

cows, they saw the huge speckled bull along with them. They were terrified by his size; he was as big as three bulls of the eastern world put together. They threw their milk pails on the ground and ran back to the palace. They told about the bull, and half the people of the kingdom were gathered around the field before dinner time, gazing with awe and wonder at the huge animal.

The king of the eastern world had a very beautiful daughter, who was under *geasa* never to leave the palace unless her eyes were covered. If she removed the veil from her eyes, she had to marry the first man she saw, even though he were only a beggar. Needless to say, the king was afraid that she might have to marry somebody of lowly birth; so he always put the veil over her eyes when she went outside the palace.

News of the wonderful speckled bull reached the king and of the half of the kingdom who were watching him. So he made up his mind to go to see the animal for himself. It was his custom to take his daughter with him when he was going anywhere, and he couldn't take her where large crowds were assembled. So he sent a messenger out to the field to order the people to go away, because he and his daughter were going to see the bull. The people had to do as they were told, of course, and as soon as they got the order, they scattered east and west. Then the king was told that all was ready.

He and his daughter, who was wearing her veil, walked toward the field. There was the speckled bull. The king had never seen an animal like him. He was as big as twenty of his own bulls. He was so filled with wonder that he thought it fit that his daughter should see the bull also. He looked around him, and as there was no man in sight at any point, he decided to take off the daughter's veil. As soon as she laid eyes on the bull, she fell in a faint at her father's feet. He couldn't understand what in the world had come over her. She lay in the faint for a while, and he thought that she might die on his hands. But she soon recovered, and her father asked her what had happened.

"O, you ought to have had more sense than to bring me to a place like this!" she cried.

"Why is that?" he asked.

"You knew well," said she, "that I was under *geasa* not to gaze on any man's face, except your own, without having my veil on."

"But you don't need any veil in this place," said the king. "There's no man here only the cattle and this speckled bull that everybody is wondering at. I thought that you should see the bull as well as anybody else."

"But I don't see any bull," said she.

"What do you see, then?" asked her father.

"I see a king's son," said she.

"A king's son," said her father. "I fear you must have lost your senses, or your eyes are affected since you fainted. Stand still for a while until you recover."

"Standing still won't do me any good," said she. "I see a king's son out there in front of me, and he's the finest man that a young girl, or an old woman either, ever laid eyes on."

"That's nonsense!" said the king. "How could a man be there?"

"Place your hand on my left shoulder," said she; "and I'll guarantee that you'll see something that will open your eyes for you."

He placed his hand on her shoulder and saw before him the finest and most handsome man he had ever seen. The moment he laid eyes on him, the king decided that here was the one man in the world whom he would like his daughter to marry. He was wondering how he could get a chance of speaking to him. Then, no sooner had he removed his hand from his daughter's shoulder, than he saw the huge wild speckled bull once more. The daughter said that she would go to speak to him herself; so the pair of them walked over to the middle of the field. The bull did not move until they were within speaking distance of him. Then the king put his hand on his daughter's shoulder again, and they both began to chat with the king's son. They conversed for a long time, and the upshot of it was that the king asked him would he marry his daughter.

"I will, and welcome!" said he. "But the way I am, I won't be of much use to her or to any other woman."

"Well," replied the king, "it may not be long more until you are free from your *geasa*. My daughter here was also under *geasa* and now she is free from them. She has met a king's son who has promised to marry her."

The marriage day was fixed. The people's wonder about the speckled bull grew less. And so the marriage took place. Whatever kind the *geasa* on the king's son were, they allowed him to be a bull by day and a man by night, or a man by day and a bull by night. On the day that they were married, the king's son asked his wife which would she prefer, and she said she would like best if he were a man by night.

"Very well," said he. "I'll be a man by night."

When night fell, he came to the palace, where his wife was, looking the finest man in the world, well dressed from head to feet. Nobody in the world would believe that he was a bull by day. The king and his wife had the greatest welcome for him; they got ready a great feast, and all ate and drank their fill. He went to bed with his wife and slept his fill until morning—what he hadn't done for a long time. He was up as soon as the sun rose and as soon as he had eaten, out he went and joined the cattle in the field as a bull. He grazed among them until sunset; then he made a man of himself and went back to his wife. She was overjoyed to see him. To make a long story short, he kept coming and going in that manner for some years. His wife loved him more and more, and she used to be heartbroken when he left her each morning.

Now at that time, every king had a druid, who knew everything in the world. The king of the eastern world had one also, and he made known his knowledge and remedies only once every seven years. The reason for this was that he did not wish to worry the king by telling him more often about things that were to happen. When the seven years were almost up, the king thought it a suitable time to ask the druid if there was any remedy in the world which would remove the *geasa* from his daughter's husband. He told the druid the whole story.

"I understand," said the druid. "Both your daughter and her husband are in a difficult position, but if you and he do as I tell you, his *geasa* will be over, and he will be a man for ever more. Tell him to start fighting with the other cattle the next day he is grazing; they will all gather about him and half-kill him. His left horn will be broken and the fighting will stop. You must act quickly! As soon as you see the broken horn hanging from him, you must run to him and catch hold of the horn. Inside the horn will be a small drop that looks like water. You must place the little drop in a vessel. Then turn away from the bull and go to the other side of the field. Have a small red cloth in your pocket. You must take this out and hold it toward the bull. He will be so mad when he sees the cloth that he will rush toward you immediately. 'Tis then you must be wide-awake! When he comes near you, you must throw the drop at him, between his two eyes. If you succeed in that, his *geasa* will be over. If you don't, he will kill you."

"Upon my soul!" said the king. "All that is more easily said than done. But I'll try it. 'Twould be better to be dead than to see how my poor daughter is suffering, seeing her husband go off as a brute beast every morning."

"If you succeed in doing what I have told you," said the druid, "you and your daughter will live happily for the rest of your lives." He then answered all the questions that had been troubling the king for the past seven years and gave him advice for the seven years that lay ahead. They parted then, and they would not meet for seven years more.

When the daughter's husband came home from the field that evening, they ate their supper, and the king told him what the druid had advised him to do. The king's son was very satisfied with what he heard and told the king to go to the field next day.

"You must be very careful not to come too close to.me." he said. "I have only my own animal sense when I'm a bull, and I might kill you."

"Don't worry about that," said the king. "I'll do my best to mind myself. I'd prefer to die, in any case, rather than be looking at you as you are."

They all went to bed that night. Next morning the king's son rose early and went off to the field as a bull, as he did each morning. The king got up too and prepared to go out into the field. He told the cow-herd to drive all the cattle into the field where the bull was and even to drive in strange cattle which the bull was not used to and he would start to fight with them. The herd did as the king told him. As soon as the bull smelled them, he lifted his head and gave one roar that shook the whole kingdom. He frightened some of the old people in the kingdom so much that they died with the terror. Others of them died in their beds. As the king drew near the field he was very much afraid, but he would have to face the battle to remove the *geasa* from the speckled bull.

The fight started between the bull and the cattle. They made hard places of the soft places and soft places of the hard places. They drew wells of water from the green stones, and there wasn't a young or an old person in the kingdom that wasn't running into holes and caves with the dint of terror. Every blow that the bull gave to the cattle knocked an echo out of them as if the two sides of the world were being struck together. The bull was dashing them together until late evening. The day's end came, and the little birds of the wood were going to rest for the night. By that time, the bull was tired. When the herd noticed that, he went to another field, where there was a big strong bullock which he had not yet shown to the bull. As soon as the bull saw the newcomer, he rushed at him and broke off his left horn at the base. He lost his strength then. But he had already killed a lot of the cattle, and there was so much blood spilt that it would reach to the mouth of a man's shoes all over the field.

The king was standing outside the fence, and he saw the horn hanging down from the bull's head. He ran toward him, snatched the horn free, and took it to the other side of the field. The drop was in it still, and he poured it into a small vessel that he had for it. The bull was recovering by this time, and when the king saw this, he pulled the red cloth out of his pocket and began to shake it toward the bull. The bull let a wild roar out of him that shook rocks and trees, lifted up his tail, and rooted up as much clay with his two front legs as would cover half a townland. He ran towards the king, who, knowing it was his only chance, took courage and threw the drop against his forehead as he made for him. It was God's will that he struck him on the right spot.

No sooner did the drop touch his forehead than there stood before the king the finest young man he had ever laid eyes on.

The *geasa* had gone. The young man shook hands with the king and thanked him for his bravery. They both went to the palace. The king was so overjoyed that he completely forgot about his cattle that had been killed. There was great rejoicing in the palace that night.

The young husband rested for some days, and then he decided that it was time for him to return to his old home to look after his mother and to get rid of his stepmother. He knew well all that had happened, and he would not rest until the evildoer had been punished. The king offered to give up his throne and his kingdom and all his wealth to him, so that he and his young wife would lack for nothing.

"I'll accept that and welcome," said the young man, "but I can't stay any longer just now. Tomorrow morning I must set out for Ireland to see my mother and remove the *geasa* from her."

"Well, since that's what you want to do," said the king of the eastern world, "I won't ask you to stay here. But I will send a fleet of ships and men with you to fight your way, in case of need."

"I'm grateful to you," said the young man; "but I won't take either fleet or men along with me. If I can't make my way myself, I won't ask anyone else to fight for me. I have come through worse trials than this, and I hope I won't meet anything that will overcome me."

As soon as the day dawned the next morning, he was up and ready for the journey. But his wife refused to let him out of the palace unless he allowed her to accompany him. He had to yield. They took with them to the shore plenty of food and drink and a magic wand. They put their baggage in a small boat that was there and bade farewell to the king. They hoisted their bulging swelling sails to the tops of the straight masts, turned the prow of the boat toward the sea and her stern toward the land and never stopped or stayed on their course until they sailed in near the palace of the king of Ireland There was a big strand where they reached shore, and the husband told his wife that she had better remain on board; he would make no delay. He would only take the *geasa* off his mother. She agreed to do this.

What should be taking place at the palace but a christening! And the whole kingdom was gathered there. Nobody recognized him; neither did he tell anybody who he was. He started to enjoy the fun as much as everybody else. There was drinking and music and storytelling; there was no shortage of storytellers there. At last the stranger was asked to tell a story. He began, and what did he start telling but what had happened to himself from the day he was born up to that time. The stepmother, who was guilty of all that, was sitting listening to him, and as he told his story, she quickly guessed who he was.

When he had finished his story, "Now, people," said he to the company, "I'll leave the decision to ye as to what punishment the woman who did that should get."

Some suggested this and others suggested that. The question was then put to the stepmother. She said that she should be put up on the highest chimney top of the palace, faced towards the wind, and given no food but whatever small grain the wind might blow to her and no drink but whatever drop of rain she could catch on her tongue.

"You have passed judgment on yourself," said he.

He gave order that what she had suggested should be done to her immediately, and so it was. He then went out into the yard with his magic wand and struck the stone which was his mother. The next moment she rose up as well as she had ever been. He wet her with tears and dried her with kisses and silks and satins. He took her to the shore, where his own wife was waiting for him in the boat. He put her aboard and hoisted his sails as he had done when coming, and left goodbye and his blessing to Ireland. He never stopped until he had brought his boat near the palace of the king of the eastern world. He dragged it up to the top of the strand, and they all went toward the palace.

The king was anxiously waiting for their return, and he was delighted when he saw them coming with the young king's mother with them. A great, pleasant, and friendly feast was prepared, and the king invited the whole kingdom to it. That feast lasted a year and a day, and the last day was better than the first. Before it ended, the king placed the crown on the young man's head and his wife became queen. His mother became a noble lady, and girls were appointed to attend her as long as she lived. They had no shortage of wealth or money, and they spent the rest of their lives happy and contented until they died.

I can't say what happened to the woman that was left on the chimney top, but if she suffered what was laid down for her, she well deserved it and nobody would have any great pity for her.

And now, you have got the start and the finish of the story that my father used to call "The Speckled Bull and the King of the Eastern World."

Part III
Saints and Sinners

The Boy Who Became Pope

A very long time ago, there was a pope and he died. Nobody could be elected to take his place except the person toward whom the pope's chair moved, of its own accord, as he entered the room where it was. A message was sent to every priest and bishop in the world, asking them to come to Rome to see whom God would choose as Pope. They came from everywhere, but it was to no avail. The chair did not move toward any of them.

Time passed. There was a young priest in Ireland, and he made up his mind to go to Rome. He got ready, and one day he set out on his journey. He traveled on and on until he was tired. Night fell, and he went into a small house by the roadside. There was nobody in the house except a man and his wife and their only son. They had a thousand welcomes for him and asked him to sit down. He did and asked if he could stay until morning. They were delighted and told him that he could. He began to chat with the man of the house. The man asked him where he was making for, and he told him.

The woman of the house got a fine meal ready for them all; the poor priest was very hungry. He sat at the head of the table, and the man and his son sat by the side. Before starting to eat, the priest said the Grace Before Meals, and as he did so, the young boy laughed. The priest told the father not to stop him, as the father was very angry and about to strike him. They ate and drank their fill, and when they had finished, the priest said the Grace After Meals. The boy laughed out loud again.

"You have no manners, son," said the father. "If you don't behave yourself, I'll break your neck."

"Let him be," said the priest. "Let him have his way. That's the only sense he has."

That passed off until it was time to go to bed. Then the priest asked the boy why he had laughed while he was saying Grace.

"Well," said the boy, "it wasn't at you I was laughing at all. I'll tell you why I laughed. When you were saying the Grace Before

Meals, I could see the Angel of the Right Hand fighting with the Angel of the Left Hand. The Angel of the Right Hand knocked the other down into the ashes of the fire and won the fight. And when you said the Grace After Meals, the same thing happened. That's what made me laugh."

"You are clever, my lad," said the priest. "Go to bed now, and I will take you with me tomorrow."

They all went to bed then. The priest rose early next morning, and when the breakfast was eaten, and the priest was getting ready to leave, he asked the people of the house would they allow the boy to go with him.

"Well," replied the father, "we have only him, and we don't wish to part with him."

His wife said the same thing.

"I promise that, if ye let him go with me," said the priest, "I will take good care of him, and nothing will happen to him until we return again."

The man of the house didn't like to refuse the priest; so he let the lad go with him. The priest and the boy traveled on together and passed over a big, high mountain. On the very top of the mountain they came upon a clump of nettles growing.

"Can you tell me, boy, why a clump of nettles should be growing here in the heart of the mountain?" asked the priest.

"I can," said the boy. "There was a church here at one time, but it has now disappeared. You will hear more about it later."

They walked on and on, and when the dark night was falling, they came to a gentleman's house far into a glen.

As they approached it, "We will stay here until morning," said the priest. "It is too late to go any farther. I'll go in first to find out if they will let us stay until morning."

"Put a mark on your finger, before you go in," said the boy, "or you will forget all about me."

The priest put a mark on his finger and then went in. The poor boy remained outside. The gentleman himself opened the door when he heard the knock. He invited the priest into the parlor, and soon he was sitting at the table for a meal. As he sat down, the priest noticed the mark on his finger and suddenly remembered the boy.

" 'Twas true for you, poor boy," said he. "I had forgotten about you."

He rose from the table immediately and went out to the boy.

"Well I knew that this would happen," said the boy. "You almost completely forgot about me."

The priest took him into the house, and they all sat down to the table. They ate a hearty meal, for they were in need of it by that time. When they had finished, the gentleman told them that his daughter was dying and asked them could they cure her by any means. The two of them went to see her. She was very ill. The priest had no cure to offer; so he asked the boy had he any idea what was wrong with her.

"I know very well what ails her," said the boy. "I will tell you. When she was receiving her first Holy Communion, the Host fell from her lips on to the floor of the church. That church has fallen since, and no trace of it remains except the clump of nettles that we saw today. There is no cure in store for her until she receives that Holy Communion again."

"The two of us will go there tomorrow to search for it," said the priest.

Very well! They stayed in the big house until morning and set out immediately for the mountain. They never stopped or halted till they reached the clump of nettles on the top. They searched high up and low down until they found the Host. They took it back with them to the big house as fast as they could. When they reached the house, the priest gave the girl the Holy Communion, and she got up out of bed completely cured. Once she had received the Host, there was no more wrong with her. When the gentleman saw that his daughter was as well as she had ever been, he was delighted. He offered them a lot of money, but the priest would not accept a penny. He told the gentleman to give it to the boy, and he did.

They said goodbye to all in the house and set off on their journey again. They never stopped traveling until they reached Rome. They went to a lodginghouse. Next morning the priest told the boy to remain there until he returned. The priest then went to where all the other priests were, but he did no good. The chair did not move toward him. He was not the one to be Pope.

He met another priest then and told him about the poor boy he had with him since he left Ireland. He said that the boy had knowledge from God and that perhaps he should be allowed in to where the chair was. He might be the chosen pope. The two priests returned to where the boy was and took him to where all the other priests were. The moment he entered the room, didn't the chair move toward him! It was he who was to be the Pope. All those who were present were filled with surprise, but it was no wonder at all. He was a holy saint.

The priest who had brought him to Rome was delighted that he had got on so well. He returned to Ireland, but the boy never came back. He was in the best service. The priest called in to visit the boy's father, on his way, and told him where his son was. The poor father was very sad that his son did not return to him. His wife went out of her mind. May God preserve us all!

•21• The Man Who Struck His Father

There was a man called Shea living at Ventry. He was poor and hadn't a sod of land, so he used to go from place to place to earn his living. Every night he would visit houses in Ballincalla and Ballyaglisha, for company's sake with a companion. This fellow was constantly talking of going to America when he had his "passage" earned.

"Wait another year for me," said he to Shea one night, "and the two of us will hit the road together."

"I will, and two years," said Shea, "if you come."

"I'll come without fail," said the other.

When the two years were up, they traveled to Queenstown by jingle and took lodgings in the town for the night. They went into a public house and spent a while talking there, the Ventry man and the Ballincalla man. The publican had a widowed sister who had another public house nearby where she sold meal and flour and things like that. The widow sent her servant girl to the brother's shop for some soap, but when she had got the soap, the girl didn't leave. She remained there watching Shea and admiring him. She had fallen in love with him. He was so handsome. When she finally went off home, her mistress was scolding her for delaying so long, and the girl told her that she had seen the finest man she had ever laid her eyes on.

"I couldn't take my eyes off him!" said she, and she started to describe him to the widow.

"Well, since he's as fine as all that," said the widow, "go and invite him down here until I see him. And tell my brother to come too."

"My mistress would like the three of ye to go down to her place, and she'll stand ye a drink," said the girl when she went back to the brother's public house.

"Do ye hear that?" said the brother. "Come along! I'll bet that my fine sister has laid eyes on you, Shea."

"I won't go at all," said Shea.

The other two were ready to go, but Shea refused for a while, until at last they got him to go with them. As soon as the widow saw him, she put a pint of whiskey on the table in front of them.

"Now," said her brother, "if 'tis a fine man you want, here he is, as fine as anyone could lay eyes on."

"I'm thinking he's all that," said the widow. "If he stays here with me, I'll marry him as he stands, and he'll get all I have in money and property."

Shea refused to stay, but they kept on pressing him until they softened him, and he finally agreed.

His companion sailed for America next morning, and Shea stayed and married the widow. Time went by, and Shea didn't send a line of a letter home to his father and mother. They were at home, wondering why he wasn't writing to them. At the end of a year, when no letter came, his father made off to the companion's people in Ballincalla and asked them was it long since they had a letter.

"'Tisn't so long," they said. "We got one about a fortnight ago."

"I'm wondering is that son of mine alive at all?" said the old man.

"He's alive below in Queenstown and married there," they told him.

"That's something I didn't know then," said the old man. "He must be dead. If he were alive, he'd write to me."

There it was. He returned home and told his wife the account he had got and where their son was. The wife said he must be dead and buried.

"I'll find out whether 'tis true or not before long," said the father. "I'll walk all the way to Queenstown to find out if he is there as they are saying. Get me some food for the road."

"I will," said the wife.

He stuck the food into a rough pack on his back, took his stick in his hand, and set out. He slept a night here and a night there until he made off Queenstown. The trouble then was to locate his son. He met a policeman and asked him if there was a man by the name of Shea living in the town.

"What's he to you?" asked the policeman.

"He's my son, if you want to know," said the old man with his pack on his back.

"If you're any relation of that man, you need never again go looking for alms," said the policeman. "He's as rich as any man in this town. I'll show you his house and welcome."

He took him within sight of the house and pointed it out to him. The old man went toward it. It was a summer morning, and the son was dressing himself upstairs after getting up. No sooner did he see his father coming to the door like a beggar man, than he ran downstairs, snatched a whip from the side of the door, and rushed out. He put his hand out toward his father and drew four blows of the whip on him as hard as he could.

"Be off with you now," said he; "and don't come like a beggar man to your son's door again. Go somewhere else."

"So that's the way you treat me." said the father. "I'm giving you notice that many a day will pass before you see me again. That's my thanks for rearing you since you were a child."

The old man turned on his heels and never stopped till he reached Ventry, leaving the son where he was. He was sad and sorrowful at what the son had done to him.

Coming on toward Michaelmas, the priest announced that there would be a "station" in the son's house. When the day came, the two priests were hearing confessions—one at either side of the fireplace. The people were farther down in the kitchen. One of the priests noticed that Shea, the man of the house, was allowing the men to move past him toward confession, while he himself remained in the same place. The priest rose from his chair, approached Shea, and asked him if he was going to confession. He replied that he was.

"I have been watching you since we started hearing this morning," said the priest; "and you have let everybody else get ahead of you. What have you done that you do not go to confess your sins yourself?"

"I won't go to confession until you have finished the others," said Shea.

"Very well," said the priest.

When the priest had finished hearing confessions, he asked Shea if he wished to go up to the room with him to make his confession. Shea said that he did. The priest took him to the room and asked him what wrong had he done. Shea confessed that he had struck his father.

"I cannot give you absolution," said the priest. "The devil has you on a chain, because you have committed a mortal sin. Think of your father, who reared you since childhood, and the way you treated him when he went to your house. Eat your breakfast with myself and the other priest now, and as soon as you have finished, go straight to the bishop. We will leave here first; you must set out for the bishop the moment we have gone. If you don't, your soul will be damned."

"I'll do what you say," said Shea.

They ate the breakfast, Shea sitting at the foot of the table, while the two priests gave him advice.

His wife did not know until that day that it was his father he had struck.

"If I knew that it was your father who was outside that day," said she, "I'd be far from letting you strike him. I'd have treated him kindly and well, seeing that it was my first time meeting him."

Shea put some money in his pocket as soon as he had eaten and set out on his journey to the bishop. He confessed his sin to him but got no absolution.

"You must go to the Pope in Rome as fast ever as you can," said the bishop. "Your soul is damned. It was a mortal sin for you to act that way toward your father."

"May God help me!" said Shea.

It was then that great fear of death came upon him. He set out on his long journey to Rome with plenty of money in his pocket and everything else that he needed. He never stopped until he neared the Pope's palace. Every bell in the palace began to ring as he approached the door.

"There is either a saintly man or an unholy one or a damned soul coming toward us," said the Pope. "There isn't a bell in the monastery that isn't ringing."

Shea was admitted and was asked who he was or what he wanted. He said that he wanted to go to confession to the Pope. He was told that his request would be granted and welcome. The Pope came out and asked him how many priests and bishops he had passed on his journey who could have heard his confession as well as himself. Shea confessed his sin to the Pope.

"I cannot give you any absolution or forgiveness for your sin any more than the others could," said the Pope. "The devil has you on a chain on account of what you did to your father. It is a great pity that a young man like you should be damned at the end of your life. Didn't you realize what a sin you were committing? I cannot either absolve you or give you Holy Communion, although you have come a long journey. But," continued the Pope, "a young priest will be ordained here in my monastery next Monday morning. Such newly ordained priests have greater power of forgiveness than I have. Try to be the first to go to confession to him. I will give you a room here until Monday morning, and I will help you to get to him before anybody else. There are twelve paralyzed people who will be trying to throw themselves on their knees in front of him after his ordination, hoping that he will cure them. But I will put you before them all."

"I am thankful to you," said Shea.

The Pope took him to a room, and there he remained praying for two or three days. The Pope came to him on Sunday evening and placed him by the door through which the newly ordained priest would pass next morning.

"Be on your two knees here in front of him and ask him for confession," said the Pope.

"I will," said Shea.

The young priest came to the door after his ordination, and when he opened it, Shea was on his knees in front of him.

"What are you waiting here for?" asked the priest.

"I want to confess my sin to you and get Holy Communion, if you please," said Shea.

"I couldn't have heard your confession until I became a priest but I will hear it gladly now."

He took Shea to his own room and heard his confession.

"If you promise to carry out the penance I will impose, I will give you Holy Communion now," said the priest.

"I will do any penance you give me," said Shea, "to atone for my sin."

"Now," said the priest, "there are many crossroads between Rome and Queenstown, are there not?"

"Many's the one," said Shea.

"At the first crossroads that you come to on your way home," said the priest, "you will meet a *piast* that will be screaming terribly. You must not pass the *piast* until you have licked it three times with your tongue. At the second crossroads you reach, you will meet a *piast* seven times more terrible. You must lick this one three times with your tongue also. At the third crossroads, you will meet a *piast* seven times as frightening as the other two altogether. You must lick the third one three times with your tongue also. Until you have done that, you will not have atoned for the mortal sin you committed."

"I promise to do all you have ordered," said Shea.

The priest then gave him Holy Communion, and he set out on the road back toward Queenstown. His sin had been forgiven by the priest. He had not gone far when he came to a crossroads. There was a *piast* in front of him, screaming and wanting to eat him.

"There's little good in you!" said Shea. "I had better not go near you."

He made his way into a field at the roadside, passed the *piast*, and came out again at the other side. He walked on along the road until he came to a crossroads where he met a second *piast* seven times worse than the first.

"The one I met a while ago was good compared with you," said Shea. "I had better jump in over the fence and pass you before you eat me alive."

He jumped into the corner of a field and came out on the road beyond the crossroads without going near the *piast*. When he reached the third crossroads and saw the third *piast*, he was terrified that it would eat him alive.

"Whatever about the first two, you are easily their master," said Shea. "I had better slip past you."

He did so.

"Here I am now!" said he. "I have passed the three of them and have gained nothing. It is better for me to go back again, in God's name, and do what the holy priest told me."

Back he went by every shortcut to the first crossroads. He licked the *piast* with his tongue three times. It made no move.

"Thanks be to God!" he cried. "What a fool I was to pass it the first time."

At the second crossroads he licked the *piast* three times, and it never moved.

"That's still better." said he. "I almost lost my chance."

When he licked the third *piast* three times, it knotted itself around his neck. He took his silken handkerchief out of his pocket and covered the *piast* with it. He felt a great weight upon him, and he lost his energy and strength. He turned back toward Rome, where the Pope was, and he could hardly walk. He went into the first house he met at the edge of the city and asked the woman who owned it if she kept lodgers. She said that she did.

"Are you looking for lodgings?" she asked.

"I am," he said. "I have made a long journey since morning and I'm very tired. Show me my room and my bed."

"Very well," said she.

She took him down to a room, the window of which looked out onto the street.

"This is your room, and there is your bed," she said. "And here is the key if you wish to lock the door."

"I think I'll go to bed," said Shea. "I'm terribly tired."

"Do as you wish," said the woman.

He lay down on the bed.

There was a servant girl in the boardinghouse, and later on in the day, whatever look she gave, she saw that the room was as dark as if it had no window at all. She tried to open the door, and when she looked in, she gave a loud scream.

"What ails you, you little fool?" said her mistress.

"O Virgin Mary!" cried the girl. "The room that was as bright as the sun itself is now so dark that nothing at all can be seen in it."

"What are you saying?" asked the woman.

"Come down here and see for yourself," said the girl.

The woman went to the room, and no sooner did she look in than she shouted to the girl, "Run for the priest as fast as you can."

The girl ran out the door. The priest she called happened to be the same one who had been ordained the day before. She told him to come quickly because he was wanted. When he came to the house, he asked who was sick. The woman told him that nobody was sick, but there was only a stranger below in her room, and her room was gone.

"Show me the room," said the priest.

She pointed it out to him. He took out his book. The whole room was full of black flies from ceiling to floor. The priest read prayers from his book until every single fly came out through the door, and the room became as bright as the sun. The priest went in. Not a thing was left on the bed, no flesh, no blood, only Shea's four bones.

"Now," said the priest, "all is well. The devils of hell have consumed his flesh and blood, but I have saved his soul."

Shea was buried in Rome and never returned home.

That's the story as I heard it.

There was a friar long ago, and he was silenced by the Pope. He had no means of livelihood as a result; so he traveled from place to place. In due course, he came to this country. He went to the top of Errigal Mountain to do penance for his sins. After he had been there for awhile, the evil spirit came to tempt him further. He gave the friar a court and castle on the top of that lonely mountain where there had never before been a shed or a house. The devil enticed the friar to go to live in the castle and told him that all the food and drink he required would come to him. All he would have to do would be to sit down and eat it. And so it happened. The friar went on living there, unknown to everybody. The only thing known about him was that he had gone to the top of Errigal to do penance. That was all. Years passed by.

An Anagry man had an only son, who was very fond of card playing. He used to be at them night after night. Not only that, but he carried a pack of cards about in his pocket. One night, as he was returning from card playing as usual, he met a red-haired girl—as nice a girl as he had ever seen.

"Have you a pack of cards on you?" she asked.

"Of course I have," said he.

"We'll play a game, then," said she.

"For what stake?" he asked.

"Whichever of us loses will belong to the other," said she.

They played a game, and the girl won.

"You belong to me now," said she, "and you must give me a promise to that effect in your own blood."

"How can I do a thing like that?" he asked with a laugh.

"Draw some of your blood with a pin," said she, "and write your name on this."

She handed him a piece of paper. He did as she had ordered and gave her back the paper. She put it in her pocket. Then she pulled out another paper with writing on it, put it among the cards in the pack, and left him. He shoved the cards into his pocket and made his way home, heavy of heart, and trying to puzzle out what it all meant. He went to bed and didn't get up next morning at the usual time.

His father noticed the cards on the windowsill and muttered to himself, "It is ye that have led him astray."

At that moment, he caught sight of the paper among the cards. He pulled it out and looked at it and immediately saw that it had not been written by human hand. In he went to the son's room and roused him.

"What sort of writing is that you brought home last night?" said he.

"That's none of your business, " replied the son.

"If that's the way with you, you'll stay no longer in this house, unless you go to see the priest," said the father.

The son took the writing to the priest, but he wasn't able to read it, and that being so, the son could not return to his father's house. With the writing in his pocket, he walked on, not knowing where his way led. As he passed by the side of Muckish Mountain, he caught sight of three priests, who were coming down the hillside after a day's hunting. He stopped until they came up to him. He handed the writing to one of them and asked him to read it. He could not. Neither could the second. He gave it to the third priest and asked him could he read it at all, as it had him in a trap. The priest examined it closely and said that there wasn't a priest in Ireland who could read it save one.

"His name is Big Friar O'Connor," said he. "He was in college with me."

"And where is he now?" asked the young man.

"That I don't know," said the priest; "but you may meet him yet."

The young man walked on, with a curious feeling in his heart and mind. When he reached the foot of Errigal, he said to himself that he would climb to the top as a penance. Up he went, walking awhile and climbing awhile, until he came to the very top. He wandered about. There was nobody in sight. And then he caught sight of the nice castle. He went to the door, knocked and entered. Inside was a big man seated by a large fire, who looked as if he had every comfort. The man got up and gave a great welcome to the visitor and told him to sit down. He then told him that he had been living there for seven years, and that nobody had ever visited him until now. He seated the young man at a table laden with the best of food, and he ate his fill for he had taken no food since he left home.

When the meal was over, the young man sat by the fire. He saw that the big man had a very sharp, intelligent face. He handed the writing to him and asked him could he make any sense of it. The big man examined it for awhile, and then went to the table and wrote a letter.

"Come outside with me now!" said he. "Your writing is in this letter also. And now," said he, "you must follow this letter wherever it goes until it stops. Hand it to the person you meet when it stops. And have your ears open to see would you hear anything that would be of help to me."

He threw the letter on the ground, and the wind blew it along. The young man followed it, whatever direction it took—around the shore of Loughsalt—until finally it reached a crossroads. There it stopped. The young man rushed to the spot and saw a huge hole with steps leading down into the ground. Down went the letter and down went he after it until it stopped at a gate. He knocked at the gate and a big black fellow came out to him. He handed the letter to him, and the fellow read it. Then he shouted to the red-haired, cardplaying girl to come out, but she didn't come. He shouted to her a second time, but she stayed where she was.

"Well," said he, "if I have to shout for you again, I'll put you into the fiery bed of boiling lead that's waiting for Big Friar O'Connor when he dies."

At that, out came the very girl that had played cards with him when he was returning from Anagry. The black fellow handed the writing to her and ordered her to give up the writing she had got in his own blood from the young man. She gave it to him.

He turned on his heels and never stopped till he reached the castle on the top of Errigal. Then he told the big man what he had heard, and how it had frightened him.

"Well, I'm the friar they were talking about," said the big man. "I am Big Friar O'Connor. You have helped me greatly by coming here. Give me the writing in your own blood."

The young man gave it to him. The friar washed and cleaned it carefully and then tore it into small pieces.

"Now take these and swallow them, and your own blood will be in your veins again."

The young man did so.

"Now," said the friar, "take the iron knife, the axe, and the saw and edge them well on that stone outside."

The young man did as he was told, and when he had finished, the friar came out to him.

"Would you be willing to accept this castle and all that is in it and live here for the rest of your life?" asked the friar.

"I wouldn't accept it, if it were a hundred times as fine," said the young man.

"I knew that would be your answer," said the friar. "Wait now until I get my book and vestments in the castle."

He went in and returned, carrying a box. He opened it, and inside were his book and vestments safe and sound. He took out his stole and put it around his neck.

Then he took up the book, saying, "May the grace of God be again upon us." He opened the book and started to read. At that moment, the castle disappeared from view, leaving no trace that it had ever been there. There was a flash of fire that scorched the whole mountaintop. The friar placed his book and stole in the box once more and closed it.

"Now," said he, "you must cut my body up into three pieces."

"I'll do no such thing," said the young man.

"You will have to do it," said the friar. "The axe will cut what the knife won't cut, and the saw will cut what the axe won't cut. When you have that done, be sure to bury me where the wild birds won't get at me."

He took off his clothes, and the young man divided his body into three parts, as he had been ordered to do. When he had done so, he was seized with terror and ran down the mountainside as fast as he could. After awhile, he looked back and saw the birds gathering about the friar's body. He realized that he had done wrong; so he ran back again. On reaching the place, he saw that the friar's body was whole and sound, as if it had never been touched. The friar gave a snore, then another, then a third, and woke up.

"You have saved me!" said he. "Let us leave this place immediately."

He put on his clothes and took up his box, and they both left the top of Errigal. Down the mountainside they went until they reached a glen.

"I see smoke from a house over there," said the friar. "Near it is a church and a graveyard; so it may be the presbytery. We will go to it, as I want to see a priest and make my confession."

When they reached the house, the priest took them into a room.

"Now," said the friar, "both of ye go into the kitchen while I examine my conscience for confession."

The priest and the young man sat by the kitchen fire for a while. They could hear voices in the room where the friar was, as if somebody were conversing with him. The priest listened. The talk was in Latin, and the priest understood every word that was being said. Soon there was a shout to call the priest to the room. The friar was seated in a chair, looking at a picture of Our Saviour, which was hanging on the wall in front of him. The priest knew that it was the picture which had been talking to the friar. The priest then heard the friar's confession and gave him absolution. The friar then told him that he was dying and asked to be anointed. He asked the priest to keep the young man in his house as long as he lived—that he would be good company for him when he had to go out on sick calls at night.

"It is he who has saved me from the everlasting pains of hell," said he.

The friar then died, and the priest waked and buried him. He kept the young man in his house until his father heard that he was there and came one day to find out how he was. The priest told him the whole story; what the boy had done and what he had suffered.

"He must stay here for the rest of his life," said he.

"Well, if that's the way," said the father, "he's better off with you than with me, and let it be so."

That's the end of my story!

• 23 • *How God's Wheel Turns*

The wheel turns, they say, and ill luck is on one side of it.

A poor scholar came to a farmer's house one evening and asked for lodgings. The farmer said he could stay and welcome. He got a good supper, and the two of them spent a good part of the night talking. The poor scholar had great learning and, faith, the farmer wasn't bad either. The farmer asked questions that the other man couldn't answer—maybe even the farmer himself couldn't answer them.

As they chatted, the farmer finally asked, "Could you tell me what God is doing at this very moment?"

"That's a very hard question to answer," said the poor scholar. "I'd want time to think over it. Wait until the morning, and I might have the answer for you."

"That'll do fine," said the farmer.

They went to bed, and when they got up in the morning, they ate a good breakfast.

"Now," said the poor scholar when they had eaten, "the question you put to me last night was a very hard one. But, what do you think? Didn't I solve it in my sleep."

"Well, what was God doing then?" asked the farmer.

"He was making a wheel. That wheel turns very slowly, and the man that was on top yesterday will be at the bottom to-morrow."

"You have answered it well," said the farmer.

"I may have even a better answer for you the next time we meet," said the poor scholar.

He left the farmer and traveled on until he reached a gentleman's house. This gentleman had a young family rising up, and he took in the poor scholar to teach them. He remained there until he had scholars made of them.

"I'm very thankful to you," said the gentleman. "You have spent a long time traveling about, and the best thing you can do now is to settle down and have a home of your own. I'll give you a place for the rest of your life, if you wish to remain here."

The poor scholar thanked him and said that he would stay. The gentleman gave him a house and a piece of land, and he got married and settled down there. He got on well. One evening as night was falling, he was standing in the doorway when he saw a small grayhaired old man coming toward the house with a bag on his back.

When the old man approached, he spoke, "Would you let me stay till morning? I'm weary from the road."

"I will and welcome," said the poor scholar. "Come in. Throw aside the bag and sit by the fire."

The old man made his way in and sat down by the fire. The poor scholar told his wife to get supper ready for him, and when he had eaten, they started to chat. The poor scholar asked him where he came from, how long he had been on the road, and so on.

"There was a time, and 'tis little I thought that I'd be the way I am," said the old man. "I had a fine place of my own once, but I gave it to my son, and in less than two years I was coming in the way of his wife in whatever corner of the house I'd be. She finally ordered me to take my bag with me and get out. I have been on the road ever since."

Who was he but the farmer who had given the poor scholar lodgings some years before!

"Well," said the poor scholar, "whether your life is to be long or short, you are to stay here in my house and you will want for nothing. Do you remember the question you asked the poor scholar the night you gave him lodgings? He told you he would have an even better answer to it the next time ye met."

"I remember it well," said the old man.

"Well I'm the poor scholar who was with you that night. You were strong and independent at that time, but see how the wheel has turned with ill luck on one side of it."

The old man had not recognized him until then. He remained with the poor scholar for the rest of his life, and had a good time until he died.

· 24 · The Man Who Was Rescued from Hell

There was a widow, and she had only one daughter. Her husband died when the child was young; so the mother had to travel long cold roads in search of alms to provide for her daughter. She saved pennies and half-pence and farthings until the child was a young girl, hoping to have something put by for her when she would marry—if she lived.

By the time that she had a small dowry put together, the daughter had grown to be a beautiful girl—kind, gentle, honest, and sensible. All the young men in the place were trying to be friendly with her, but it wasn't every young man would suit the old widow. She wanted a husband for her daughter who would own a good farm of land and be firmly established, as she had a good dowry. One night the widow spoke to her daughter.

"Isn't it time for you, daughter," said she, "to be thinking of settling down? I am old and spent now, and my days are in. I would like to see you married in your own little house before I leave this world."

"Do you think so, Mother?" said the daughter. "Have you any husband in mind for me?"

"I have a certain man in my mind," said the widow. "I know him and his people well. He has a good farm, and he's well off. We had better make a match for you to marry him."

"Very well, Mother. I'm satisfied with whatever you say."

The match was made, and when Shrove came, they were married. There was no fear but the husband had got a good wife. She was able to sew, to knit, to do the housework, and even to work on the land, for she had been working for farmers since she grew up. The widow had gone to live in the house with her daughter and the husband. So the years went by until the husband came home one evening. His wife knew by his rough manner that he was displeased about something. She went over to him.

"What's wrong with you, Séamus?" she asked. "You are seldom as grumpy as you are today. Something is troubling you."

"There is," said the husband. "'Tis hard enough for me to support you and look after you not to have your mother as a load on my back."

"May God help us!" said his wife. "My mother won't be a burden on anybody for long. Her life is nearly over, and you shouldn't upset her now."

"She won't stay on here," said the husband.

"My mother had it hard when she was young," said Máire, the daughter; "and now, when she deserves some little comfort at the end of her days, she's to be thrown out of here to travel the same long white roads with nobody to take care of her if she is to be separated from me. But I have one request to make," said Máire.

"What is that?" asked her husband.

"You must give me time to make a dress and a coat for my mother to wear before she leaves the house."

"Very well," said the husband, "but don't be long with it."

"You must promise to give me my own time for it," said Máire. "I'll start at it, and she may be taken off by death before 'tis ready."

He consented to allow the widow to remain in the house until the garments were ready. Máire went off and got seven pounds of wool. She took them home and started to comb and tease and roll the wool before spinning it into thread. She spent a year turning each pound into thread—seven years in all, trying to delay the work. One day her husband came in; his face was red with anger.

"Is it trying to make a fool of me you are, Máire?" he said.

"No, indeed," she replied. "I have secured these seven years for my mother, and now I have her clothes ready for her. Seven years ago today I made the bargain with you. Now I have the garments ready, and my mother will bid you goodbye."

Máire washed and got ready the old woman and put on the dress and coat. She then placed a small cloak about her.

"You are ready to be cast forth now, Mother," said Máire, "but you won't go alone. Whichever road you take, I will take the same road. You have cared for me since my youth and you trudged the long roads for me. I will now go the long roads with you until death takes you from me."

She threw on her cloak, took her mother by the hand, and left without saying goodbye to her husband. They traveled along, spending a night in some house like any poor people would. The old widow was always given the best of any food Máire got. At last they were far from home among strangers. Late one evening, Máire saw a fine looking house some distance from the road.

When they reached it, she said, "Mother, we are tired from the road. Come with me to this house, and I may get some work there for your sake. I won't ask for any wages—just a room and food for two of us. We can be helping each other."

"You're tired out and tormented from me, daughter," said the old woman.

"Indeed, I'm not," replied Máire. "You cared for me far longer than I have done for you."

She took her poor mother's withered little hand and led her toward the house. When they reached the door, Máire saluted the people of the house gently, and they did the same.

"Would you be willing to give a night's lodging to myself and my old mother?" she asked the woman of the house.

"Yes, with my heart's welcome. Come in." said the woman.

They went toward the fire and seated themselves in one of the small corners. Then they shyly ate the food that was given to them. Next morning Máire spoke to the woman of the house.

"I'm a young, strong woman," said she, "and I'll be able to do any housework you give me. I won't ask you for any payment—only a little room for my mother and some food for her. I will look after her if she gets sick, and if she dies, I will be with her to lay her in the coffin."

"There's plenty work here for you, good woman, and you are welcome to it," said the woman of the house. "I badly need someone like you."

So the bargain was made. Máire fixed her mother up in a small room at the back of the house, and each morning as soon as she got up and said her prayers, she went to her mother's room.

"How are you after the night, Mother?" she would ask.

"I'm well, daughter, if you are," the old woman would reply.

"I'm well too, Mother," said Máire.

She would then go off to her work until the time came to give her mother some food. A couple of months went by like that, and the people of the house became very fond of Máire. She was handy and expert at her work and knowledgeable about the house. Then one evening, as she was returning from the well with a pitcher of water, she thought that she caught sight of a fine, young, handsome *strapaire* of a man standing by the fence in front of her. She had never seen him since she had come to the house, and she was surprised.

"You're a stranger here," said the young man to her.

"I am, sir," she replied; "and you're a stranger to me too. I haven't seen you around here since I came."

"I haven't been here since you came," said the young man. "But I have come to you now to see would you be good enough to do something for me. If you don't tell anyone about me for a year and a day, I will be restored to life and health again. I was the only child my parents had, and I was taken from them by death while still young. I have been suffering and suffering, as I was not a Christian. If you don't tell anyone about me for a year and a day, things may be better for me."

"I will keep your secret even to my death," said Máire, "and I'll do all in my power for you."

"Now," said the young man, "when you are getting ready for bed tonight, you must tell the woman of the house, as you call her—she's my mother—you must tell her that you will have to leave because you are not satisfied with the little bedroom you have. The bedroom which I had before I died has been closed ever since; my mother wouldn't allow it to be opened or let anyone into it. Tell her that you and your mother will leave if you're not given the room which is locked as a bedroom."

"I'll do that," said Máire.

"Goodbye now. I'll see you again," said the young man.

He vanished from her view, as if the ground had swallowed him, and she didn't know was it east or west he went. The woman of the house was wondering what was delaying her. When Máire went in, she said that she was tired of the little bedroom she had. It was too small and uncomfortable and gloomy. She asked for the room that was idle.

"It is going to waste as it is," said Máire; "and I would like to have it. It will be good for my health and more comfortable than the small room I have now."

"Young woman, it is great daring and courage you have to ask such a thing," said the woman of the house. "That's the room in which my only son died; it was his bedroom. His bed is still there and all his belongings, and the key hasn't been turned in the lock since the day he was carried out of it. 'Tis you have the presumption to ask for it now."

"I'll be leaving so," said Máire.

The woman of the house thought better after a while, and she calmed down.

" 'Tis hard to turn down a good servant girl for anything," said she. "The room has been idle long enough, and 'twill have to be opened sometime. I may as well let you have it."

She found the key, wherever is was, and opened the door. The room had a cold damp smell, as neither door nor window had been opened for a long time.

"It wants to be aired and tidied up," said she to Máire. "You can look after that yourself."

"I'm very thankful to you, mistress, for doing this for me," said Máire.

She was the girl who was well able to brush and clean and scrub it. The bed was already there, and she left everything as it was. She aired the bedclothes under the sun, and when bedtime came, she got into bed. But if she did, she wasn't long there when about midnight, she thought she heard the door opening easily, and someone came in. She rose up on her elbow and saw the same *strapaire* of a man, who had been talking to her outside at the fence that evening. He saluted her, and she replied. He pulled a chair to the bedside, and they started to talk in a quiet, friendly, sensible way for an hour or more. Then he left her. She felt lonely then, for she thought that she had never seen a young man like him before. Still, she was a married woman, and she did not wish to have anything to do with another man, as her own husband was still living. She was foolish, for he hadn't been very good to her, indeed.

The days and weeks and months went by at full gallop. After six months or so, the mistress noticed that Máire had changed, that something was wrong with her. It seemed to her as if she were bearing a child. Still, she said nothing, but she had a suspicion that if it were so, her own husband was to blame. So they began to quarrel and weren't very friendly, for she had a grudge against him. The mistress was full of envy and jealousy of Máire, thinking that she had something to do with her husband. Nobody else noticed anything strange about Máire. Each morning, she would go to her mother to wash her and make her comfortable, before she did any work about the house. Her mother had not to depend on anyone else.

That was good and it wasn't bad. Máire worked away as usual, pretending nothing and carrying her child in her womb. However, one morning everybody else in the house was up out of bed, and there was no sign of Máire. The woman of the house was in an evil mood, talkative and scolding Máire for not getting up and saying that there must be something wrong with her.

"Go up," said she to another servant girl who was in the house, "and see what's wrong with that hussy. There must be something wrong that she's not getting up today."

When the girl went to the room door, she couldn't open it. It was locked as usual. She looked in through the keyhole, and what did she see but a fine, handsome, nice, young man sitting on a chair by the bedside, and Máire sitting up in the bed with a baby to her breast, as if she were feeding it. Back down ran the girl with terror in her two eyes.

"Oh, mistress, mistress!" she cried. "Such a thing. She is sitting up in bed with a baby at her breast, and there's a *strapaire* of a gentleman sitting on a chair at the bedside, and they're talking.

Come along and put your eye to the keyhole, and you'll see them for yourself."

The woman of the house went up and looked through the keyhole.

"Oh! My child! My child!" she cried, for she recognized the young man as her own son.

She drew back without saying another word.

A few days later when Máire was able to get up and unlock the door, the servant girl went to her and said, "The mistress wants you to let her use the room for a couple of days and nights. There's something hidden in this house, and we hear that a search will be made for it. If it is found in the house, we will all be arrested. Would you please let her hide it in a corner of your room for a few days? She'll be very thankful to you."

"Very well," said Máire.

What did the old lady do but disguise herself in straw that was covered over with a cloak, tied about with straw ropes, and carried into Máire's room. There she was set up in the corner like a statue until the danger would be over. She made no sound of any kind. She could see Máire getting into bed with the baby. When midnight came, she could see through a hole she had made in the straw the young man coming in through the door. He sat down on the chair beside the bed and started to talk to Máire. The poor mother lost patience, and no wonder. Nature was too strong for her. She tore off the cloak and the straw, jumped out on the floor, ran to her son, embraced, and kissed him.

"Oh, shame, shame, shame, Mother!" he cried. "That's a hateful thing you have done to me. Had you waited until I had been coming here for a year and a day, I would have been as well as I had ever been. But now, I must go back to suffer in hell for seven years more."

"You won't go, son," cried the mother. "I have a hold on you."

"I don't think you can keep me, Mother," said the son.

"Well, I'll try," said his mother.

Next morning she got ready, but 'twas useless for her to try to deal with the demons of hell. She set out on the road, following the son's directions, but she hadn't gone far when she was pulled about and scratched by the demons of hell. She hadn't a hair on her head or a bit of her skin sound when she reached home again.

"See how you are now, Mother!" said her son. "I knew well that you wouldn't succeed."

"She was never much good at anything," said her husband. "I'll try my own hand at it."

"You won't succeed either, Father," said the son.

"I'll try, anyway," said he.

So off he went, but short as the mother had gone, the father went even less far. He had to turn home again.

"I knew well, Father, that neither of ye could do it," said the son.

"I'd go to hell in your stead, except for my mother and my child," said Máire.

"If anybody could do it, it is you, Máire," said the young man.

"I wouldn't be slow to go," said Máire, "but ye would have to mind my mother."

"My hand and word to you that your mother will be well cared for as long as she lives," said the man of the house. "And if she dies before you come back, she will be well looked after, as regards wake, funeral, and burial. We'll follow her orders. And your child too will get good care."

Máire rose and put on her clothes with a special belt that she had about her waist.

She kissed the child tenderly and then went to where her mother was. "Goodbye, and my blessing on you now, Mother," said she. "I'm going on a long journey, and we may never see each other alive in this world again. But the man of the house has promised that you will be well cared for and given Christian burial if you die."

"May my blessing and the blessing of God be with you, daughter," said the mother. "I must put up with it."

She bade a special farewell to the young man, and as she was leaving, he took a ring off his finger. "Now," said he, "as you are setting out on this task, here is a ring for you. Put it on your finger. And when you reach where you are going, if ever hunger comes upon you, all you have to do is to look at this ring. There is all the food and drink you need in it. But you mustn't touch any food or drink you get in that place."

"Very well," said Máire.

She said goodbye to them all and set out on her journey. As she came near the gates of hell, the pains and troubles of the souls within began to grow less, it seemed to them. Their sufferings were not so great once she arrived, and they all had great love and respect for her, and no wonder. She worked away at whatever she was given to do. (All we can do is tell the story as we heard it.) When mealtime came, Lucifer brought her a dish of food and set it in front of her.

"That's your food now, and eat it!"

"That's good," said Máire. " 'Tis time."

No sooner had Lucifer left than Máire placed the dish of food in front of Caesar, a big brute of a dog, that was tied by a chain at the side of the room. It didn't take him long to devour the dish and the food. Máire turned aside and got all the natural food and drink she needed from the magic ring. Things went on like that until the seven years were up. It seemed only like seven days to Máire, for she had plenty of company and lots to look at. God between us and all harm! May God never allow us or those who are listening to us into hell! On the last day of the seven years, Lucifer came to her.

"Well, my dear girl," said he. "Your seven years are up today."

"They are," said Máire. "And now I want my pay."

"Your food and your pay will be put against each other," said Lucifer.

"I have taken none of your food from the day I came here until today," said Máire. "Caesar over there can bear witness to that."

"Nobody lives without food," said Lucifer.

"Caesar will tell that he ate all the food I was given during the seven years," said Máire.

Caesar spoke, "The girl is telling the truth," said he. "She didn't eat a bite of any food that was brought to her for the past seven years. I ate it. She should get her pay."

"Well, what pay do you want?" asked Lucifer.

"All I want," said Máire, "is the heaviest load I can carry out of hell of the souls that are in greatest torment here."

"You'll have to get them," said Lucifer.

She began to collect the souls and to gather them to her, while they cried out "Take me with you! Take me with you!" They screamed as they struggled to get near her—each hoping to be rescued, God help us! She kept on until you couldn't touch any part of her body with a pin from the sole of her foot to the crown of her head—so many souls were clinging to her. Her load was a heavy one when at last she turned her back on the place below. Glad she was, I'm thinking.

When she had gone some distance, she met a man striding swiftly toward hell. She recognized him when he came near her. He was her own husband, the man who had banished herself and her mother.

"Where are you going, good man?" asked Máire.

"To the place where I deserve to go," he replied.

"I'm sorry for you," said she. " 'Tis an old saying that we must return good for evil. See can you hold on to any part of me, and I'll try to save you."

She helped him up in some way and carried him along with her by the help of God. She traveled on and after awhile she met a man on the road. The gentleman spoke to her and she replied.

"That's a heavy load you have, poor woman," said he.

" 'Tis that," said Máire.

"Would you sell it to me?"

"I would, if I thought the buyer worthy of it," said Máire. "Who are you?"

"I am Saint Michael," said he.

"I won't sell it to you," said she. "Well though you may deserve it, I have bought it far more dearly myself."

She left him there and continued on her way. She met a second gentleman, who spoke to her and asked her what load she was carrying and would she sell it to him.

"Who are you?" she asked.

"I am Saint Matthew," he replied. "I would like you to sell the load to me."

"Indeed, I won't!" said she. "Much as you deserve it, I have bought it far more dearly myself. I have earned it for seven years, and if I sell it, it will be to some buyer who is more deserving than you."

He left her, and she kept on her way with her heavy load, poor woman. She met a third man, and they saluted each other.

"That's a heavy load you're carrying, poor woman," said he.

"It is, sir," said she, "but I'll try to keep going."

"Would you sell it to me?" he asked.

"I would," said she, "for I'm getting tired of it, if I thought the buyer worthy of it. Who are you that's wanting to buy it?"

"I am the King of Sunday," said he.

"Ah, you are the right buyer," said she. "Dearly though I have bought them, you have bought them still more dearly. I give them to you as a gift."

"You have done well," said he.

Each of the poor little souls flew off from her in the form of a snow-white dove.

"You have done well, and you are on the right road," said he. "Your mother was buried yesterday. She made her confession and was anointed and got a Christian burial, after having been well cared for while you were away. Now," said he, "the father of your child will be getting married tomorrow night. He is taking another to be his wife, for he never thought you would return from the place you went to."

"I'd like to go to his house," said Máire.

"You'll be in time, if you start off now," said he.

I'd say he gave her his blessing, and it helped her. It was he who had been helping her from the start.

She walked on and on until she neared the house where she had left her mother. She met an old beggar man near it and she spoke to him.

"Where are you making for, old man?" she asked. "The evening is getting late."

"I'm going to a wedding house, young woman," said he. "The young man there is getting married tonight, and there's no show but the feasting that will be there."

"I suppose so," said she. "The pair of us had better go there together. If I get anything good at the bottom of the kitchen, you'll get your share of it. You might be better off in my company than by yourself. Let's go together, and we'll have a good night. Nobody will notice us."

"Very well," said he.

They set off toward the farmer's house. (I may as well call it that!) There were people there from the east and beggars from the west, and such commotion you never heard. It was the rule at that time that the young pair didn't get married until the end of the night, when the daylight was coming, be it priest or minister that was there. (I suppose there were Catholics and Protestants there at that time.) The house was full of people. There was drinking and fun and dancing, of course, with no thought at all for the woman who had gone to hell.

Máire and the old man went in and sat down shyly at the bottom of the house on a seat that had been placed there for the poor people. She glanced around her, saying nothing and taking in everything. What wrung her heart most of all was to see her son, now a hardy *garsún* seven years old, whom she had left behind. It would make anybody's heart rejoice to see him; he was so pleasing in appearance. He kept moving about among the crowd like any child of his age until finally he reached where the old man and Máire were and stood gazing at them.

"What looking have you, dear child, at this old man and myself beyond all the rest in the house?" asked Máire. "But now since you have taken notice of us, go up to where your father is and tell him there's a poor woman and an old man sitting at the bottom of the house, and that the woman would like to have something to drink. She's very thirsty."

The boy went off in great excitement to whatever part of the house his father was in.

"Daddy," said he when he found him, "there are two poor people in the bottom of the kitchen, and the poor woman asked you to send a drink to herself and the old man. They are dead from the thirst, and they haven't had a bite or sup all the evening, although they have come a long way."

"No poor person will be hungry or thirsty in my house," said his father, getting to his feet.

He took a drinking vessel and filled it with whatever kind of drink was going round the house.

"Take that to the poor woman who asked for it, my boy," said he.

"I will gladly," said the boy.

Off he went with the vessel and never stopped till he reached the poor woman who had spoken to him.

"Here you are, little boy!" said Máire.

"I am," said he.

She took the vessel and drank two or three mouthfuls from it. Then she turned to her companion, the old man.

"Drink the rest of this, good man," said she, "but leave the dregs for me. You are short of breath and in need of a good drink, but a little will do me. Drink it up now, for you may not get any more tonight."

The old man took the vessel from her and threw most of what was in it back his throat, leaving about a glassful behind. He handed the vessel back to her, and she thanked him. She then pretended to drink the rest, but she took only a small sip. Unseen by anybody, she slipped the ring from her finger and dropped it into the vessel.

"Now, my child," said she to the boy, "take this vessel back to your father and don't give it into anybody else's hand. When you give it to him, say that he is to drink the health of the poor woman in memory of this night seven years and seven nights ago."

The boy took the drinking vessel to his father.

"There's still a drink in this, Daddy," said he, "and the traveling woman wants you to drink her health in memory of this night seven years and seven nights ago."

The father started and thoughts raced through his mind. When he came to himself, he put the vessel to his lips to drink, but if he did, the ring fell into his mouth. He caught it and looked at it. 'Tis then he was really disturbed.

"So that's how it is," said he. "Come along, my boy," said he to his son. "Take me to where the poor women are, and show me the woman to whom you gave the drink."

The boy walked very proudly in front of his father till he stood in front of the poor woman.

"That's she, Daddy; that's the woman I gave the vessel to."

"That's she, all right," said his father. "She was the woman that day and for the past seven years; the woman who bought me and saved me, at the risk of her health, from pain and torments. Here she is now at the bottom of the house, while another is in her stead at the top. But it won't be so. Get up!" said he, taking her by the shoulder. "Wrong has been done, but it is not too late to set it right."

He took her up to her room, where the clothes which she had left behind still were as she had left them.

"Put on these clothes now," said he. "Your dress is ragged and torn, and no wonder, but I won't have you that way."

When she had dressed and combed and tidied herself, he led her from the room and stood in the center of the floor.

"Friends!" said he. "High and low though you be. All is well now. You have your share," said he to the father of the girl he had been going to marry. "You and your daughter have not lost your honor, and she will get a husband any day. I have my own wife now. She belongs to me, and I to her, for what I am worth. I will pay the cost of the wedding here tonight, and nobody can complain. We will spend the rest of the night happily. I have my wife."

That satisfied everybody. If they were surprised and amazed, 'tis little wonder. That a woman who had spent seven years in hell should come back from the other world to join her husband!

They were married and lived a long, comfortable, happy life together until the son whom she had borne before she went to hell was reared. God blessed them and him, and he grew to be one of the strongest and most graceful men in the district at the time.

·25· *The Hour of Death*

The old people used to say that in the olden times everybody knew the exact time when he would die.

There was a man who knew that he would die in autumn. He planted his crops the previous spring, but instead of building a fine firm fence around them, all he did was to plant a makeshift hedge of a few rushes and ferns to guard the crops. It so happened that God (praise and glory to Him!) sent an angel down on earth to find out how the people were getting on. The angel came to this man and asked him what he was doing. The man told him.

"And why haven't you a better fence than that makeshift to protect your crops?" asked the angel.

"It will do me," said the man, "until I have the crop stored. Let those who succeed me look after their own fences. I'll die this autumn."

The angel returned and told the Almighty what had happened. And from that day on, people lost foreknowledge of the hour of death.

Part IV
People of the Otherworld

The Fairy Frog

There was a girl here long ago, and one day she was herding cattle. She was looking around her, and she noticed a very large frog jumping past her on the ground. She looked at the frog for a while, wondering at its size, for she had never seen one so large.

"I hope you won't give birth to your young until I am present," said the girl as a joke.

She returned home in the evening. Later on that night, a gentleman came to the house, riding on a horse. He stopped at the door and dismounted. He asked was the girl within, and he was told that she was.

"Well," said he, "I want her for a short time tonight, and I will bring her back safe and sound."

The people of the house were very surprised that a gentleman should come to the house, asking the girl to go with him. They didn't know under heaven what he wanted her for, and they weren't very anxious to let her go with him. She herself was slow to accompany him.

"She may as well come with me," said he, "and I give my hand and word that I will bring her back safe and sound before long."

The girl went with him. He put her up on the horse behind him and galloped off, telling her not to be afraid; she had no need to worry, he said. They traveled on until they reached a fairy palace. They dismounted and went in. The place was full of people—men and women everywhere—but she recognized nobody. They passed through several rooms, and at last he led her into a small room where there was a fire and a bed. On the bed was a woman, who was giving birth to a child. The poor girl was very frightened, as she didn't know where in the world she was. The man told her not to be afraid, that there was no danger, and that she would be home soon again.

The girl wasn't long in the room until the child was born. There were two other women attending the woman in the bed, and when the child was born, they opened out the fire and put the child in at the back of it. They left it there until it was burned to ashes. The girl was watching what happened. The women then collected the ashes and put them into a kind of dish that was in the room.

"You can go home now," said the man when it was all over. "I'll take you with me. You may as well give her some present, before she leaves," said he to the woman in the bed.

"I'll give her a present," said the woman, handing her a purse of money and a shawl.

Before she left the fairy palace, she saw the people who were leaving the room where she was putting their fingers into the dish that contained the ashes of the child and rubbing them to their eyes as they left.

"By heavens! I'll rub some of it to my own eyes, for good or for evil," said the girl.

She rubbed the ashes to only one of her eyes. The man took her outside, put her behind him on the horse, and set out for her home. They came to where a huge tree was growing by the roadside, and the man pulled up his horse. They both dismounted.

"Where is the shawl the woman gave you?" asked the man.

"I have it here," said the girl.

"Go over and tie it around that big tree," said the man.

She went over and tied the shawl around the tree. No sooner had she done so than the tree split in two.

"If you had put that shawl on you, it would have split you in two, like the tree," said the man. "And now, the purse of money she gave you. As soon as you get up tomorrow morning, change all that money in different houses. Don't have as much as a penny of it in your own house tomorrow night. If you do, you'll suffer."

They reached the girl's house.

"Get off the horse now," said the man, "and don't forget to do everything I told you."

He galloped off again, and when the girl looked after him, there wasn't a trace of him to be seen.

Next morning, she took the purse of money and went from

house to house to change it. By the following morning, there wasn't a single house that had any of the strange money in it that wasn't burned to the ground.

Some time afterward, the girl went to a fair five or six miles away from her home. She was able to see many people at the fair who couldn't be seen by others at all. If she had rubbed the ashes to both of her eyes in the fairy palace, 'tis unknown what she would be able to see. She walked here and there through the fair, and whom should she catch sight of at last but the man who had come for her one night before. She walked up to him and took him by the two hands.

"Well, I'm delighted to see you," said she. "How are you?"

He looked at her.

"How do you see me?" he asked.

"I see you with this eye," said she, pointing to the one to which she had rubbed the ashes.

"Well, you'll see me no more," said he.

He pushed his finger into the socket and pulled out her eye. From that day on, she had only one eye.

·27· *The Fairy Wife*

There was a young man below in the Rosses long ago. He was living alone. One day as he was straining potatoes at the doorway, a woman came up to him, and he spoke to her.

"Come in," said he.

"I won't go in today," said she.

Next day, she came to the door again when he was straining potatoes.

"Come in," said he.

"I won't go in today," said she.

On the third day, he was straining potatoes again when the woman came.

"Come in," said he.

"Very well, I'll go in today," said she.

She went in and lived there with him. About a year later, she gave birth to a son. A good while after that, the harvest fair was to be held in Glenties.

"I think I'll go to the fair today," said the young man. "I want to meet my friends from around Glenties. I have uncles living there."

"Do, of course," said his wife.

He set out for the fair. He saw his uncles there, but instead of coming to speak to him, it was as though they were avoiding him. At last he went up and stood in front of one of them and asked what was wrong.

"What crime have I committed?" he asked. "I haven't met ye for a long time, and all ye do is avoid me."

"Why shouldn't we avoid you," said the uncle, "when we hear that you have married a fairy woman? If you had come to us first, we would have got a good wife for you, and you needn't have taken up with her at all. Now," said the uncle, "I'm going to buy a knife for you to kill her with when you go home."

The uncle bought a knife for him. The young man took it home, but even if he did, he had no wish to kill her. There was a field of corn near the house, and as he passed it on his way home, he threw the knife into it as far as he could. His wife was sitting in the kitchen when he got home.

"Well, how did you put in the day?" she asked.

"Very well," said he.

"What humor were your uncles in?"

"Good," said he.

"You should tell the truth," said she. "They were ·in bad humor. One of them told you you had married a fairy woman, and that if you had gone to them first, they would have picked a good wife for you. And didn't he buy a knife for you to kill me with?"

"He did, surely," said the husband.

"And you threw it away from you into the corn?"

"I did."

" 'Tis well that you did," said she. "I'm going to leave you altogether now, and you can go to your uncles, and let them pick a wife for you."

She left and took the child with her.

"Now," said she, as she was leaving, "it won't be long until you marry again. Every night when you are going to bed, I want you to leave a light burning and some food on the table for me. The child and myself will come to eat it."

And so it happened. It wasn't long after till he got married. Late one night when he and his wife were in bed in the kitchen, she turned her head and saw the woman and her child having a good meal. Then they left. Some time later, she saw the woman and child at the table again. The woman in bed gave a laugh that echoed through the house. Then the woman at the table spoke.

"That's a laugh that you will cry for yet," said she.

She left the house and never came back.

The husband was well off and wanted for nothing. But after a while, all his cattle began to die on him, and in the end, he was left with only a mare and foal. The foal was almost reared. One day when he was putting them out to graze, the mare galloped over a cliff and was killed. All he had then was the foal. He took her and put her on an island to keep her from harm.

When the foal was a year or two old, the man said to his wife one day, "I think I'll go for the foal today and take her to the fair and sell her."

He took the foal off the island. As he was taking her along the road to the fair, he came to where there was a cliff at the side of the road. As they were passing by, a door opened in the cliff, and a boy came out.

"What are you asking for the foal?" said he.

The man named the price.

"I'll give you five pounds for her," said the boy.

"That's not enough," said the man.

"Take her to the fair then," said the boy, "and if you are offered more for her, take it. If you don't get more, come back this way, and I'll give you the five pounds."

He reached the fair with the foal and kept her there till the evening. But if he did, he got no offer more than five pounds; so he decided that the first person that had made him that offer should get her. He brought the foal back home the same way. The boy was waiting for him and he gave him the foal.

"Come in now, and I'll give you the money," said the boy.

He went in and saw his first wife sitting near the fire. As the boy was giving him the money, she spoke.

"Give him five pounds more," said she.

The boy did so.

"And five more now," said she.

The boy obeyed.

The man knew well that she was his first wife.

"Go home now," said she. "You have cried enough now for the laugh your wife gave the last night I was in your house. Go home now and buy cattle and sheep with the price of the foal. That's your son, who bought her from you. It won't be long until you are well off again."

He went home and bought cattle and sheep with the price of the foal, and it wasn't long till he was as rich as he had been before. He prospered from day to day and was snug till the day of his death.

• 28 • *Fairy Money*

There was a man here in Teelin many years ago, and people said that he had fairy money for a long time. This is how he got it.

He was in the church at Carrick one Sunday. The Mass had only begun when he felt a kind of weakness coming over him, and he had to leave the church. He walked down the street when he recovered, and when he was outside the hotel, he met a gentleman. They started to chat in a friendly way.

"You are not looking well. Is there anything wrong with you?" asked the gentleman.

"There is," said the man from Teelin. "I was at Mass in the church and a kind of weakness came over me and I had to leave."

The gentleman put his hand in his pocket and handed him a florin. "Go into Éamonn's public-house and take a good glass of whiskey; it will do your heart good, and you'll feel better."

The Teelin man thanked him, and the stranger went off and was seen no more. The Teelin man went into the public-house and asked for a glass of the best whiskey in the house. He told them about the weakness that had come over him, and they gave him a good drop of whiskey. He paid for it with the florin which the gentleman had given him, and Éamonn Haughey gave him some change. He put the change into his pocket, drank the whiskey, and left.

Next day when he was going fishing, he was short of tobacco, so he went to the shop. When he put his hand into his pocket to pay for the tobacco what did he find there but the same florin which the gentleman had given him. He pretended nothing, but handed it in payment to the shopkeeper for the tobacco and received some change. That evening at the end of his day's work, he was returning home tired, hungry, and wet and went into the publichouse for a half-whiskey to warm himself. When he put his hand in his pocket to pay for it, he found the florin there again. He was greatly surprised and didn't know what to do. Still he pretended nothing.

He went on like that for a good while, buying all he needed and always getting the florin back again. He was getting rather worried; still he said to himself that if it was something bad, he wouldn't have got it at all. His main worry was about the man who had given him the coin; he might not be a man of this world at all. He feared to go out on the sea in his boat carrying the coin and didn't know what to do with it.

After a long time, he went into Éamonn Haughey's publichouse in Carrick and asked for a glass of whiskey. When paying for it, he found the coin in his pocket.

He threw it on the counter, saying, "May the devil go with you!"

He told Éamonn the whole story, and Éamonn said he was a fool not to have kept it. Éamonn went over to the till to get the coin. It had vanished, and neither he nor the Teelin man ever saw it again. Nothing would get it out of the Teelin man's head that it was a fairy man had given it to him.

· 29 · *The Children of the Dead Woman*

There was a man long ago, and he was looking for a wife. He found one, but he was only a year married to her when she died, while giving birth to a child. Her mother was anxious to have the child to rear, but the father said that he would not give the child away to anybody. He would try to rear it himself. At that time, there were old women who earned their living by minding children; so the father got one of them to look after his own child. The only people in the house besides the child were this old woman and himself. He was a very strong man. Two months went by. The old woman slept in a bed beside the fire with the cradle nearby, so that she was able to attend to the child by night and by day.

One stormy evening, the father came home from his work. He took off his boots and sat beside the fire.

He took up the child, saying, "You are doing well, my little orphan, and getting strong."

"May God give you long life," said he to the old woman. "You are minding him well, to say that he is thriving so fast!"

"You don't know what I know," replied the old woman. "Every night since she died—at least, since I came here—that child's mother comes here. She eats some boiled potatoes and drinks some milk from the cupboard. The moment she comes in, she goes over to the cradle and kisses the child. Then she warms her hands at the fire before taking the boiled potatoes and milk from the cupboard. When she has taken some food, she comes to the cradle again, takes up the child, and feeds him at her breast. Then she washes him, puts dry clothes under him, and lays him down in the cradle, kissing him. She then stands in the middle of the floor, looks up toward the room, where you are asleep, heaves a sigh, and goes out the door. She has done that every night since I came here. I see her, but I don't ask her any question."

"Had I known that," said the man, "and had I seen her, I would have held her here or failed in the attempt."

"You'll get your chance," said the old woman. "I will cough tonight when she comes. Have your ears open."

That night he did not take off all of his clothes but lay on the bed, so that he would see her when she came and hold her.

Late that night, they heard the door opening. She came in and kissed the child; then she went to the cupboard, got the dish of potatoes and the naggin of milk—naggins were common vessels at that time—and ate quickly. She then stirred up the fire and warmed herself. (I'd say she was cold.) When she had warmed herself, she went to the cradle, took up the child, suckled him, washed and cleaned him, and put dry clothes under him. Then she stood in the middle of the floor and looked up toward the room. The old woman coughed, and the woman went out the door.

"Are you awake now?" asked the old woman.

"I am," replied the man, coming down from the room.

"Did you see her?"

"I did, but I was too frightened to go near her. And I thought that if I saw her at all, I'd hold her here."

The two of them did not go to bed until it dawned. The man went next morning to the house of his wife's parents. Her three brothers were there, two of them were strong, hefty fellows, but the third was a weakling. The family welcomed him and asked him how the child was doing. He told them the child was thriving, that his mother came each night to wash and clean and suckle him.

"I saw her myself last night," said he. "She ate some potatoes and drank milk after attending to the child. Then she went out the door, and I was too frightened to move."

"Bad luck to you," said the eldest brother. "If you saw her, you could have held her. If I were there, I'd not let her go."

"Well, come over to me tonight then, and you'll see her," said the husband. "We'll see if you can hold her."

"If I see her, I'll hold her," said the brother.

They walked back to the house again. The old woman and the child were there. When they sat down, the dead woman's brother asked the old woman did his sister come every night. She said that she did.

"Well, if I see her tonight, I won't let her go," said he.

Early in the night, the dead woman's husband and brother went up to the bedroom and kept watch to see if she would come. It wasn't long until they heard the door opening. Her brother saw her as well as the husband and the old woman. She went up to the fire and warmed her hands. (I suppose she was always cold.) When she had warmed herself, she went to the cupboard, took out the dish of potatoes and a naggin of milk and ate quickly. Then she went to the cradle, took up the child, and put him to her breast. She cleaned and washed him and put dry clothes under him. Then she stood in the middle of the floor, looked up toward the room, heaved a sigh, and went out.

"Are ye asleep?" asked the old woman.

"No," they replied, as they came down from the room.

"Ye are the two most cowardly men I've ever met," said the old woman.

(I must shorten my story for you now.) The same thing happened to the second brother.

"May the devil take ye!" said the third brother. "If I were there, I'd hold her."

"Bad cess to you! You're able to do nothing," replied the two brothers.

"I'll tell ye what I can do," said the youngest brother. "If I saw my sister, I'd hold her and wouldn't let her go. If ye come along with me tonight, ye'll see that I'll hold her if I lay eyes on her."

The three brothers went to the house that night. Before it was too late, they decided to go up to the bedroom. They lay down, the youngest on the outside, so that he could easily run down to the kitchen to catch his sister. It wasn't long until they heard the door opening, and in she came. They all saw her. She ran to the fire and warmed her hands. Then she went to the cupboard and took out the potatoes and milk. She seemed to be very hungry. After eating, she sat down and took the child from the cradle and put him to her breast; then she washed and cleaned him and put dry clothes under and about him.

As she put him back into the cradle, she kissed him three times. On the other nights, she had kissed him only once. She then stood up to leave. Weren't the four men great cowards that they made no move? Just then, up jumped the youngest brother, and he put his two arms around her. She screamed and begged him, for God's sake, to let her go. In the struggle, she lifted him up to the rafters, beseeching him to release her.

"I'll be killed if I'm not back in time," she cried.

"The devil a foot will you put out of here," said her brother.

She was dragging him about, almost killing him; so he shouted to one of his brothers to come to his assistance. The pair of them struggled with her until she finally fell down on the floor in a dead faint. The youngest brother still kept his hold of her.

Next morning, her husband went with one of the brothers for the priest. When they came back, the priest prayed over her until ten o'clock, while her young brother held her. When she recovered her speech, she told the priest that that was to have been her last visit, as the fairies with whom she stayed were moving to Ulster that night. So she stayed with her husband and child, much the same as she had been before, except that she had a wild look in her eyes till the day she died. She bore nine sons to her husband after her rescue, and they came to be known as the children of the dead woman.

· 30 · The Three Laughs of the Leipreachán

There was a farmer long ago, and he used to get up very early in the morning and go out to see how his livestock and crops were after the night. One fine morning when he went out, he heard a noise as if somebody were hammering. He looked around and saw a huge mushroom growing. He was surprised at its size and went to take a closer look at it. What should he see under the mushroom but a *leipreachán*, who was making a pair of shoes. People say that the *leipreachán* is a shoemaker. The farmer ran and seized hold of him.

"I have been a long time looking for you," said the farmer; "and you'll never leave my hands until you tell me where I can get riches."

They say that when the Danes were in Ireland, they hid a lot of money in the earth, and only the *leipreachán* knows where it is.

"Oh, I can't tell you that," cried the *leipreachán*. "I don't know where they hid it."

"You'll have to tell me," said the farmer, "or I'll cut off your head."

"Well, I can't tell you," said the *leipreachán*.

The farmer brought him home and put him into a trunk. He left him there for seven years. One day when the farmer was out walking by the shore, he found a balk of timber washed in by the tide. He sold it to another man, and when he returned home, the *leipreachán* laughed inside the trunk. The farmer didn't take any notice of this, but when the seven years were up, he took him out of the trunk.

"I'll put you in for seven more years," said he, "and, if you don't tell me where I can get riches, I'll cut off your head."

"Do, if you wish. I can't tell you where you'll find it," said the *leipreachán*.

One day soon afterward, a poor man who was passing by came in. The farmer was at his breakfast, and he invited the poor man to sit down and eat something.

"No, thank you. I'll be going," said the poor man.

He hadn't gone far when he broke his leg. The *leipreachán* laughed again, but the farmer took no notice. When the second seven years were up, the farmer went to the trunk again and took out the *leipreachán*.

"If you don't tell me where I can get those riches, I'll cut off your head," said he.

"Do, if you wish. I can't tell you." said the *leipreachán*.

The farmer locked him in the trunk once more. Some time after that, the *leipreachán* overheard the farmer saying that he was going to a fair. Now at that time, anyone who had money used to hide it in the earth, fearing it might be stolen from him. There were lots of thieves in those days. (Indeed, we have some, even today.) When the farmer was getting ready to leave, he went to the hiding place to get some of his money. Weren't the thieves watching him taking it! He went off to the fair, and when he returned home, the *leipreachán* laughed. The farmer jumped up and took the *leipreachán* out of the trunk.

"That's the third time you have laughed since I caught you," said he. "What made you laugh each time?"

"There are many things which a person would be better off for not knowing," said the *leipreachán*.

"Enough of that coaxing talk," said the farmer. "Tell me why you laughed."

"Well," said the *leipreachán*, "you remember the day you found the balk of timber at the edge of the sea?"

"I do," said the farmer.

"That balk was full of money, and the man to whom you sold it has been rich ever since."

"That's true enough," said the farmer. "Now, tell me why you laughed the second time."

"Ah, let me go," said the *leipreachán*.

"I won't until you tell me," said the farmer.

"Well," said the *leipreachán*, "you remember the day a poor man came in and you invited him to eat something, and he refused? When he turned down the food, he turned down his luck, and he hadn't gone far when he broke his leg. Had he waited for a bite of food, the danger would be over."

"Tell me now about your third laugh."

"I won't. Better for you not to know," said the *leipreachán*.

They started to argue, and finally the farmer took hold of the *leipreachán's* head and told him that he'd sweep it off unless he told him why he laughed the last time.

"Very well," said the *leipreachán*. "When you were getting ready for the fair, you went to the hiding place in the field to get some money. You took some of it with you. But there was a thief watching you, and when you had gone off to the fair, he went to the place and stole the rest of it."

The farmer jumped up, and out he ran to search for his money. He went around like a madman from one place to another. If he didn't know that it had been stolen, he mightn't have lost his reason.

There was a man one time, and his name was Rory O'Donoghue. His wife was a great woman for knitting stockings, and Rory's job was to go from town to town, selling them.

There was to be a fair in Macroom on a certain day, and Rory left home the evening before with his bag of stockings to sell them at the fair next day. Night came on him before he reached the town. He saw a light in a house at the roadside, and he went in. There was no one inside before him but a very old man.

"You're welcome, Rory O'Donoghue," said the old man.

Rory asked him for lodgings for the night and told him that he was on his way to the fair at Macroom. The old man said he could stay and welcome. A chair that was at the bottom of the kitchen moved up toward the fire, and the old man told Rory to sit on it.

"Now," said the old man, "Rory O'Donoghue and myself would like to have our supper."

A knife and a fork jumped up from the dresser and cut down a piece of meat that was hanging from the rafters. A pot came out of the dresser, and the meat hopped into it. Up rose the tongs that were at the side of the hearth; they pulled out some sods of turf and made a fire. Down jumped the hangers and hooked the pot over the fire. A bucket of water rose up, and water was poured over the meat. The cover jumped onto the pot. A wickerwork sieve filled itself with potatoes, threw them into the bucket of water, and washed them. The potatoes then rose up and went into a second pot. The knife and fork went up to the first pot and the lid rose up. Up came a plate from the dresser. The knife and fork took out the meat from the pot and put it on the plate. The hangers took the pot off the fire and hung the pot of potatoes on it. When the potatoes were boiled, they strained off the water into the sieve. A tablecloth spread itself on the table. Up rose the sieve and spread the potatoes out on the table. The plate of meat jumped onto the table and so did two other plates as well as two knives and forks. A knife and fork cut the meat into two portions and put some on each plate.

"Get up, Rory O'Donoghue," said the old man. "Let us start eating!"

When they had eaten their supper, the tablecloth rose up and cleared off what was left into a bucket. Rory and the old man rose from the table and sat at either side of the fire. Two slippers came up to Rory O'Donoghue and two others to the old man.

"Take off your shoes, Rory, and put on those slippers," said the old man. "Do you know, Rory, how I spend my nights here? I spend one-third of each night eating and drinking, one-third telling stories or singing songs, and the last third sleeping. Sing a song for me now, Rory."

"I never sang a song in my life," said Rory.

"Tell a story, then."

"I never told a story of any kind," said Rory.

"Well, unless you tell a story or sing a song, you'll have to go off out the door," said the old man.

"I can't do any of the two," said Rory.

"Off out the door with you, then," said the old man.

Rory stood up and took hold of his bag of stockings. No sooner had he gone out than the door struck him a blow on the back. He went off along the road, and he hadn't gone very far when he saw the glow of a fire by the roadside. Sitting by the fire was a man, who was roasting a piece of meat on a spit.

"You're welcome, Rory O'Donoghue," said the man. "Would you mind, Rory, taking hold of this spit and turning the meat over the fire? But don't let any burnt patch come on it."

No sooner had Rory taken hold of the spit than the man left him. Then the piece of meat spoke.

"Don't let my whiskers burn," it shouted.

Rory threw the spit and the meat from him, snatched up his bag of stockings, and ran off. The spit and the piece of meat followed him, striking Rory O'Donoghue as hard as they could on the back. Soon Rory caught sight of a house at the side of the road. He opened the door and ran in. It was the same house he had visited earlier, and the old man was in bed.

"You're welcome, Rory O'Donoghue," said the old man. "Come in here to bed with me."

"Oh, I couldn't," said Rory. "I'm covered with blood!"

"What happened to you since you left here?" asked the old man.

"Oh, the abuse I got from a piece of meat that a man was roasting by the roadside," said Rory. "He asked me to turn the meat on the spit for a while, and 'twasn't long till the meat screamed at me not to burn its whiskers. I threw it from me, but it followed me, giving me every blow on the back, so that I'm all cut and bruised."

"Ah, Rory," said the old man. "If you had a story like that to tell me, when I asked you, you wouldn't have been out until now. Lie in here on the bed now, and sleep the rest of the night."

Rory went into the bed and fell asleep. When he awoke in the morning, he found himself on the roadside, with his bag of stockings under his head, and not a trace of a house or dwelling anywhere around him.

•*32*• *Doctor Lee and Little Aran*

Long ago, and a long time it was. If I were there then, I wouldn't be there now. If I were there then and now, I would have a new story or an old story, or I would have no story at all. In any case, however well off I am tonight, may ye not be half so well off tomorrow night.

There was a man named Lee to the west of us here in Carna, in the townland of Letterdeskert. He had a boat, and he was always out in it on the sea. When he came to shore in the evening, he used to tie the boat up at the harbor at Cornarone. He was an only son, but there were several sisters of his in the family. It is they who used to do the farm work when he was at sea.

One day when he was going to Galway by boat, he thought that the boat touched a rock to the east of the Head. He got a start when the boat turned on its side at a spot where he thought there wasn't a stone or a rock or any talk of such. He jumped to his feet and took hold of a big wooden cross, which he had in the boat for taking seaweed. He looked down over the edge of the boat, and what did he see but the dry land with heather growing on it. The moment he touched the land with the wooden cross, the boat floated.

He sailed on, but he hadn't gone far when the sea rose up behind him as high as a hill. It would swamp the boat or even a big ship, if she were there. He had three sods of turf beside him where he sat as he steered the boat. He took up one of them when he saw the huge wave and threw it against it. The sea grew as calm and still as it had ever been. He sailed on, but he hadn't gone far when he saw another towering wave following him. He thought that it would swamp the whole world. He bent down, took another sod of turf, and threw it as hard as he could against the wave. The sea fell and became as calm and still as it had ever been. He continued on his way with a nice breeze that filled his three sails. For the third time, the sea rose up behind him, and as the wave came toward him, he didn't know under God what to do. He gave himself up for death as he bent down for the third sod of turf. He threw it against the wave, and when it struck, the sea fell and grew as calm as it had ever been.

That was good, and it wasn't bad. He sailed on, with a kind of fear and worry on him all the time. After awhile, he saw a huge sea approaching for the fourth time. The previous waves were small as compared with this one. He was certain that he could not survive it. The only thing he could do under God was to put his hand into his pocket, pull out his knife, open it, and throw it at the wave as it came near him. The sea fell, as calm as it had ever been. He kept on his way, still afraid, and finally reached Galway. There he took his cargo on board and returned home. He told his adventures to his father and mother and sisters and everybody.

That was good, and it wasn't bad. A good while later, there came a day when he wasn't using his boat at all. He owned a number of cattle, and he said to himself that he should go to cut some heather as bedding for them in the cow house. He went off to the hill and cut a basketful of heather. When he had almost finished the work, he felt a kind of sleep and faintness coming over him. The next moment, he was carried off into the air as he slept. When he awoke, he didn't know where he was. He found himself in a house, lying near the fire. At the other side of the fire was an old man, who spoke to him.

"You had a long sleep," said he.

"I had, and I don't know why it came over me," said Lee.

He put his hand into his pocket and pulled out his pipe, as he wanted a smoke.

He had a flint stone to "redden" the pipe with, like all the smokers at the time, and when he was about to use the flint stone, the old man cried out, "Oh, for God's sake, don't take my house or my kingdom from me, my Little Aran! Don't put me wandering the roads, not knowing where to go! Leave me my kingdom! Put that flint stone back into your pocket, and 'redden' your pipe at the fire there on the hearth!"

Lee put the flint stone back into his pocket and "reddened" his pipe with an ember from the fire.

"Now," said the old man, "there's a reason for everything, and that's why you're here. Will you do something for me?"

"I'll do anything I can for you or for anybody else who asks me," said Lee.

"Come up to this room with me, then!" said the old man.

Lee stood up and followed the old man to the room. When they entered, Lee saw a bed, and lying on it was the most beautiful woman he had ever seen. She was moaning and complaining. The old man told him to go over and look at the knife which was plunged into her right breast. The woman begged him, for the sake of God and the Virgin Mary, to pull out the knife. He walked over to her and was filled with remorse when he saw that it was his own knife, which he had thrown against the wave. He pulled it out, and immediately she rose up as well as she had ever been.

"Now," said the old man, "you had better marry this woman and stay here with us."

"Indeed, I won't," said Lee. "There's no use in my saying that I will, because I can't stay. I have several sisters at home, but I am the only son my parents ever had. My father is weak now, and I want to stay with my sisters until I see them settled down."

"Stay here!" said the young woman. "There's no need for you to leave. If you do, you'll inherit all this kingdom of Little Aran forever."

"I won't stay," said Lee.

"Well, we won't let you go without giving you a present," said the old man. "We know that you couldn't avoid throwing that knife. Any man in danger must do all in his power to save himself."

The old man left the room, and it wasn't long till he returned with a book.

"Here is a book for you," said he. "You must not open it for seven years. And there won't be a doctor under the sun anywhere that'll be half as good as you. But, for all you have ever seen or ever will see, don't open it until the seven years are up."

"I'm thankful to you," said Lee. "I won't open it, if I can."

The old man went out, and by his magical power, he took Lee with him and left him back on the hill beside his basket of heather. Lee lifted the basket on his back, took the book under his arm, and walked down the hill by the side of Knockakilleen and Letterdeskert to his home at Cornarone, where he kept his boat moored. He threw the basket of heather into the cow house, went in home, and put the book a-keep.

A year went by, and Lee did not touch the book. So did a second year, and he did not open it. Everyone in the townlands around was urging him to open it, but he said he would not until the seven years were up. Just as the third year was ending, a cousin of his, who was very dear to him, fell ill. When the cousin was dying, everybody was at Lee to open the book to see if it had any cure for the sick man. He was so fond of this cousin that he finally went to where the book was hidden. He opened it and read through it until he found the remedy which cured him. However, only three years' share of the knowledge in the book was readable; the rest of the pages had melted and turned as black as soot. He could not make any use of them. Still, there wasn't a doctor in County Galway or in Connacht or even in all Ireland who was half so good as Doctor Lee. He cured many people and finally left Letterdeskert and traveled before him, curing both lowly and noble. He never returned, and we are sure that it must have been that the young woman took him off to Little Aran and that he is still there.

May the dear blessing of God and of the Church be on the souls of the dead, and may we and this company be seventeen hundred thousand times better off a year from tonight. This story is quite true. I know the townland of Cornarone. I was often there. I know where Lee had his house and where he used to moor his boat. It isn't very many years since he lived there. 'Tis a true story, indeed, that happened in Carna in Conamara.

·*33*· *The Child from the Sea*

One day in the olden times, a fisherman from Errismore was fishing for gurnet. The day was very fine, and fish were plentiful. Toward evening, the fisherman felt a great weight on his line and thought that he had hooked a heavy fish. He started to haul it in, and when he had it on board, what had he caught but a male child! His hair was as red as the coat of a fox. The hook was stuck into his cheek. The fisherman was very proud of his catch. The boy ran up under the forward thaft of the boat and stayed there.

The fisherman took him home, but as soon as he let him down on the floor, the boy rushed in under a bed, and even a man with a pitchfork couldn't get him out. There he stayed until the following day. They tried by every means to get him to eat and drink, but it was no use. The man went to the priest and told him what had happened.

"You must take him out again, as close as you can to the spot where you caught him," said the priest, "and put him back into the sea again."

The fisherman took him in the boat next day and rowed toward the place where he had caught him. When they were near the spot, the boy gave a big laugh. He jumped, legs up, out of the boat, dived down like a cormorant, and was seen no more.

·34· The Big Cat and the Big Rat

There was a poor man in Galway many years ago, and he worked each day for himself and his family in a house which he had built down near the Long Wall. One morning, when he came in for his breakfast, his wife and children were before him. He sat down to the table to eat, but he was barely seated when in came the largest rat that anybody had ever seen. She jumped onto the table and started to eat the breakfast as though she belonged in the house. She was so terrible looking that no one in the house made any attempt to drive her away; in fact they drew back from her, until she had finished the meal. When she had eaten, she jumped off the table and went out.

"We have little chance of escaping with our lives," said the man of the house, "seeing that she comes in so boldly. If she comes again, I'm worried about what she may do."

When the man came home to his dinner, the food was ready for him on the table. He had only just sat down when in on the floor came the rat, jumped up on the table, and started to eat the food with him. The man and his wife said they had enough, so frightened were they. When she had eaten her meal, the rat jumped off the table and went out.

"May God help us!" said the man. "That rat won't leave us tills she kills all in the house. What will we do?"

When evening came, and the man returned from work, the supper was put on the table. Just as the family were going to sit down, the rat came in. She gave a lively jump onto the table and started to eat as quickly as she could. The man of the house ate hardly anything, he was so much afraid of the rat. When she had eaten her fill, she jumped off the table and left.

"We're finished now or never, God preserve us!" said the man. "We were poor enough already without this thief coming to us."

Next day, the rat came as before, so the man of the house said the best thing to do was to go in search of a cat. He and his wife found a nine-month-old cat and brought him home. He was a fine strong animal. The man told his wife, regardless of how she got it, to give the cat plenty of milk, to strengthen him, in the hope that he would drive away the rat or frighten her.

When the rat came in next day, the cat was sitting on his haunches on the hearth. When he saw her, he moved his tail and hunched his back. The rat saw the cat and slinked sideways up to him. The fight began, but it wasn't long until the cat was mewing pitifully as he tried to escape from the hold and claws of the rat. For a quarter of an hour, the rat tore him fiercely and almost killed him. Finally the cat escaped to the farthest corner to get away from his enemy. The rat calmly jumped on to the table and began to share the food with the man of the house. When she had eaten enough, she went out the door quietly. The cat came out from the corner and lay down on the hearth, covered with wounds. The woman of the house fetched a large dish of milk and gave it to him to drink. When he had drunk his fill, he started to lick himself near the fire. Then, when he had warmed himself, he went to the door, looked carefully out, to see whether the rat was anywhere near, and, finding that she wasn't, went off out of sight around the corner of the house.

When the man of the house returned from work in the evening, the first thing he did was to inquire whether the cat had come back. He was told that he hadn't.

"We're done for now, God help us!" said he. "'Tisn't for our good, but to kill us, that that thief of a rat has come here."

When the supper was laid on the table, he sat down to eat but, no sooner had he done so, than the rat came in, jumped up on the table, and started to eat alongside him. When she had eaten enough, she jumped to the floor and went out.

"I'm certain that we'll meet our deaths through that rat," said the man. "She'll be with us until she kills all in the house. We have no chance now since the cat left us."

The rat kept on coming for three nights and three days, but there was no trace of the cat. Early the fourth morning, when the man opened the door, he saw the biggest cat he had ever seen, or ever would see, and with him was the man's own cat. The big cat entered as soon as the door was opened and gave a mew.

The small cat did the same. They went toward the fire; the big one stayed on the hearth, and the small one jumped onto a seat.

"Go out and bring in a quart of milk for the cats," said the man to his wife.

He felt great courage when he saw the big cat with the small one. Very well. The two cats drank the milk, and when they had enough, each of them went to the side of the fire and began to lick themselves. The man sat down to the table to eat his breakfast when it was ready. As soon as he did so, in came the rat. When the big cat saw her at the threshold, he twirled his tail and got to his feet. The small cat jumped up and ran off in terror of the rat, remembering the clawing and bites he had got from her; he left the two of them to face each other.

As soon as the rat caught sight of the big cat, she sidled up to him. The cat advanced toward her. Then both jumped and attacked each other on the middle of the floor. Such tearing and clawing and murdering there never was before. They spent a long part of the day fighting inside the kitchen. Then they went out into the yard and fought up and down by the Long Wall three times, through the long summer day. The sun was just setting when the cat killed the rat. He went back to the house, wounded and torn. The woman gave them both a dish of milk. When they had drunk their fill, they sat at either side of the fire, warming themselves. After a while, the big cat went to the door and mewed. The small cat did the same. Then the big one went out, followed by the small one, and not a trace of either was seen from that day to this.

May we be seven thousand times better off a year from tonight.

·35· *The March Cock and the Coffin*

There was a house in this townland, in which I am telling my story, and a man lived there with his wife and children. The man worked every day not far from the house, and whenever he looked toward the house, he would see a coffin descending from the sky on the side of the house. At the same moment each day, the March cock, which was in the house, used to jump up, shake his wings, and crow loudly. Then he used to try to fly up on the gable, and if he couldn't do that, he would settle on the chimney and keep crowing until he banished the coffin.

That went on for three weeks or so, and the man saw it happening each day. The woman of the house came to hate the cock on account of its crowing. Then one day, when the man was in the field, he saw the coffin coming down on the side of the house. The cock was inside in the house and he jumped up, shook his wings, and started to crow. The woman was so annoyed that she took up a wooden mallet and threw it at the cock to drive him from the house, so that she wouldn't be listening to him. She hit the cock on the head and killed him with the blow. The coffin remained where it was. The man was worried and he went to the house and found the cock dead.

"Who killed the cock?" he asked.

"I did," said his wife. "My head was split from his crowing day after day. I threw the mallet at him to drive him away, but I struck him on the head and killed him."

"My seven thousand curses on you!" said the husband. "You killed the cock and you killed me too!"

He lay down on the bed, and in three days' time, he was dead.

That's as true a story as was ever told. It happened here in this townland, and the house where the man and the cock were can still be seen by anybody.

The dear blessing of God and of the Church on the souls of the dead! And may we be seventeen hundred thousand times better off a year from tonight—ourselves and all who are listening to me.

· *36* · Seán na Bánóige

A long, long time ago, long after the "Danes" were driven out of Ireland, there was a poor farmer living in the townland of Bánóg in the parish of Lispole. His name was Seán O'Shea. He was married and had a houseful of children. Everything was going against him, the poor man. He was getting low prices for what he had to sell, and he had to work very hard.

One day he came home from the field, his heart and his health broken. He gave a sigh as he sat down on a chair.

"Do you know what I'm thinking of doing?" he asked his wife.

"I don't, Seán," she replied. "When a person is poor and tormented, many things come into his mind."

"I'm thinking of leaving here and trying my fortune somewhere that I can get work and earning. Yourself and the eldest lad will keep the place going. Whatever I earn won't be kept back from ye. I'll always be sending ye something to help ye along."

"May God help us!" said his wife. "What'll we do, if you leave the house?"

"I'm tormented and heartbroken from the world," said Seán; "and I can't bear it any longer. Let ye carry on with the place, and I'll be off as soon as I get ready."

His mind was made up. A week later when he was ready for the road, he took hold of his stick and bade them goodbye.

"Work hard now and help each other as well as ye can," said he. "I won't hide from ye anything I earn."

His poor wife was lonely after him, and the children were crying. Still, he had to leave them. He set out and faced the long road ahead of him, staying a night here and a night there. At one place he'd get an offer of work; at two other places, he'd be refused. He kept on traveling till he reached Cork and walked about, meeting with no success, till he made off Cork Harbor. There was a three-masted ship moored at the quay, and a lot of men were putting cargo aboard for Lochlainn. He spent a good part of the day watching them at work, and when he was tired of that, he noticed a fine man some distance away. He asked the workmen who he was.

"That is the captain of the ship, Captain Mackey," they told him.

"Two Irishmen should understand each other," said Seán. "I'll go to have a chat with him."

He went over to the captain and saluted him respectfully, as one should a stranger.

After talking for a while, the captain said, "What sort of a man are you that you don't take a hand at the work with the men? I'm anxious to have the ship loaded and want all the hands I can get, for 'tisn't always the tide and wind are suitable for a heavy ship like mine."

"Where are you bound for, sir?" asked Seán O'Shea.

"For Lochlainn," said the captain.

"You wouldn't be slow to help a poor man like myself, would you?" asked Seán. "I haven't a penny to my name and have no way of earning a living. I left my wife and family behind me in West Kerry to see if I could help them. Would you ever give me a chance and take me on as a sailor? I'd work as hard as I could in every way, for I have no money to pay for my passage."

"Very well, I'll help you," said the captain. "Lie in there with the workmen."

Seán started to work very happy, and he ate and drank with the men until the cargo was on board. Then, when the captain got a suitable tide and wind, the ship sailed out from land. If the wind was against them sometimes, it was favorable at other times, so they finally reached Lochlainn.

"Now," said Seán O'Shea to the captain, when they landed, "you won't want me any longer. You have been very good to me, and if God gives me courage, there's no danger that I'll forget to reward you. I may get work somewhere, and we'll meet again, maybe."

"Don't worry about that," said the captain. "What I did was small. 'Tis only right to help anyone in trouble."

He bade goodbye to them and traveled through the country. It was a rough, furzy land, and poor Seán had very little in his pocket to enable him to go into a public house or hotel to fill his belly with a good meal. He went through the poorest part of the country first to see if he would gain anything by it. Late in the evening, he saw a small, little hovel shaped like a mushroom with a chimney in the center. It had a very untidy appearance.

"You don't look to be much of a place for a poor hungry man to get a night's lodging," said Seán. "Still, I'll have to try you."

He drew nearer to the house and entered. He looked around, and if he did, he saw two old men, the likes of whom he had never seen before. They were thin and shriveled and covered with beard and rags and had prominent teeth.

As soon as Seán stood inside the door, one of them said, "Here you are, Seán O'Shea from Bánóg. You are welcome!"

"God of miracles! And how do you know my name? Or how did the person who told you my name know it? I'm thankful for the welcome," said Seán.

"Sit up here near me," said the old man. "You're tired and worn out after your long travels."

"I am, my good man," replied Seán. "I'm finding all this strange, and I'm a bit afraid, too."

"Don't be afraid at all. Sit up here. You're welcome in this house."

Seán sat up to the fire slowly enough, and whatever look he gave around, what should he see but a very old woman as shriveled and hairy as the men, sitting in the far corner. She had two long front teeth that reached the floor, and she looked as if she'd swallow him into her stomach in one bite.

"Don't be a bit afraid!" said the same old man. "We cannot help being as we are. Get up, Sibyl, and get a bite of food ready for the stranger. He's hungry."

The old woman got up and shook herself. Miserable and ugly and wild though she looked, she wasn't long getting something to eat and drink ready for Seán, and the poor man was in need of it by that time. The food didn't taste too bad, although Seán wasn't at his ease. When he had eaten his fill, they spent the evening and some of the night talking, but the other old man— they were brothers—never said anything. Late at night, they went to bed, but if they did, 'twas little Seán slept with the fright. Next morning 'twas the same way; the second brother and the old woman said no word. She looked to have no welcome for Seán at all, though she got the food ready for them.

He stayed there a few days with them. One day, he noticed a still smaller hovel some distance away shaped in the same way as the one they were living in. It didn't appear to have any opening in it, but there was what looked like a flagstone in what might be a doorway. It was as firmly fixed as iron, and Seán couldn't knock any stir out of it.

After he and the talkative old man had walked about a bit, the old man said, "Wouldn't it be a good thing for us to go hunting awhile? You'll be able to have a view of the countryside and take a walk. Come along."

"There's nothing I'd like better," said Seán. "I'm tired of sitting. But what about you? How will you be able to walk?"

"Oh, I'll walk all right, my boy. The walk is good by me, no matter how I look."

They took with them whatever hunting gear they needed and set out. For a long part of the day, they saw no game, no rabbit or cat or hare or deer or eagle. But, while on the way home, they met one sample of game which Seán thought very queer—a mouse. This mouse was the size of a cat. The old man fired at it and killed it.

"Thank heavens, we have something by our day," said he.

He took home the dead mouse and very proud of his kill he was. By the time they reached home, they were in need of some food.

"Come, Sybil," said the old man. "Cook this mouse for our dinner."

'Tis she wasn't long at it. She had good practice it seemed. She skinned and gutted the mouse and got it ready for the pot. Its flesh would just fill a saucer—that's what our mice here wouldn't do. When the dinner was ready, the flesh was put on the table and the three of them sat down. Now Seán would normally eat all that was on the table by himself, but hungry and all though he was, he was slow to eat the flesh of the mouse. Still, he was afraid to refuse the old man, fearing he would get angry or turn against him and 'twas unknown what would happen then. So he ate it as sweetly as if it were bacon he had in his mouth. No sooner had he swallowed it than he gave a hearty laugh.

"What ails you now, my good man?" asked the old man.

"God bless me!" said Seán. "There isn't any money or treasure hidden in any part of Ireland from corner to corner that I don't know where it is."

"That's a fine thing to know, my boy," said the old man. "But you don't know the half of it yet. Wait till we drink a drop of the soup of the mouse. Give us a drop of it, Sybil."

She poured some of the soup into a little vessel and gave some of it to Seán and some to the old man, *moryah*.

"Swallow that now, and 'tis then you'll have all the knowledge," said the old man.

Seán drank it to get the knowledge, but no sooner had he swallowed it, than he knew as little about the hidden treasure as he did when he came into the house.

"By the dickens, if I'm not as blind about the treasure as I ever was," said Seán.

"I knew that would be the way, my good man," said the old man. "I knew that no Irishman could keep a secret. That knowledge would have brought you to the gallows. You are better to be the way you are than to run that danger."

"Well, for my part, I'd rather have knowledge of something that would help me at the end of my life than be as blind as I am," said Seán.

"You're better off as you are," said the old man. "You won't be poor later on, if you do a good deed for me. We'll live here together for another while, maybe a couple of months, until your ship is ready to sail for Ireland with a cargo of timber. You are a good man and a courageous one, and you may be able to help me yet. I know that there is a *lios* on your farm—in the corner of a field. All the money you and your family will ever need is in that *lios*, if you can lay your hands on it. When you return home now, you must get a big basket of turf and light a fire near the door of the *lios*. Have a quarter of mutton ready to put roasting on it when it is blazing. You must also have with you a nice, well-edged axe. When the test comes, you will show how good a man you are. There's nobody inside the *lios*—only a cat. As soon as she smells the roasting meat, she will get a craving for it and come out. You must stand somewhere at the side, so that she won't see you. When she has eaten her fill of the meat, she will want to lie down near the fire and go to sleep. That's when you must get to work, Seán. Steal up to her with your axe in your hand, and give her one blow between the head and shoulders. Be sure not to let the head rejoin the body again. Throw it a good distance away. The *lios* will be free from the spell as soon as the cat is killed.

"Go into the *lios* then. On your left, you will find a room, and you will see a mirror, a piece of soap, a razor, and a towel on a table. Take hold of them carefully, and don't forget any of them! You mustn't breathe a word about all this to anyone. When you have got the things, turn to the right, and you will come to a small room the southwest corner of which has a flagstone with a brass ring attached to it. Lift up the stone by the ring, and under it you will find three jars of gold. Take them away with you, and they will free your wife, your family, and yourself from poverty. Come back here to me then without much delay and bring me the things from the *lios*. That's when I'll be able to reward you properly for your work."

"There's one thing troubling me," said Seán. "I'm still as poor as I ever was. The ship's captain, who was so generous and kind to me, hasn't got any reward for it. I promised to repay him, and here I am now returning to him as poor as ever."

"You won't be so," said the old man. "Go out and pull the ring on the flagstone in the other little hovel and see what happens."

Seán went out, but, alas, if there were twenty Seán O'Sheas there, they couldn't knock a stir out of the flagstone! He went in to the old man.

"I couldn't knock a budge out of it," he said.

"Take me by the right hand, and I'll go out with you."

"Bad scran to you," said Seán. "Well you were able to walk for the past month!"

"That power of walking has left me for the present," said the old man. "But 'twill come back. Do as I tell you."

Seán helped him out to the little hovel, and as soon as the old man pulled the ring, the flagstone came out easily.

"Take a look in there now," said the old man. "Take one of those jars, and you'll have enough for the road and enough for the captain, and God won't let you want for the rest of your life."

Well, Seán was singing "Dómhnall na Gréine" then. He was independent of them and was thinking that he might have the gold in the *lios* at home for himself as well. When it drew near the time for his ship to sail back to Ireland, Seán said goodbye to the three old people.

"Don't fail me now, Seán," said the old man. "I have every trust in you. You were sent to help me."

"I'll keep my promise to you till the death," said Seán. "If I fail you, you can call me a blackguard."

"Very well," said the old man. "Success to your journey!"

Seán packed away his money carefully, and 'tis he was in high spirits as he set out on his journey. His courage was far higher than when he came. When he reached the quayside, he met the captain.

"You're here again, my good man," said the captain.

"I am, sir. I want to make another journey to Ireland, if you take me on board."

"I've no objection. Come on," said the captain.

He took Seán to his cabin. There Seán pulled out his purse and gave him a fistful of the fine yellow gold. There was no shortage of it.

"Take that," said Seán. "I gave you my hand and word that if I had any luck, I'd pay you well. There's plenty for both of us, thank God."

They sailed east and west with the wind, and toward the end of the year, Seán reached Cork Harbor once more. He went ashore, dressed himself up in a fine suit of clothes with shoes, hat, and overcoat, and set out for home. He walked and walked till he reached Bánóg. His wife was standing at the door before him.

"It is Seán, and it isn't Seán, said she. "The Seán that's coming isn't the Seán that left me. The man that's coming is a gentleman, and still he resembles Seán in appearance in every way and has the same smile. How could Seán get to be like that? 'Tisn't he at all."

Then, when he came near her,

"In the name of God! Is it dead or alive you are?" said she.

"Alive, my girl!" said he. "Don't you know if I was dead, 'tisn't like this I'd be looking?"

When he went inside the house, she threw her arms around him, the poor woman, and started to cry with the dint of joy.

The children gathered round, some of them dancing, some shouting, and all of them full of happiness that their father was home again. He spent two or three weeks doing jobs about the house and farm. He noticed that his eldest son had grown a lot while he was away.

"He's a fine able man now," said Seán to his wife.

"He's that," said she. "We were helping each other, trying to keep the house going, hoping to God that you'd return sometime."

After a couple of months, Seán had all his preparations ready for the *lios*. He bought a nice, edgy axe in the town of Dingle as well as a quarter of mutton. He hung up the meat when he brought it home, so that neither the cat nor the dog could get at it. His wife was wondering what all the goings-on were, or what he was doing at the *lios*. He brought a couple of baskets of turf—there was no shortage of that—and lighted a fine big fire about seven yards from the door of the *lios*. He kept an eye to it till it was fine and red. Then he laid the quarter of meat to roast at the edge of it where the cat could easily get at it if she came out. Then he went aside where he could have a view of the fire and the door of the *lios* and of the cat, if she came out. He could easily get at her from where he was.

The meat wasn't too long roasting, and a fine smell rising from it and going all over the parish and everyone wondering what Seán O'Shea was doing, when a monster of a big black cat slipped out of the *lios*, sniffing and smelling all the time until she came to where the meat was roasting. She put her claws into it and dragged it out to the edge of the ashes. Then she started to eat and to eat, and she kept on eating till she put two bellies on herself. When she had plenty eaten and was ready to burst, didn't she lie down, stretch out her four legs, and fall soundly asleep.

"Things are going well for me," said Seán in his own mind. "May God help me to do the rest of the job!"

He took hold of the axe, stole up to the cat in his bare feet, and with one jump struck her a blow in the neck that cut off her head. The head give two or three hops, but if it did, Seán was on his guard. He gave the head a crack of the axe that sent it spinning a good distance and kept it from getting near the body.

He went into the *lios* and looked about him. As the old man in Lochlainn had told him, there was a small room with a table, and on it were the little mirror, the razor, the soap, and the towel. He rolled them up in the towel and tied a cord around it, so that they couldn't fall out. Then he turned to his right, and there he saw another small room.

"Everything is coming right for me," said he in his own mind.

He entered the room, went to the southwest corner, and there was the flagstone with a brass ring on it. He took hold of the ring and raised the stone. His eyes nearly jumped out of his head when he saw the three jars of gold underneath.

"Thanks be to God, I have done my work now," said he. "I'm rich! Pity the man that doesn't travel."

He took the jars home carefully with him.

When his wife saw him coming, "Where were you since, Seán?" she asked.

"That's none of your business, little woman," said he. "Take all that's offered to you. Everything is fine now, but I'll have to leave ye in a little while. Even so, there will be no hunger on ye after me, and I hope to return, with God's help, later on."

They ate their meal together, very happy.

"Now," said Seán, "come down to the room with me till we make a hole under the bed in the corner of the room. I have something to put a-keep there that will provide for yourself and the children and myself for the rest of our lives."

Her two eyes opened wide when she saw what he had after his work. They dug a deep, safe hole for the gold, and you may be sure that they closed it up well; no one could find it.

"Now," said Seán, "tomorrow morning I'll have to make another journey. I don't know if I will succeed or not, but if I don't, you and the children won't see a poor day after me. Take good care of yourself and the children, and don't be short of anything. If God spares me, I won't be long away."

Next morning he got himself ready for the road. There was little to stop him. He had plenty of money in his pocket, a fine suit of clothes on his back, good shoes on his feet, and a nice hat on his head. He said goodbye to them and set out. He knew the way well, and when he reached Cork Harbor, he made off the

ship and the captain. When they were ready to sail, he spoke to
the captain.

"I have the journey of the Eight-legged Dog ahead of me," said
he. "I have been over to Lochlainn and back, as you know, and
I have to go there again and come back. You have been a gentleman to me, and I hope you'll let me go with you again this
time."

"You're very welcome," said the captain.

Seán went on board and enjoyed his trip very much till he
arrived in Lochlainn. He was in good spirits. A poor man is a
great pity without courage or gaiety. But Seán was independent
now; his pockets were full; he was good company for anyone
he'd meet. When the ship docked, Seán set off. He didn't want
any guide, for he knew the way well. He walked on and on until
he made off the hovel. It was the same as ever, and the three were
seated round the fire, as they were the first day that Seán came
to them. The old man saw him coming in the door.

"A thousand welcomes for you, O'Shea," said he. "I knew you
had it in you to do that task. Good is the name for what you have
done. And now when you have some food, you'll do one more
thing for me, and everything will be fine for us."

Seán ate and drank in their company. Then the old man said,
"Sybil, get some hot water."

Sybil got up, fetched some hot water, and left the vessel down
on the middle of the small floor.

"Come here now, Seán, and shave me with that razor you
brought," said the old man.

Seán grasped the razor, and there was no need to edge it. He
took out the little mirror, the soap, and the towel also. The razor
had to have a good edge on it to cut through the thick growth
of beard that had grown in the hundreds of years since the Danes
had been in Ireland. He made a good job of the shaving, although
when he took up the razor first, he thought he'd never be able
to bare the old man's jaws. No sooner had Seán given the last
touch with the razor just below the ear than the fleece of hair
which was on the old man's head fell off him in one piece, like a
covering of shellfish off a rock. The old man stood up, after
being shaved and washed by Seán, and he had become a young,

pleasing, handsome man of about thirty years of age. The magic spell which had been on him had gone.

"I haven't spoken to you up to now, my good man," said the second old man, "and I wonder, since you have the power in your hand, would you help me too?"

"There's no job I'd like better for the rest of the evening than to be clearing the old feathers off ye," said Seán.

The second old man got up and went slowly down to the little seat in the center of the floor. Seán wasn't long at him, and when he had shaved him, the great fleece of hair on the old man's head fell on the floor like a cluster of shellfish. When Seán had washed and cleaned him, he stood up, and when Seán looked at him, he thought he had never in his life seen a finer young man.

"A thousand thanks to you. Good indeed is what you have done," said he to Seán.

"Take pity on me too, my good man," said Sybil.

"Don't!" said the first brother. "Little welcome she had for you the first day you came."

"Ah, don't say that," said Seán. "I must return good for evil. A good deed never yet went astray. As I have the power in my hand, I won't leave her covered with her old feathers any longer."

Down she went to the little seat. Seán wasn't long lathering her and giving her the edge of the razor here and there. And when she was shaved and cleaned, there wasn't a young man in the parish that wouldn't fall in love with her. She looked to be only about thirty years of age.

"That's done now," said the first brother. "Good indeed is what you have done."

"It is good," said Seán; "and I'm proud and glad to have been able to do it.

"We have been under a spell here for hundreds of years," said the first brother, "and the means of removing it was in the *lios* near your house. We'd have been here till the end of time only that God sent you to us. Now we'll be with you always, either here or somewhere else."

Seán spent a year or more with them in comfort, for instead of the little hovel they had up to then, they had now a beautiful pleasant house which was good enough to receive anybody, high or low. It was the happiest year of Seán's life. He went hunting and fowling with the two young men all over Lochlainn. And as for the young woman with her lovely dresses and fine yellow hair, she got the best of meals ready for them.

I don't know whether the three of them traveled back to Ireland in the ship with Seán. I'd say they remained in Lochlainn. The spell was gone off them; they were able to do everything for themselves, and they had no shortage of anything they wanted. When Seán was about to leave them, the first brother gave him two jars of gold and told him to "knock soup and music" out of it in return for the great service he had done to them. They were now in the bloom of youth and health and could go out among the people instead of being three miserable creatures without means of living or comfort.

Seán was kind of lonely leaving them. He said goodbye and made for the quayside where his ship was getting laden for Ireland. He traveled in her to Cork Harbor and never stopped until he reached Bánóg. The house was clean and tidy, and the children had grown up during the three or four years since he had first gone to Lochlainn. He wasn't long home when he bought a fine farm of land some distance from Bánóg and put plenty of cattle and sheep on it. All the people around who had known him were wondering where he got the money that put him on his feet and made him so independent. From that time on, he and his family had all they needed, and so had his grandchildren. I don't know whether any of his descendants are still at Bánóg. I suppose there are, but if there are, I don't know them. Whether there are or not, Seán himself did well.

That's my story, and if there's a lie in it, let there be. 'Tis long ago I heard it from my father. He had the world of stories. I had a lot of them, but alas, my memory is gone and my mind is astray now, and I can't help that.

The Queen of the Planets

There was a man and his wife long ago. The husband had the blessing of everybody, but his wife had the blessing of nobody. She was so hardhearted. The husband was the first to die, and only that the neighbors were so grateful to him, he couldn't be buried at all, the day of the funeral was so wet and stormy. His wife died some time afterward, and she got the two finest days that ever came out of heaven for her wake and funeral. The people were greatly surprised at this, seeing that she had nobody's blessing. Their son then said that he would not sleep a second night on the same bed or eat a second meal at any table until he found out why it was that his father, who had everybody's blessing, got a bad funeral day, while his mother, who had nobody's blessing, got a fine day.

Off he set on his travels. He was a good distance from home when he came to a house, and he got lodgings there for the night. It was the house of a widow who had three daughters. After a meal, the widow asked him where he was going and he told her the whole story.

"Well," said she, "if you get the answer to your questions, would you find out why no man wants to marry my eldest daughter? They all want to marry the other two, but they won't even look at the eldest one. I don't know why it is."

"I have enough troubles of my own," said the young man, "without taking more on my shoulders, but if I get any word for you, I'll bring it back."

He left the house next morning and traveled on until the night came on him. He came to the house of a smith and got lodgings for the night. The smith asked him where he was going, as the widow had, and he told him about his father and mother.

"If you can at all, will you try to bring me some account of what's causing my troubles?" said the smith.

"What troubles have you?" asked the young man.

"Well," said the smith, "I'm working here in my forge from

morning till night, from Monday to Saturday, and I can't save a penny. I'm as poor as ever at the end."

"I'll do my best," said the young man, "but I don't suppose I'll ever return again."

He took to the road again the following morning and walked on during the day. He got lodgings in a farmer's house for the night. As they were sitting near the fire, the farmer asked him where he was going, as the other two had done. He told him his story about his father and mother.

"If you can bring me any word, I hope you will," said the farmer. "There's a part of the roof down there at the door, and the rain is always coming through. I have called in the best thatchers, but they can't dry it."

"I have plenty of troubles now to find out about," said the young man. "I'm getting no answer to my own questions, but everyone inquires about his own. I'll do my best, and if I get any news for you, I'll bring it back and welcome."

He set out again the next morning and traveled on during the day with no house meeting him. Night was coming on when at last he saw a light in a house some distance from the road. He made for the house and found the door wide open before him. The kitchen was large and clean and warm; a fine fire was on the hearth, and a big chair in front of it. But there wasn't a sign of a person anywhere. He sat down on the chair, and after a while, in the door came a beautiful woman. She saluted him courteously and kindly, and he answered her in like manner. She prepared a meal for him, and 'twas no trouble to her. He sat down and ate his fill. She then gave him water to bathe his feet in, after his walk. He sat near the fire again, chatting with her. She was as affable a woman as he had ever met.

When they had talked for a long time, she said that it was time for him to go to bed, that he was tired after the day. His room was at the end of the kitchen with a door through which he could see the kitchen from his bed. There was a large pot of water, almost boiling, on the fire. He stretched himself in bed, but tired and all though he was, he didn't fall asleep. It wasn't long till he could see that the pot was boiling over the kitchen fire, but the woman left it there. Then he could see her putting her head down into the boiling pot. She went down, down, down, until all he could see was her two feet sticking up over the rim of the pot. Finally, they too disappeared as well, and not a bit of the woman could be seen. He could see all this clearly through the room door as he lay in the bed. I need hardly tell you, 'twasn't of sleep he was thinking. He was wondering at, and terrified by, what he was seeing. When he thought she was long enough in the boiling pot to be melted away, up she rose out of it again, bit by bit, as she had sunk into it, as much alive as she had been before. The man was frightened out of his wits. He thought he'd be next for the pot himself.

She then got a rope, made a noose at one end, and threw it over one of the rafters of the kitchen. She stood on a stool, put her head into the noose, and hanged herself. There she was, kicking as she hung, until she finally made no move. When he thought that she must be quite dead with her tongue protruding from her mouth, out from the noose she came as live and energetic as she had ever been.

She next fetched a razor and cut her throat. The blood ran as it would from an ox, until she dropped on the floor and lay there kicking her heels and complaining and moaning. At last she lay quite still.

"She's finished now or never," said the man below in the bed to himself.

After she had lain on the floor for a while, she stood up again as sound and live as she had been before. The man's thoughts were in a whirl, wondering what was best for him to do. Everything that he had seen was so strange.

It wasn't long till she started another trick. She went and fetched a bag and put it on the table. She pulled the table out on to the center of the floor and started to count the gold and silver coins that were in the bag. She kept at this for a long time, until she had a lot of it counted; then she collected it all together and put it back into the bag.

She next got a silken dress, put it on, picked up a book, and spent a long time reading it. Just as long as she had spent in the pot, in the noose, on the floor with her throat cut, and counting the coins. After reading the book for a time, she came down to the room to the man.

"Are you asleep?" she asked.

He gave no reply.

"I know that you're not asleep," said she. "Far from sleeping you are. You saw," she asked, "everything I did tonight?"

"I did."

"Did you ever hear mention of the queen of the planets?"

"I did," said he.

"I am she," she said. "You saw how long I spent in the boiling pot?"

"I did." -

"That's the death which is in store for any child who came into the world during that time. And you saw how long I was hanging?"

"I did," said he.

"That's the death which is in store for any child born during that time. You saw the time I spent lying on the floor, my throat cut and bleeding?"

"I did."

"That's the death which is in store for any child born during that time. You saw how long I spent counting the money?"

"I did."

"That's the way of life which is in store for any child born while I was counting. And you saw how long I spent reading the book?"

"I did."

"That's the way of life which is in store for any child born during that time. I know what brought you here—to find out about your father and mother. Nobody was ever unthankful to your father. He had the blessing of everybody. His purgatory lasted only during those two wet, stormy days of his funeral. Your mother never got a blessing from a poor person, and all that was in store for her was the two fine days of her funeral. Now, tomorrow you will meet your mother with her mouth open, while two mastiffs pursue her. Here is a brazen apple. You must throw it toward her, and unless it goes straight into her mouth, she will devour you to prevent you from bringing home news of her plight. Tell the widow who is worried about her eldest daughter that if the daughter takes her to Mass two Sundays on her back, everybody will have a high opinion of her. Tell the smith that no luck ever followed those who toil from early on Monday morning until late on Saturday night. As for the farmer, tell him to give back the straw thatch that he stole for his roof, and his house will be dry."

The young man spent that night in the woman's house and set out for home next morning. He had not traveled far when he saw his mother coming toward him open-mouthed and pursued by two mastiffs. He threw the brazen apple toward her, and it went into her mouth. Down she fell on the road, in the form of a lump of jelly, and the two mastiffs ran off. He traveled home, giving the queen's advice to the farmer, the smith, and the widow on his way. They all followed it and prospered ever after.

That's an account for ye of the queen of the planets.

· 38 · *Seán Palmer's Voyage to America with the Fairies*

Seán Palmer—he lived in Rinneen Bán. He had a small farm and owned a fishing boat—he fished during the summer season. He was married and had three children growing up. Now Seán was very fond of tobacco—he was a very hard smoker and would prefer to go without his meals any day than to go without a smoke of his clay pipe, and at that time shops were few and far between. The country folk had to depend on huckstering egg-women who visited them once a month perhaps, to buy their eggs, to supply their various household needs—tobacco, soap, needles, pins, etc., which they exchanged for the housewives' eggs. They sold tobacco for a penny a finger. The middle finger of the right hand from the top to the knuckle was the measure. It was called "a finger of tobacco."

Now it so happened that on this certain occasion to which our story refers, the egg-woman who used to visit Rinneen Bán was not as punctual as was customary with her, and Seán Palmer had to go without his usual smoke. As with all heavy tobacco smokers, this enforced abstention from the nerve-soothing weed had a very serious affect on Seán's usually active and industrious disposition. For two days he sat on the hob by the kitchen fire, grumbling and grousing and cursing the egg-woman roundly for her delay in supplying him with his favourite weed.

On the evening of the third day, after he had made about the twentieth trip from the hob to the kitchen door in the hope that the egg-woman would sooner or later make her appearance, he spoke thus to his wife: "Mary," said he, "I can't stand it any longer! The end of my patience is exhausted. I think I'll set off to Seán [Murphy] The Locks for a finger of tobacco. There will be no living in this house with me if I have to spend the night without a smoke of tobacco."

Seán The Locks kept a little shop about a quarter of a mile to the south of the present village of Waterville—there was no village then—and sold tobacco and groceries.

"The potatoes are boiled, Seán," said his wife, "and you may as well sit over to the table and eat your supper before you start off."

"Yerrah, woman," said Seán, "I cannot see the table, nor can I see the potatoes. I am stark blind for the want of a smoke. I will start off this very minute for Seán The Locks' shop, and the potatoes can wait until I come back."

He arose from his seat on the hob, grasped his blackthorn stick, and set off for Seán The Locks' shop, dressed only in his sleeve-waistcoat and flannel drawers. He had neither shoes nor stockings on his feet, as men wore shoes only when going to Mass or to the local town on a fair or market day at that time. As he approached the quay—there is a little quay on the roadside at the bottom of Rinneen Bán, where fishing boats came to shore and landed their catches of fish—it is how there were two men on the road before him, standing, and he made toward them.

"That is Seán Palmer," said one of the men to the other. "I know what is the matter with him, and where he is going. He has no tobacco," said he, in Seán's hearing. They knew Seán was listening to them.

When Seán came within speaking distance of the two men, he saluted them, and they returned his salutation.

"I presume you have got no tobacco, Seán," said one of the men; "and do you see those two men down there? Go down to them and you will get your fill of tobacco from them."

There was a little boat pulled up alongside the quay below, and two men in her. Seán hesitated for a moment.

"I suppose it is rather late to go to Seán The Locks' shop, now," he said, "and my supper is on the table, awaiting my return. Even if I only got one pipeful from them, sufficient to satisfy my craving till morning, I'd be very well pleased." "Go on down," said one of the men, "and you'll get plenty tobacco."

Seán went down to the quay and stood on the pier. The boat was pulled close in beside the quay. There were two men in her. Seán addressed them very politely and said he would be ever so grateful if they would kindly give him a smoke of tobacco.

"That you shall get, and plenty, and to spare," said one of the men. "Step into the boat and be seated. Come in," said he.

As Seán was stepping into the boat, he chuckled with delight at the idea of having had such good luck.

"By gor," said he to himself, "isn't it I that have struck the good luck. It is an old saying, and a true one, that a hound let loose is better than a hound on the leash."

"Here you are, Seán," said one of the men who was in the boat, "take that and smoke to your satisfaction," handing him his own pipe, which was red [i.e., lighted] and in full steam.

Seán took the pipe from him, thanked him, and sat on the center thwart of the little boat, puffing great blasts of smoke from his pipe. He was almost enveloped in tobacco smoke. He sat there puffing eagerly at the pipe, oblivious of his surroundings and oblivious of everything like a man in a trance. "Oh, man alive!" said he to himself. "Isn't it the oil of the heart. 'Tis the grandest pipe of tobacco I have ever smoked in my life."

It was not very long until the two men in the boat made a sign to their two companions who were still standing on the road-way, bidding them to come down and get into the boat at once, and so they did, and no sooner had they stepped aboard than the sails were raised close to Seán's ear, and the order was given:

"To sea with you boys!" and the little boat shot out from the quayside and away to sea with her.

"By gor," said Seán to himself, "you have high notions like the poor man's cabbage (an old saying or cant-word), whatever destination you are bound for."

Neither Seán nor any of the four boatmen spoke a word for some time nor interfered with one another in any way, and in the meantime the boat was racing along, skimming over the surface of the sea like a shot from a gun, and it was not very long until Seán saw lights—the lights of houses he presumed.

"Yerrah," said Seán to one of the men, "are not those the lights of Lóhar houses?"

"Och! God help you," replied one of the men. "Wait awhile and you shall see much finer houses than your Lóhar houses."

"By the cross of the ass," said Seán, "surely they are the Lóhar houses, and there is Rinneen Bán to the west."

"Och! God help you," said another of the men. "Do you not know where you are now. You are beside New York Quay!" said he. "See the ships and the people and the grand houses. Step ashore now, Seán," said he.

Seán stared in confusion at the sight that met his eyes, and it took him some time to regain his usual composure. However, he stepped ashore, as he was bade to do by the man in the boat, and he mixed with the crowds of people on the quay, but they were all complete strangers to him. He knew none of them, and he imagined they were all staring at him.

"Oh, good heavens," said he to himself, "no wonder they are all staring at me with nothing on me but my sleeve-waistcoat and my flannel drawers and without a shoe or a stocking on my feet. Why did I not put on my frieze coat when I was leaving the house."

A man passed close by him as he stood there on the quay, gazing at the crowds. "Upon my conscience," said the man as he passed him by, "but that fellow bears a very close resemblance to Seán Palmer of Rinneen Bán."

"By heaven," said Seán to himself, "that fellow certainly is in America. Andy Pickett from Rinneen Bán. Sure I knew him well before he came over here, and if he is in America, I am in America also. I suppose he did not recognize me."

"Make no mistake about it," said one of the men who brought him over in the boat. "You really are in America. Now, Seán," said he, "you have a brother here in New York, have you not?"

"I have," said Seán, "but New York is a big place, and how could a poor greenhorn like me find out where he lives."

"Never mind," said the man, "come along and we shall find him."

Two of the men accompanied Seán, and the other two men remained in charge of the boat. They walked along through the main streets of New York, Seán and his two companions, until they came to one of the side streets. The two men suddenly stopped in front of a tenement.

"Your brother Paddy lives in this house," said one of them to Seán. "Knock at the door and tell the people of the house that you want to see Paddy Palmer."

Seán did as he was bade. He knocked at the door, and one of the servants came in response to his knock.

"Does Paddy Palmer from Rinneen Bán live here?" Seán asked the servant.

"Yes, he does," the servant replied. "Come right in to his room." Seán followed the servant upstairs to an upper room. "This is his room, now," said the servant. "You can step right in," and he left him.

Seán stepped into the room, and when Paddy saw him dressed in a sleeve-waistcoat, flannel drawers, and without shoes nor stockings on his feet, he thought he belonged to the other world —that he was dead and that this was his spirit which had come to visit him.

"Good heavens, Seán!" he exclaimed. "Was it how you died?"

"No, faith," replied Seán, "but I am very much alive."

"And when did you come to America?" asked Paddy.

"I landed on the quay about a quarter of an hour ago," Seán replied.

"And when did you leave home?" asked Paddy.

"I left Rinneen Bán about a half hour ago," said Seán.

"And what brought you over, or were there many people on the boat coming over?" asked Paddy.

"Wait a minute until I tell you my story," said Seán. "I ran short of tobacco, and I started off just after nightfall for Seán The Locks' shop to get some tobacco, and when I reached Rinneen Bán Quay [repeats his experience]. As I stood there on the quay, gaping at the crowds as they passed to and fro, Andy Pickett from Rinneen happened to pass by. 'My soul from the devil!' said he, as he passed along. 'That fellow resembles Seán Palmer from Rinneen Bán very closely!'"

"Well, one of the men asked me if I had a brother here in New York. I said, yes, I have. So they brought me along here."

"Sit down just for a moment until I order some supper for you," said Paddy; "and while you are eating. I'll go out to the store next door and fetch you some tobacco, and when I come back I shall give you my best suit of clothes. You look terrible in those old duds you are wearing. I can buy myself another new suit tomorrow."

Seán sat down when the supper came and started eating, and he had just finished as Paddy came back, carrying a fairly large box of tobacco under his arm.

"Now Seán," said he, "you have a half-year's supply of tobacco in this box," putting his hand in his trousers' pocket at the same time and producing a bundle of dollars. "And here are a few dollars for you," said he, "which I intended sending you at Christmas, but as you happen to be on the spot now, you will save me the trouble of sending it along to you."

'Pon my word, he gave him a very good present, Paddy did.

"Well," said Seán, "you have given me a very decent present, Paddy, and I am very thankful to you, and now I must be going. The two men are out there on the street waiting for me; so I cannot delay any further."

Paddy wrapped up his best suit in a sheet of brown paper together with the box of tobacco and handed the parcel to Seán.

"Goodbye now, Seán," said he; "and God speed you."

Seán stepped out into the street. His two companions of the boat were standing there waiting for him.

"My word, Seán," said one of them; "you have not fared too badly by your visit."

"By my soul!" replied Seán. "You bet I haven't. I have a bundle of dollars to the value of seven pounds together with a large box of tobacco and a fine suit of clothes!"

"Give me the bundle now, Seán," said the man, "and I will put it on the boat." Seán handed him the parcel and the man set off toward the boat with it; and said the other man, addressing Seán: "Seán," said he, "haven't you got a sister up in Boston?"

"I have, by gor," said Seán. "I have a sister somewhere in the States—probably in Boston."

"Yes, she is in Boston," replied the man, "I know the house where she lives, and if you wish to visit her, I will accompany you there, and we shall find her out. The other man will catch up with us. Come right along," said he.

"By my soul," said Seán, "I'd like very much to see my sister Kate. Why shouldn't I?"

They started off and reached Boston in less than no time. As they were going through the city of Boston, Seán's companion stopped suddenly in front of one of the houses in the main street, in front of the door.

"Well, Seán," said he, "here we are in Boston, and your sister Kate lives here in this house. Go over and knock at the door and inquire if she is in, that you want to see her."

Seán went over and knocked at the door. The door was opened by a middle-aged woman, in answer to Seán's knock. "Whom do you want to see?" the woman asked.

"I want to see Cáit Palmer," said Seán.

"I am Cáit Palmer," said she.

"Good God, Cáit," said he, "do you not know your brother Seán from Rinneen Bán."

"Yerrah, Seán," said she, "and when did you die?" She thought that it was from the other world he had come, when she saw the sleeve-waistcoat and the flannel drawers on him, and he barefooted.

"By my soul!" said Seán, "I am not dead. I am very much alive," said he. "I have come all the way from Rinneen Bán to see you. I have been down in New York with Paddy since I arrived in the States, and he will tell you the whole story when you meet him."

"Wisha, Seán," said she, "and when did you leave Rinneen Bán?"

"I left there about suppertime tonight," said he. "I started off for Seán The Locks' shop to get some tobacco; but it would take too long to tell you the whole story now. Paddy will tell you all about it when you see him. I had supper with him down in New York. God bless poor Paddy. He was very kind to me. He gave me a big box of tobacco, a grand new suit of his own clothes, and a bundle of dollars to take home with me."

Cáit opened her purse and handed him a twenty-dollar bill.

"Here, Seán," said she, "take that. It is all the money which I have got on me at present; but I shall not forget you at Christmastime. I will send you a check at Christmas."

Seán bade his sister goodbye and stepped out into the street, where his two companions were still standing, waiting for his return.

"Well, Seán," said one of the men to him, "how did you get on with your sister Cáit?"

"By my soul!" replied Seán, "I did very well. She gave me a twenty-dollar bill."

The three then set off again for New York, and as they were approaching the city, Seán stopped suddenly. "Good heavens!" he exclaimed. "Where is my pipe? It must have fallen from my mouth, or I must have left it behind in Boston. I should have handed it back to the man who gave it to me, and now it is lost, and what a fine pipe it was."

"Never mind about the pipe," said one of his companions. "Don't worry about it, we shall get another pipe."

As they were going through New York, one of the men said, "By the way, Seán, I suppose you knew Cáit 'Strockaire' O'Shea from the top of Lóhar?"

"I did indeed," said Seán. "We were very close friends before she emigrated to America. As a matter of fact, I had a great notion to marry her at one time."

"Would you like to see her?" asked the man. "She lives here in this lane. I know the house where she lives."

"Ah, I don't think I should," said Seán. "My clothes are very shabby, and I would feel ashamed to meet her in this rig-out."

"Don't let that prevent you from seeing her," said the man who asked the question. "I'll run down and fetch your new suit from the boat, and you can exchange it for your old duds. We are in no hurry. We have got plenty of time."

The man started off for the boat and was back again with the new suit to Seán in less than no time.

"Come along now, Seán," said he, "and peel off every stitch of your old clothes from the skin out and put this suit on you."

He handed Seán the suit, and the other companion took Seán aside. He took him into a dark corner of the alley, and Seán put the new suit on.

His two companions then directed Seán to the house in the lane where Cáit "Strockaire" O'Shea lived. Seán knocked on the door and was admitted by Cáit, who recognized her old neighbor as soon as she laid eyes upon him. She gave him a *céad míle fáilte* and asked him how long was he in America and when he came over.

"I have been here during the past few years," replied Seán. He did not want to let her know that he had only just come over that night. "And I am going back to Ireland again," said he; "so I decided to call to see you before I go back."

"That was very kind of you indeed, Seán," said she; "and when are you sailing for Ireland?"

"I am sailing this very night," replied Seán. "I shall be leaving in a few hours time."

"Ah, Seán," said she, "had I known in time that you were going back to Ireland, I would have booked my passage on that boat along with you."

She opened her purse and handed Seán a fifteen-dollar bill. "Take this little present to my brother Con," said she—her brother Con "Strockaire" O'Shea, who lived in the top of Lóhar —"and here is a little gift for yourself," said she, handing him a five-dollar bill. "You can drink my health on the boat when you are crossing. By the way, Seán," said she, "did you marry ever since?"

"I say marry to you," replied Seán. He gave her no direct answer.

"Perhaps, Seán," said she, "we may both splice it up yet."

"You could never tell," replied Seán as he bade her goodbye, "stranger things might happen."

Seán stepped out into the street, where his two companions were still standing waiting for him.

"Well, Seán," said they, "how did you get on with Cáit 'Strockaire'?"

"We got on fine," replied Seán. "We had a very pleasant chat and she gave me fifteen dollars to take home to her brother Con, who lives in the top of Lóhar, and five dollars for myself, to drink her health going over on the boat."

"Come along now, Seán," said his two companions, "our time is running short. We must make off the boat."

They started off for the quay—New York Quay—and they made off the boat, and the other two men were waiting for them at the boat, where they had left her. They told Seán to come aboard, and he did. They spread their sails by the quayside and loosed the mooring rope.

One of the men spoke in a low tone to the fourth man, who was at the steer, "There is no time to spare now. Give her all the canvas she can take." And the little boat bounded out from New York Quay like a falling star.

They were not very far out to sea when Seán felt the missing pipe being shoved between his teeth.

"My soul from the devil," he exclaimed; "is not this the missing pipe?"

"Never mind," said one of the men, "but see if it is still red, and if it is, puff away at it to your heart's content."

The pipe was still red, and soon Seán saw the puffs of smoke coming out of his mouth. "Ah," he exclaimed, "it is an old saying and a true one that a lucky man only needs to be born."

That was well and good, and it was not very long until Seán saw land appearing in the distance, and very soon he was able to distinguish the houses on the mainland.

"Bless my soul," said he to one of the men. "Are they the Lóhar houses which I can see in the distance?"

"Yes, they are," replied the man.

"Well, I give this little boat the lead for good speed," said Seán. " I thought we were only a few miles out from New York, and here we are now within a few oars' length of Rinneen Bán quay."

The boat swept in toward the quay like a rushing wave, her forward part resting on dry sand.

"Step out of the boat, Seán," commanded one of the men; "you are landed safe and sound on Rinneen quay."

Seán took up his parcel and stepped ashore, and as he turned around to thank the crew, there was no trace or tidings of the crew or of their boat to be seen anywhere, as if the sea had swallowed them up.

As Seán walked up to the road from the pier, he heard the cocks crowing in the houses above. When he reached home, he knocked loudly at the kitchen door.

"Get up and open the door for that rascal of a father of yours," said Seán's wife to her eldest daughter. They had retired long since and were sound asleep. "He has spent the night card playing in Seán The Locks' shop, I presume."

The little girl got up and opened the door, and when she saw the strange man dressed in an elegant Yankee suit, the likes of which she had never before seen, complete with panama hat, and wearing a pair of well-shined glacé kid shoes, she shrank back in fear before the stranger and rushed back to the bedroom, screaming and calling her mammy that there was a strange man in the kitchen. Her mother got out of bed, dressed, and came up in the kitchen. She knew Seán at once, of course—Seán had thrown some bog deal on the fire in the meantime, and it lighted up the kitchen.

The wife looked at Seán for some time and surveyed him from head to foot, and when she recovered her composure, "Good lord, Seán," said she, "where have you been all this night or where did you get that fine suit of clothes which you have on your bones?"

"I did," replied Seán, "I got it over in New York from my brother Paddy."

She looked at him again more closely. She thought he had lost his reason.

"And see here again," said he, "as proof that I have been in New York, see this fine box of tobacco which I got from Paddy. A full half-year's supply," said he. "And see here again," said he, putting his hand in his trousers' pocket and pulling up a fistful of dollars. "There's some money which he gave me to take home with me. I was up in Boston also, and I visited my sister Cáit and she gave me some money, and on the way back to New York, I visited our old neighbor Cáit 'Strockaire' O'Shea from the top of Lóhar—and 'tis she that is looking fine and strong—and she gave me a twenty-dollar bill to bring home with me to her brother Con and a five-dollar bill for myself to drink her health coming over on the boat."

Seán's wife took up the tobacco box and examined it. She had a little education and was able to read and write, and she saw the words "New York" in large characters on the lid and the date of the month on which the tobacco was packed.

"By gor, Seán," said she, "your story is a true one. This box came from New York sure enough, but how in the name of heaven did you manage to get there and back again and in such a short time too?"

So Seán told her the whole story, as I have already told it to you, and next morning when Seán got up out of bed—he didn't get up too early, I suppose, as he felt tired after the voyage of the previous night—he ate his breakfast and dressed himself up in his grand new suit of clothes, shoes, and panama hat, and strolled out around the little farm. And when the neighbors saw the well-dressed stranger, they were wondering who he was. Nobody knew Seán when he was dressed up in the suit of fine clothes. After awhile they approached closer to Seán to find out who he was. It was only then that they recognized Seán.

In the course of time letters came from America to Seán's neighbors in Rinneen Bán and the top of Lóhar—from Andy Pickett and Cáit "Strockaire" O'Shea, telling them that they had seen Seán Palmer in America and that they had spoken to him.

So that is now the story of Seán Palmer for you, and the tobacco, and his voyage to America with the fairies.

Part V
Magicians and Witches

• 39 • The Sailor and the Rat

Long ago there were people who were able to banish rats, if they were doing damage. They used to have a charm for it, called the charm of the rats.

There was once a sailor on a ship, and he had a very fine, costly suit of clothes in a trunk. One day when he opened the trunk to put on the suit, or to air it, what did he find but that it was torn and eaten to rags by a rat.

He made no delay but took out his razor and laid it edge upward on the deck. The razor was not long on the deck when out came a rat, rubbed its mouth along the edge of the razor and kissed it. Then it ran back to where it had come from. Other rats followed, one by one; each of them rubbed its mouth along the edge of the razor, kissing it, and then ran away again. After a few score of them had done that, there finally came out a rat, screaming loudly. She went up to the razor and rubbed her neck along its edge, until she fell dead beside it.

The captain of the ship had been watching what was going on from the first rat to the last, which had cut its throat on the razor. He went straight to his cabin, took out his book, and called the sailor to him. He paid him whatever wages were due to him and ordered him to leave the ship.

"You could have done that trick to any man on board," said he, "as easily as you did it to the rat."

• 40 • The Girl and the Sailor

Long ago a lot of women and girls used to go to Catherciveen to sell buttermilk. There would often be ten or twelve churns of the milk at the Cross and great demand for it.

I heard that one day the women and girls were at the Cross as usual selling the milk. Among them was a girl from Rinnard, who had a churn in a donkey cart. She was standing in the cart with a measure in her hand to sell to anybody who came to her. Below at the pier, a ship was tied up while her cargo was being unloaded. Two of the crew walked up toward the Cross where the women were, and one of them turned to the girl from Rinnard and asked her what price the buttermilk was.

"A penny a quart," said she.

"All right," said the sailor. "Give me a quart of it. I'm thirsty."

She handed him the quart of milk, and he gave her a penny. He put the saucepan to his mouth and drank the milk while the other sailor looked on. When he had finished, he handed the saucepan back to her. He was standing near the cart in which she was, and he wiped his mouth with a corner of her apron. The two sailors then went off down the street. What did the girl do but jump off the cart and away with her down the street after the man who had wiped his mouth with her apron. She left the ass and the cart and the churn behind her. Some relatives of hers who were on the street tried to stop her and get her to return to the cart, but if they did, she paid no heed to them. Whenever the sailors went into a public house, she followed them and stood near the sailor who had touched her apron. It was idle for her relatives to try to separate them.

Later on in the day, a relative of hers heard what had happened. He went along the street and into a public house where the three of them were standing at the counter. The girl had her back to him when he entered. He went up behind her, took out his knife, and cut the string of her apron. It fell on the floor. No sooner did it fall than the girl went off out the door of her own accord and went back to her cart and churn.

The man who had cut the strings picked up the apron, took it into the kitchen, and shoved it into the center of the fire. He stood there until it was burned.

All that were at the fair couldn't separate her from the sailor until the apron was taken off her. May God guard us all!

The Four-leafed Shamrock
and the Cock

There was a great fair being held in Dingle one day long ago.
'Tis a good many years ago, I think. All of the people were
gathered there as usual. Whoever else was there, there was a
showman there, and the trick that he had was a cock walking
down the street ahead of him, drawing a big, heavy beam tied
to his leg. At least, all the people thought that it was a beam,
and everyone was running after him, and as he went from street
to street, the crowd was getting bigger all the time. Each new
person who saw the cock and the beam joined in the procession.

Then there came up the street a small old man carrying a load
of rushes on his back. He wondered what all the people were
looking at. All that he could see was a wisp of straw being
dragged along by a cock. He thought that everybody had gone
mad, and he asked them why they were following the cock like
that.

Some of them answered him, "Don't you see the great wonder?" they said. "That great beam of wood being dragged after
him by that cock, and he's able to pull it through every street
he travels and it tied to his leg?"

"All that he's pulling is a wisp of straw," replied the old man.

The showman overheard him saying this. Over to him he
went, and he asked him how much he wanted for the load of
rushes he had on his back. The old man named some figure—to
tell the truth, I can't say how much—but whatever it was, the
showman gave it to him. He would have given him twice as
much. As soon as the showman took the load of rushes off the
old man's back, the old man followed after the crowd, but all
that he could see was the cock pulling a heavy beam tied to his
leg. He followed him all over Dingle.

What happened was that the old man had a four-leafed shamrock, unknown to himself, tied up in the load of rushes. That's

what made what he saw different from what the people saw, and that's why the showman paid him three times the value for the rushes. He told the people, and they gave up the chase.

I heard that story among the people, and it could be true, because the four-leafed shamrock has that power.

•42• *The Black Art*

A man and his wife were living in Malinmore long ago, and they had an only daughter, a young girl. As with every couple of that kind, the daughter was the apple of their eye.

One day the father was cutting turf at Rossmore. When dinner-time came, the mother sent the girl with food, consisting of some broth in a wooden dish, to her father. There were only wooden vessels at that time. The father sat down at the edge of the bog to take his meal. It was a fine day, and the two of them were looking out over the sea. It wasn't long until a large sailing ship came into view, making for the mouth of the river.

"Isn't that a fine large ship?" said the little girl to her father.

"It is, indeed!" said he.

"I wonder—where is she going to?" said the girl.

"I'd say she is making for Killybegs."

"Well, if I wished so now, she would never reach there, big and all as she is," said the girl.

"Shut up, you little fool!" said the father. "What could you do to a ship that's out on the sea? Have sense in what you say."

The girl made no reply and waited until her father had finished his meal. Then she took the dish to wash it in the pool of water in the bog. When she had done that, she started to play tricks with the dish in the water. The father was lighting his pipe and took no notice of what she was doing; he thought she was only washing the vessel. Soon she spoke to him.

"Look now, father, and see what I can do with that ship," said she.

The father looked out to sea and saw that the ship, which

should have been making for the river mouth, was coming straight for the cliffs below them.

"Who taught you how to do that?" he asked.

"My mother," said she.

"And what are you going to do to the ship when you get her near the shore?" he asked.

"As soon as I get her near enough to the rocks, I can turn this dish upside down, and the same will happen to the ship on the sea," said she.

"I see," said the father. "And you tell me that it was your mother who taught you this?"

"She did, indeed," said the girl.

At any rate, the girl let the ship go free, and it floated out to the open sea again. The little girl took the dish home, and her father passed no remark on whether what she had learned from her mother was good or bad. That night, when he returned from the bog, he cleaned and washed himself well and put on his best suit of clothes. He left the house that night, and wherever he went, his wife and daughter never saw him again for the rest of their lives. He was angry to learn that he had married a woman who practiced the black art. Had she not taught some of it to her daughter, he would never have found out. But the girl had let the cat out of the bag, and that left her without seeing her father any more. Wasn't it strange, whatever place he went to, that he was never seen again?

Part VI
Historical Characters

·43· Daniel O'Connell and the Trickster

There was a man living at Carhan, near Caherciveen, in the time of Daniel O'Connell. He was poor and he had a large family. One day he was selling two pigs—a white one and a black one —at Tralee fair. A buyer asked him how much he wanted for the white one, along with the black one. The poor man thought, and no wonder, that the buyer wanted only the white pig; so he named the price. The buyer immediately marked both pigs and took from his pocket only what had been asked for the white one.

"What do you mean?" asked the poor man. "You only inquired about the white pig."

"That's a lie!" said the buyer. "Didn't I ask you how much you wanted for the white one along with the black one?"

The poor man could do nothing but give him the two pigs for the price of one. He returned home and told his story to his wife and to all the neighbors. It wasn't long till it spread all over the district, and everybody was sorry for the poor man. He told his story to Daniel O'Connell, who had great sympathy for him.

"We'll get our own back on that buyer later on," said O'Connell. "Are you willing to cut off the lobe of your right ear?"

"I am," said he.

O'Connell cut off the lobe of the man's right ear, put it into an envelope, and took it home. He asked the poor man to accompany him to Tralee next day to play a trick on the buyer.

"He has a tobacco shop in Tralee," said O'Connell; "and we'll call into him. After a while, you must take out your pipe and take a whiff or two from it. I will then pass the remark that you don't smoke very much, and you must reply that you would smoke seven times as much, if you had the tobacco. I will then say that I'll give you all the tobacco you want."

The following day, they both went to Tralee and went into the tobacco shop. The poor man pulled out his pipe, "reddened" it, drew a few whiffs, and put it back into his pocket.

"You don't smoke very much," said O'Connell to him.

"I'd smoke seven times as much, if I had it," said the poor man.

"Well, I'll give you plenty of tobacco," said O'Connell.

He ordered the buyer to give the poor man as much tobacco as would reach from his toe to the lobe of his right ear and asked how much it would cost.

"Eight shillings," said the buyer.

"That's agreed," said O'Connell.

The buyer then began to measure the length from the man's toe to the lobe of his right ear, but when he reached the ear, he found that the lobe was missing. He pretended nothing.

"We have caught you!" said O'Connell. "That's not the lobe of his right ear. It is back in Carhan, if you know where that place is. So you must measure from his toe to Carhan!"

The buyer was dumbfounded. He could say nothing. Then O'Connell ordered him to pay the man for the black pig, and he would not insist on the tobacco at all. The buyer paid the money, and even something extra, and went off to his kitchen, covered with shame. And no wonder!

·44· *O'Connell Wears His Hat in Parliament*

When Daniel O'Connell was going forward for election as Member of Parliament (in London), an English member said that if O'Connell sat in the House of Parliament, he would shoot himself.

O'Connell was elected, and the first day he sat in the House, he kept his hat firmly on his head. He was ordered to remove it, but he asked to be allowed to keep it on, as he had a bad headache. Permission was granted. Next day, he wore his hat again, as his headache hadn't improved, The third day, he wore his hat again, and kept his head bent down, as he still had the headache. On the fourth day he entered the house with his head in the air and his hat on, and everybody knew that his headache had left him. He was asked how his head was, and he said he felt fine.

"Won't you remove your hat, then?" they asked him.

"I won't" he replied. "Whatever passes three days in Parliament becomes law!"

So he kept his hat on and did so all the time he was a member, although everybody else was bareheaded.

He kept looking around him, and somebody asked him, "How do you like this house?"

"I like it well," he replied, "but I'm greatly surprised that it doesn't collapse with a perjurer inside it."

The man who had sworn to shoot himself heard the remark, and he went out into the yard and shot himself.

·45· *The Smell of Money for the Smell of Food*

There were six young fellows visiting a town one day. One of them suggested that they go and eat some food. They had some drinks before that. They went into an hotel, and one of them ordered a meal for them all. Each was to pay his own share. A pound of meat was placed in front of each of them. One of the fellows told the woman to take away his own meat, as he wasn't going to eat it at all.

"I won't," said she. "It was ordered, and you can eat it or leave it."

He ate a small bit of bread and took a cup of soup or tea, whichever it was. Tea wasn't very plentiful at that time. After the meal, each of them went to pay his share, but this fellow wanted to pay only for the bread and the soup or tea. As they were about to leave, the woman snatched this fellow's hat at the doorway. He asked her to give it back to him, but it was no use. They started to argue about it, but she remained firm.

Daniel O'Connell was walking along the street when he heard

the argument and saw the young fellow bareheaded. He stopped and asked what was the trouble.

"This is the trouble," said the fellow. "Five others and myself came in to this woman to get a meal. One of us ordered a pound of meat for each. When she put the meat in front of me, I said I wouldn't have any and wouldn't eat it. She told me to eat it or leave it. I didn't taste the meat at all; so I didn't want to pay for it."

"If this fellow didn't eat the meat," said O'Connell, " 'tis strange that he should have to pay for it. Give him back his hat."

"He didn't have to eat it," said the woman. "The smell of my meat filled his belly."

"You may be right in that," said O'Connell. "I have always heard that all a woman needs to do to get an excuse is to glance over her shoulder."

O'Connell took off his own hat, put his hand into his trousers' pocket, and threw a fistful of silver into the hat.

"Come over here now," said he to the woman. "Place your nose over this money and take your time smelling it. Fill your belly well with it."

She was taken aback by that.

"Does that satisfy you?" asked O'Connell.

She was covered with shame and made no reply.

"Give him his hat quickly, said O'Connell. "You have got as good a bargain as you gave."

That ended the matter. The fellow got his hat and went off.

·46· *The Heather Beer*

People say that the Danes were able to make the sweetest of beer from the tops of the heather. But the Irish people could not get the secret of it from them, although they tried their best.

When they were routing the Danes out of Ireland, they killed the most of them until there were only two left alive, a father and son. The Irish made up their minds to try to get the secret of the beer from these two, or it would be lost for ever. So they said to the pair that were left that whoever of them would give up the secret would be let go free.

Then the father spoke, and he said,

"If that's the way things are and if only one of us will be let go alive, let ye kill the boy, and I will tell ye how my people made the beer from the heather."

The son was put to death, and then the father was asked to tell the secret.

"Well," said he, "I asked ye to kill the boy first, because I was afraid that ye would get the secret out of him, if I died before him. Since he's dead now, I want to tell ye that ye won't get from me the secret ye are trying so hard to get. Ye'll never get it from me. Do what ye wish with me."

The father was put to death, and the secret was never found since.

•47• *The Man Who Lost His Shadow*

A man named Brasil bought an island from a Danish chieftain, but the chieftain had to go back to Lochlainn before the bargain was completed. Brasil had to travel to Lochlainn after him to get the papers from him. He spent a long time looking for him here and there, until at last he was directed to the chieftain's castle. Brasil went in and found the chieftain sitting at a table which was covered with all kinds of documents. The chieftain welcomed him and gave him food and drink. Brasil then told him that he had come from Ireland to get the papers dealing with the agreement.

"I have them here," said the chieftain. "But maybe you would like to stay here in this place with us. I promise that you will be well off—better off than you would be at home."

"Oh, I wouldn't stay at any price," said Brasil. "Give me the papers and let me be off."

"Very well," said the chieftain. "But, seeing that you won't stay with us, I'll have to keep your shadow instead of yourself."

"But I can't leave that behind," said poor Brasil. "I couldn't live without it."

The Dane gave him the papers. Brasil snatched them from him and rushed out the door like a shot. But when he was passing the window, the sun cast his shadow in through the window. The Dane put a big book on top of the shadow and held it there.

It is said that nobody named Brasil has had a shadow ever since.

·48· *Cromwell and the Friar*

There was a gentleman named O'Donnell living in Ireland long ago. He was very friendly with a certain friar.

"Things will change very much in Ireland before long," said the friar to O'Donnell one day. "The English will invade Ireland, and they will have a leader named Cromwell, who will evict every Irish gentleman from his lands and settle his own followers on them. The best thing for you to do now," said the friar, "is to cross over to England. Go around England, and ask every Englishman you meet to sign in your book a promise that he will never take your lands from you. Keep on going like that until you make off to Cromwell, and ask him to sign the promise too. He's a shoemaker at present."

Very well. O'Donnell started out and never stopped until he reached England. He let on to be a fool and went around, asking everyone he met on the streets to sign the promise that they would never take his lands or house from him. He finally made off to Cromwell's house, and he went in to get a patch sewn on the side of one of his shoes. He asked Cromwell would he do the job, and Cromwell said he would. O'Donnell took off the shoe, and Cromwell patched it for him. O'Donnell handed him a guinea.

"A thousand thanks," said Cromwell. "That's good payment."

"Now," said O'Donnell, "I hope that you will sign this book, promising never to take my house and lands from me."

"Of course, I'll sign it," said Cromwell. "Why shouldn't I?"

He took the book and signed his name to the promise. When that was done, O'Donnell returned to Ireland. A few years after that, a great change took place in England. Cromwell rose very high and took the power from the king. Then he came to Ireland. He started to evict people from their lands, gentlemen and everybody—they were all the same. He killed some of them and finally came to O'Donnell's house. He knocked at the door.

"Get out of here quickly. Long enough you've been here," said Cromwell.

O'Donnell went out to him.

"I hope you won't evict me until we have dinner together," said he.

"What kind of dinner have you?" asked Cromwell.

"Roast duck," said O'Donnell.

"That's fine," said Cromwell. "I like roast duck."

He went in, and the two of them started to eat. When the meal was over, O'Donnell produced his book.

"Do you recognize that writing?" asked O'Donnell.

"I do," said Cromwell. " 'Tis my own. But how did you get it? And how did you know that I would rise so high?"

O'Donnell couldn't get out of it; he had to tell him.

"A holy friar that was here told me that a great change was to come over Ireland and that a shoemaker named Cromwell would come to put me out of my land."

"You must send for the holy friar to come to me now," said Cromwell. "And, if he doesn't, I'll cut off his head."

O'Donnell went off to the friar and brought him back to Cromwell.

"Where did you get this knowledge?" asked Cromwell.

"I got it from heaven," replied the friar.

"Well, you must tell me now how long I will live?" said Cromwell.

"You will live as long as you wish," said the holy friar.

"Then I'll live for ever," said Cromwell.

"And how long will I live?" asked an English gentleman who was with Cromwell. "Will I have a long life?"

"If you're alive after passing the door of the next forge ye meet, you'll live a long time," said the friar.

"I'll live for ever so," said the gentleman.

Very well. Cromwell didn't evict O'Donnell. He left him as he was and went his way with the English gentleman and his troop of soldiers. When they were passing the door of a forge, Cromwell stopped.

"Here's a forge," said he. "That's luck, for there's a shoe loose on one of the horses."

He jumped off the horse and went in. The smith was inside.

"Hurry up and put a shoe on this horse for me," said Cromwell.

The poor smith was shaking with terror, as he ran about from corner to corner of the forge, looking for a good piece of iron. He was afraid to choose any piece, fearing it would be bad, and he was terrified of Cromwell and his soldiers. Cromwell himself went searching too, and he spied the barrel of an old gun stuck over one of the rafters.

"This is good iron," said he.

He pulled it down and threw it on the hearth. He was a smith's son himself and he knew a good deal about forges and smithcraft. He used to blow the bellows for his father when he was a boy. He took hold of the bellows and started to blow the fire for a while. The English gentleman was standing outside the door of the forge with his two elbows leaning on the fence. A shot went off from the barrel of the gun and went clean through his body, killing him. No sooner did the gun go off than Cromwell ran out, jumped on the back of his horse, and spurred it as hard as he could on the road toward Dublin.

On the way whom should he see, walking on the road ahead of him but the holy friar. The friar ran in fear to hide behind the parapet of a bridge.

"Come out of there, you devil!" shouted Cromwell. "If I have to go down for you, I'll cut the head off you."

The friar came up to him.

"It wasn't you who saw me," said he to Cromwell, "but the man behind you on the horse."

"What man is behind me?" asked Cromwell.

"There's a man sitting on the horse behind you," said the friar.

Cromwell turned to look, and there was the devil sitting behind him. He dug the spurs into his horse immediately and faced for Dublin. From there he crossed to England and never returned to Ireland. After spending a while in England, Cromwell became restless. The King of Spain died and was succeeded by his young son, who had no great sense or judgment for ruling the country. Cromwell thought of a great plan. He wrote to the young king and invited him to England to marry his daughter. When the young Spanish king received the invitation, he sent for his advisers and told them about it.

"That's only a trick of Cromwell's," they said. "He only wants to get a foothold in this country and take it for himself. Write back to him and tell him you would be pleased with the match in a year's time. In the meantime, strengthen your army, and when it is strong enough, write and tell him that you won't marry the devil's daughter."

Very well! When the year was up, the Spanish king wrote to Cromwell to say that he wouldn't marry the devil's daughter. Cromwell was shaving himself when the letter arrived. He had one cheek shaved, and he opened the letter before shaving the other to see what the news was. When he found out what the letter said, all he did was catch hold of the razor and cut his throat. He fell down dead.

About the time that Cromwell killed himself there was a ship going into Liverpool. The captain saw, coming toward him in the sky, a fiery chariot drawn by mastiffs which cried out: "Clear the way for Oliver Cromwell!"

At the same moment, in Cois Fharaige, in county Galway, a little girl was having an argument with her mother.

"May the devil stick in your throat," cried the mother.

The girl began to choke immediately. The priest was sent for, and he began to pray, calling on the devil to leave her throat. He called a second time, and the devil appeared.

"Where were you the first time I called?" asked the priest.

"I was where Cromwell was dying," said the devil.

"Where were you the second time I called?"

"I was coming here as fast as I could."

The priest banished him into the air in a shower of fire.

·49· *Damer's Gold*

At the time Cromwell was going around Ireland killing and plundering and robbing all before him, there was an Irish chief in it. He had three big barrels—one full of gold, the second full of silver, and the third full of copper.

When the war was coming close to him, the chief was afraid that the gold and silver and copper would be taken off him by Cromwell and his men; so what plan did he think of? Didn't he get a barrelful of tallow, melted it down, and poured some of it on top of the gold, some of it on top of the silver, and the rest of it on top of the copper. When the tallow cooled down, you'd give your oath that it was three barrels of tallow that was in it. Off went the chief then and he hid somewhere, so that he wouldn't be found out.

It wasn't long till the war came as far as his castle. Cromwell couldn't get much value in the castle, only three barrels of tallow, and he didn't think the tallow of much account. He held an auction, anyway; and the devil a one he could get to bid for the tallow at all.

There was a poor man that lived in the neighborhood. He went by the name of Damer, and the trade he had was candle-making. When Damer heard that no one was bidding for the tallow, he went to the auction himself, and he got the three barrels for a few shillings.

He brought them home, and the first day he went making his candles, he put his hand down in the first barrel to take up a share of the tallow. The wonder of the world came on him when he felt the hard pieces below. He pulled up a fistful, and the sight nearly spread on him when he saw the fistful of glittering gold. He put his hand down in the second barrel and he found the silver coins. He put it down in the third barrel and he found the copper.

Damer was a very wise, shrewd, little man, and he never let on to anyone of the neighbors that he had found such a lot of riches in the three barrels. He made a strongroom with a lock and key, and he put the three barrels into it. Every day in the year then, Damer used to go into the room and spend a while there looking at the money and handling it. It used to give him great pleasure.

In the long run, he was in need of a suit of clothes, and he went to the tailor to leave a suit making. When he came for the suit after a week, the payment he had for the tailor was a fistful of gold. The tailor was so surprised that he wouldn't take the gold at all.

"I don't charge a fistful of gold for every suit I make," said he. "A pound note would do me, if you have it."

"You might as well take the handful of gold from me," said Damer. "I have more silver and gold and copper in my house than I'll ever be able to spend."

"No, I won't take your gold," said the tailor. "All I want is one look at your money."

So Damer told him to come any day he liked to see the gold and silver and copper. The tailor called to Damer's house a few days later, and he spent a while looking at the heaps of money and handling them.

"Are you satisfied now?" asked Damer.

"I am," said the tailor. "I have knocked as much satisfaction out of all that money as you'll ever be able to do, even if you live for a thousand years. You can't eat it, and neither can I. I don't see what satisfaction it can give you to be looking at it."

The tailor's talk stunned Damer.

"Wait a minute," said he. "Bring away with you all the gold and silver and copper you can carry. 'Tis of no use to me, lying there idle."

The tailor filled his pockets with the coins, as much as he could carry.

"I'll bring this much with me," said he. "'Twill support me and my family for the rest of my life. If you spend it in the same way, it may do good to someone."

Damer took the tailor's advice, although it broke his heart to part with the gold.

Part VII

The Wise, The Foolish, and The Strong

· *50* · *Secret Tokens Prove Ownership*

Long ago when times were bad, it is said that there used to be a lot of thieves stealing horses. At that time too, there used to be poor scholars traveling about.

One night a poor scholar came to the house of a man in Bally-bawn, looking for lodgings. He got the lodgings. It happened that the man of the house had a mare on the brink of foaling. After the supper, the man went out to see how the mare was and he found her uneasy. He went back to the house and told his wife and family that the foal was coming. They all ran out, and so did the poor scholar. The moon was shining. The poor scholar looked up at it, and he must have taken some meaning out of it, for he had the learning. He went into the stable.

"Is the foal coming?" he asked the man of the house.

"It is."

"Could you delay it five minutes from coming into the world?" asked the poor scholar.

"I couldn't delay it at all," said the man.

"I'd be glad, if you could," said the poor scholar. "Two men will lose their lives by that foal. But it may not be you and your son or anybody in this house."

When the foal was born, the poor scholar asked the man to slit the skin on its forehead, to put a silver coin with a cross on it inside the skin, and to sew it up again. That was done. The foal lived, and the man reared and trained him, until he was six years old. There wasn't a finer horse going into Galway.

One morning when the man went out to the stable, the horse was missing. He didn't know from Adam who could have stolen him. He went in home and told his son, saying that he would try to find who the thief was.

"I'll go along with you," said the son.

"You couldn't walk that distance," said the father. "I'll go by myself."

"I won't let you go alone. I'll go with you," said the son.

"Come along so," said the father.

The boy was young, only twelve or thirteen years of age. They set out and kept searching for most of a fortnight, until they reached some place in Leinster. A wet day came, and they passed by a forge. Not far beyond the forge, they came to an avenue leading to the house of a gentleman with a hedge along it to the road. The rain was heavy; so they walked nine or ten steps up the avenue to let the rain pass. It wasn't long until who should come along the avenue, riding one horse and leading another, but a young man. When he reached the road he turned, as if he were going toward the forge.

"One of those horses is ours, father," said the boy.

"What's that you're saying?" asked the father.

"He is," said the boy. "I recognized him. We had better go to the forge and have a good look at him—if it is he."

When they reached the forge, the young man who had passed them with the two horses was inside with the smith. The father and son stood at the door, and when the smith saw the wet clothes on them, he asked them to come up to the fire and warm themselves. They went near the fire. They never took their eyes off the horses while the smith was mounting the shoes on them. Then they went out of the forge.

"By my conscience, he's our horse all right," said the father.

"Didn't I tell you he was?" said the son.

They hid themselves near the avenue again, until they saw the young man turning in there with the two horses. Then they went to the peelers and told them all about the horse. The peelers went with them to the gentleman's house and told him that these two men were searching for a stolen horse and that they had seen him at the forge. The gentleman said that he had never stolen a horse and shouldn't be accused of it. The father and son said the horse was theirs. Two of the gentleman's workmen said that they had been working for him the day the foal was born, and it was a lie to say that he was stolen. The peelers took their word.

A lawsuit started between them. The two workmen swore that they had been ploughing with the mare shortly before she gave birth to the foal in the gentleman's field. So the judges decided that the man and his son were making false charges against the gentleman, and the two were condemned to be hanged on that score.

A cart was placed on top of another cart to form a gallows, and ropes were thrown across to hang them, one at each side. When they were about to be hanged, the farmer said that he and his son were ready to die if there wasn't a coin of cross-money between the flesh and the skin of the foal's forehead under the white spot. A knife was got and a slit was made at the white spot. The coin was taken out. The man from Ballybawn and his son were released. They had been telling the truth. The two workmen were hanged from the cart. The Ballybawn man got the foal and took him home. I don't know what happened to them after that.

•51• *The Cow That Ate the Piper*

There were three spalpeens coming home to Kerry from Limerick one time after working there. On their way, they met a piper on the road.

"I'll go along with ye," said the piper.

"All right," they said.

The night was very cold, freezing hard, and they were going to perish. They saw a dead man on the road with a new pair of shoes on his feet.

"By heavens!" said the piper. "I haven't a stitch of shoes on me. Give me that spade to see can I cut off his legs."

'Twas the only way he could take off the shoes. They were held on by the frost. So he took hold of the spade and cut off the two feet at the ankles. He took them along with him. They got lodgings at a house where three cows were tied in the kitchen.

"Keep away from that gray cow," said the servant girl, "or she'll eat your coats. Keep out from her."

They all went to sleep. The three spalpeens and the piper stretched down near the fire. The piper heated the shoes and the dead man's feet at the fire and got the shoes off. He put on the shoes and threw the feet near the gray cow's head. Early next morning, he left the house wearing his new pair of shoes. When the servant girl got up, she looked at the door. It was bolted, and the three spalpeens were asleep near the fire.

"My God!" she cried. "There were four of ye last night, and now there are only three. Where did the other man go?"

"We don't know," they said. "How would we know where he went?"

She went to the gray cow's head and found the two feet.

"Oh my!" she cried. "He was eaten by her."

She called the man of the house.

"The gray cow has eaten one of the men," said she.

"What's that you're saying?" said the farmer.

"I'm telling the truth," said she. "There's only his feet left. The rest of him is eaten."

The farmer got up. "There were four of ye there last night, men," said he.

"There were," said one of the spalpeens, "and our comrade has been eaten by the cow."

"Don't cause any trouble about it," said the farmer. "Here's five pounds for ye. Eat your breakfast and be off. Don't say a word."

They left when they had the breakfast eaten. And they met the piper some distance from the house, and he dancing on the road. Such a thing could happen!

·52· *Seán na Scuab*

Long ago there was a poor man living in Buffickle, west in Béara. He was married. He made his living by making brushes and selling them in Cork a few times a year.

After some years, the mayor of Cork died, and three men were in for the position. When the day of the election came, the three had the same votes. They went to a magistrate to decide between them, but he shook his head and said that he couldn't settle the matter. He told them to go out next morning to a certain place at the edge of the city and to tell their troubles to the first man who came along. Whoever that man named would become mayor. They did so. The first man to come along was Seán of the Brushes with a load of brushes on his shoulder. The three of them stopped him and told him their story. He listened to them and said that it would be hard to pass over two of them and elect the other. So he told them that the best plan was to elect himself as mayor. They did so. That was that.

Seán's old wife was at home when she heard that her husband was mayor of Cork with a gold chain across his chest and two gray horses drawing him from place to place. She set out and never stopped until she reached Cork. She looked about, and next day she saw Seán being drawn by two gray horses, a Caroline hat on his head, and a big gold chain hanging down from his neck. She went over to him.

"Stay out from me, old woman!" he shouted.

"Are you my husband, Seán?" she asked.

"I am," said he, "but keep away from me and don't pretend to know me. I don't even know myself!"

•53• *The Great Liar*

A young boy from this place went as a seasonal laborer to the Lagan Valley one time. He was a good worker, and his master thought highly of him.

About November, when they were digging the potatoes, the master dug up a huge potato one day.

"Did you ever see as big a potato as this at home by your father?" asked the master.

"I did, and one that was a lot bigger," said the boy.

"I don't believe you ever saw a bigger one than this," said the master.

"There was one year that my father had a lot of rotten potatoes," said the boy. "He threw them all into a limekiln that we had and filled it up. The following summer, a big potato stalk grew up out of the limekiln. It had plenty of manure in the rotten potatoes, and it grew as tall as a tree. In November, my father went to take a look at the limekiln and he found that one huge potato filled the whole place. He knocked down the limekiln and got four men to root out the potato with crowbars. He then split it into four parts and got the four men to carry them into the barn on handspikes."

"That was surely a big potato," said the master.

Sometime soon after that, the master came in one day with a cabbage head.

"Did you ever see a bigger head than that?" he asked the boy.

"I saw one that was far bigger," said the boy. "There came a year when we had very good cabbage. We had three or four bullocks, and they went to the cabbage one very wet day. One of them took shelter under one of the cabbage leaves, and when the shower was over, he shook the leaf. There was so much water on the leaf that it swept the bullock down to a stream at the bottom of the garden and drowned him."

"That was surely a big cabbage head," said the master.

A few days later, the master came in with a huge piece of cheese.

"Had your father ever as big a piece of cheese as that?" he asked the boy.

"He had," said the boy. "One summer we had a lot of milk in the house, and we had no room for it. My father dug a hole in the field and poured the milk into it to make cheese. We had a foal at that time, and one day when he was running about, didn't he fall into the hole where the milk was, and we saw him no more. Nobody saw him falling in, and we thought that he had been stolen. My father searched high and low for him but couldn't find him. Nine months afterward, my father went to take a look at the cheese, and what should jump out of it but a fine young horse!"

"That was surely a big lump of cheese," said the master. "There's a brother of mine to be hanged tomorrow at midday," continued the master; "and if anyone can save his life, 'tis you. If you do, I'll give you a hundred pounds."

"I'll have a try," said the boy.

On the following day, the boy went to where the man was

to be hanged. There was a large crowd of people there to see the hanging.

"I have something to say to ye," said the boy to the crowd. "The wrong man is going to be hanged, although there's a man here in the crowd who ought to be hanged in his stead. I'm going to tell ye a story now, and when I have it told, the man who should be hanged will call me a liar."

"Very well," said the judge. "Tell us your story until we hear what it is like."

"My father divided his farm between two brothers and myself. He gave me eight acres and asked me to do my best with it. I bought an old white horse and plowed the eight acres. When I had them plowed, I found that seed was very scarce. I'd have to go to England for it; so one morning, I put the saddle on the old white horse and rode her down to the edge of the sea. The old horse jumped out into the sea and swam until we reached England. I went ashore and bought eight sacks of fine oats at a big market that was there. I tied the eight sacks of oats on the back of the old horse and sat up on top of the load myself. Back we went to the edge of the sea, the old horse plunged in and never stopped swimming until we were back at the bottom of my father's farm again. The old horse was tired by that time, and she sank down in the sand of the shore. It looked as if her back was broken and she would never rise again. There was a holly tree growing nearby. I broke off a branch of it and shoved it into the old horse as a backbone. Up she jumped and I was able to take the oats home. Well, I planted the oats. The old white horse wasn't much good any longer; so I let her loose in the wood.

"When the oats were ready for reaping, I went one day to take a look at the crop. I had no money to pay for help, and it would take me a long time to reap it myself. I had about three or four sheaves cut with my reaping hook when a hare rose up at my feet. I threw the hook at him, and the handle of it struck into his side. Down along the trench ran the hare, and I after him, trying to get back my hook. I followed him up and down all the trenches until he ran out of the field at last. When I looked around me then, wasn't the whole crop reaped by the

hare with the hook? When it was reaped, I put it into the barn
and threshed it. I had no money to pay a man to take it to the mill
for grinding; so I remembered the old, white horse. If she was
still alive, she would take it to the mill for me. That evening,
I went to the wood to search for her. There she was, looking
fine and strong, grazing away with a huge holly tree growing out
of her. I sprang upon her back, and from there climbed the tree
to the top. Could ye guess what I found there? A red salmon
inside in its nest."

"You're a liar," shouted an old fisherman who was in the
crowd. "That's one thing a salmon never had—a nest!"

"Now friends," said the boy, "that's the man who should be
hanged and not the other."

So they hanged the fisherman. I left them there, and I don't
know what happened to them since.

·54· *The Uglier Foot*

There was a tailor in Ballyvourney a long time ago. He had very
big ankles, and the nickname the people had on him was Tadhg
of the Ankles. At that time, tradesmen traveled from house to
house, and the people used to gather in for sport and fun with
them.

One night Tadhg was sewing away, sitting on the table, and
he had one of his legs stretched out from him. The woman of
the house was sitting at the head of the table, between Tadhg
and the fire. She noticed Tadhg's big ankle.

"Upon my conscience, that's an ugly foot," said she. One or
two people laughed at this.

"Upon my conscience," said Tadhg, "there's a still uglier foot
than it in the house."

The woman of the house must have had badly shaped feet
herself, and she thought that Tadhg was hinting at her.

"There isn't an uglier foot than it in the whole world," said
she.

"Would you lay a bet on that?" asked Tadhg.

"I would," said she.

"I'll bet you a quart of whiskey that there's an uglier foot than it is this house," said Tadhg.

"I'll take that bet," said the woman.

At that, Tadhg pulled his other foot from under him.

"Now," said he, "which is the uglier, the first foot or the second one?"

"Upon my word, the second is a lot uglier," said the woman.

"Very well," said Tadhg. "Send out for a quart of whiskey for me."

"I will, indeed," said the woman.

She was glad to have lost the bet when her own feet weren't compared to Tadhg's.

· 55 · *The Blacksmith and the Horseman*

There was a man one time, and he was very strong. He was full of money, and one day he put about twenty pounds of it into a purse.

"I'll set out on my travels now," said he, "and I'll keep on going until I meet a man who is stronger than myself. If I meet him, he'll get this purse."

So on he traveled, asking everyone if they knew of any strong man, until at last he was directed to a certain smith. When he reached the forge, he pulled up his horse outside the window without dismounting.

"Have you anything in there to 'redden' my pipe for me?" he shouted to the smith.

The smith picked up a live coal with the tongs, placed it on top of the great anvil, took up the anvil by its snout with one hand and reached it out through the window to the horseman. The horseman took hold of the other end of the anvil, let the live coal slip into his pipe, and handed the anvil back to the smith. The smith put the anvil back on the block.

"My horse needs a shoe. Have you any made?" asked the horseman.

"I have," replied the smith, picking out a horseshoe. "This may do you," said he.

"Give it here to me," said the horseman. When he got it, he pulled it apart with his two hands. "That shoe was no good," said he.

The smith gave him another shoe, but he broke it in two in the same way.

"That one was no good either," said he. "Give me another."

"What's the use in giving them to you?" asked the smith.

"I'll try one more," said the horseman.

The smith passed another shoe to him.

"This will do," said the horseman.

The smith put the shoe on the horse, and when he had the last nail driven, "How much do I owe you?" asked the horseman.

"A half crown," said the smith. When the horseman handed him a half crown, the smith took it between his fingers and broke it in two.

"That was no good," said the smith. The horseman gave him a second half crown, and the smith broke it in two again.

"That was no good either. Give me another," said he.

"What's the use in giving them to you?" asked the horseman.

"I'll try one more," said the smith. "This will do," said he when he got the third half crown.

The horseman took the purse out of his pocket. "Take this," said he. "You deserve it, for you are a stronger man than I am. I had a good hold on the shoes to break them, but you had hardly any hold on the half crowns that you broke."

Notes
to the Tales

The following notes are intended to place the tales in their traditional and international context. References cite the latest revised editions of the Aarne-Thompson Type Index and the Thompson Motif-Index. Variants of Irish tales are fully listed in Seán Ó Súilleabháin and Reidar Th. Christiansen, The Types of the Irish Folktale *(Helsinki, 1963). Citations are given when applicable to other volumes in this series containing variants of tales in this book.*

PART I

ANIMALS AND BIRDS

· 1 · *The Fox and the Heron*

Type 9, *The Unjust Partner*; and compare Types 15, *The Theft of Butter (Honey) by Playing Godfather*; and 232C,* *Which Bird Is Father.* IFC Vol. 113, 17–23. Recorded by Brian MacLochlainn, collector, in October, 1935, from Antoine Ó Maoláin (58), Baile Nua, Cleggan, county Galway.

In the present story, the Irish name for the heron is Máire Fhada (Long Mary). Many other birds are known by human names in the Irish language. Type 9 is represented, in its more common form, by No. 5 in *Folktales of Japan*, a companion volume in this series.

Although Motif K372, "Playing godfather," is absent from this composite story, the tale otherwise resembles Type 15.

Motifs: K232, "Refusal to return borrowed goods"; and K343.3, "Companion sent away so that rascal may steal common food supply."

· 2 · *The Fox and the Eagle*

IFC Vol. 962, 43–47. Recorded by Ediphone, January 9, 1945, by Tadhg Ó Murchadha, collector, from Seán Sigerson (72), An Rinnín Dubh, parish of Caherdaniel, county Kerry.

This storyteller had an amazing amount of knowledge about birds, animals, and fishes, as well as tales and legends concerning them.

Ó Murchadha recorded material from him which filled thousands of manuscript pages.

For other versions of the story see T. F. Crane, *The Exempla of Jacques de Vitry*, p. 194, No. 144, and J. A. Herbert, *Catalogue of Romances*, Vol. III, p. 12.

Motif L315.3, "Fox burns tree in which eagle has nest."

• *3* • The Fox in Inishkea

Types 1, *The Theft of Fish*; and 33** *Fox Overeats, Is Caught, Feigns Death*. IFC Vol. 134, 177–82. Recorded February 27, 1936, by Pádhraic Bairéad, collector, from Conchobhar Ó Dubháin (70), Léim, parish of Kilmore, Erris, county Mayo.

Seventy-three versions of Type 1, and thirteen versions of Type 33** have been recorded in Ireland. For a seventeenth-century version heard in Ireland by an English traveler, John Dunton, see E. Mac Lysaght, *Irish Life in the Seventeenth Century*, Appendix, p. 332. A Japanese version of this tale-type is No. 1 in *Folktales of Japan*, a companion volume in this series.

Inishkea, an island off the Mayo coast, is now uninhabited. The islanders have moved to the mainland.

There are several fox tales in Ireland which are not mentioned by Aarne-Thompson in *The Types of the Folktale*. Some of them may have international provenance.

Motifs: K752, "Capture by hiding under a screen"; and K891.5.4, "Dupes deceived into falling over precipice."

• *4* • The Magpie and the Fox

IFC Vol. 702, 282–84. Recorded September 3, 1940, by Seosamh Ó Dála, collector, from Seán Bruic (84), fisherman, Tír Íochtarach, parish of Cloghane, county Kerry. Seán had heard the story thirty years before from Ned Shea (65), parish of Castlegregory, county Kerry.

Motifs include K1010, "Deception through false doctoring"; and Q261, "Treachery punished."

• *5* • Two Women or Twelve Men

Type 72*, *The Hare Instructs His Sons*. IFC Vol. 84, 201. Recorded in June, 1934, by Pádraig Ó Milléadha from Seán Ó Catháin (45), An Cnoc Buí, Baile na Molt, county Waterford.

There can be little doubt that this story was originally composed by a man as a hint to women that they are far too talkative. The jocose reason given for the loquaciousness of the fair sex is that a woman's tongue is attached to the throat by only its middle part, while a man's tongue is attached by both sides. Thus the woman's tongue can wag more freely.

· 6 · The Grateful Weasel

IFC Vol. 605, 434–41. Recorded on Ediphone by Proinnsias de Búrca, collector, from Seán MacAodhgáin (60), Gleann Gabhla, parish of Kilcummin, Moycullen, county Galway.

In Ireland, weasels were regarded with awe, as if they were uncanny animals. Instead of mentioning one of them by name, one would say "the lady" or "the noble old lady."

A common story tells how a weasel spat into a can of milk that mowers had in the meadow when she saw them approaching her nest of young ones in the hay. The mowers, seeing the nest, avoided it and did not disturb it, whereupon the weasel spilled the poisoned milk in gratitude.

Motifs: B514, "Animal fetches remedy for man"; and D1500.1.4.2, "Magic healing leaves."

· 7 · The Man Who Swallowed the Mouse

Type 285B*, *Snake Enticed Out of Man's Stomach*. IFC Vol. 308, 39–40. Recorded March 1, 1936, by Tadhg Ó Murchadha, collector, from Pádraig MacGearailt (77), Cill an Ghoirtín, parish of Dromad, Iveragh, county Kerry.

In Irish versions of this tale, the animal swallowed is usually a newt or lizard, never a snake as in the international versions. Sixty-six versions of the story have been recorded in Ireland.

Motif B784.2.1, "Patient fed salt; animal comes out for water."

· 8 · The Cat and the Dog

Type 200D*, *Why Cat Is Indoors and Dog Outside in Cold*. IFC Vol. 62, 287–88. Recorded November 12, 1931, by Seán MacGiollarnáth from Pádraic MacDhonnchadha, An Coillín, Carna, county Galway.

This etiological story is told to explain why dogs bark so much at beggars and attack them. A somewhat similar story tells how the cat bought three gifts with her money: power to see in darkness, a cozy seat near the fire, and the housewife's forgetfulness (to lock up the milk, fish, etc.).

• 9 • *The Sow and Her* Banbh

Types 106, *Animals' Conversation*; and 2075, *Tales in Which Animals Talk*. IFC Vol. 84, 250. Recorded July 12, 1934, by Pádraig Ó Milléadha, from Áine, Bean Uí Choinghialla (88), An Tuairín, Baile Mhic Cairbre, county Waterford. She had heard the tale about seventy years before from her father, a native of the same district.

The Irish words for "any more" and "always," when repeated, as in this tale, can be made to resemble the grunting of the pigs. There are many similar examples of the interpretation of animal and bird calls in Ireland.

For a Kerry version of this tale, see No. 107, "Caint Na Muc," in *Béaloideas*, XXIX (1961), 130–31.

• 10 • *The Old Crow Teaches the Young Crow*

IFC Vol. 489, 281–83. Recorded in 1937, by Pádhraic Ó Coincheanainn, from a storyteller (unnamed) at Anach Cuain, county Galway.

Motif: J1122.1, "Young crow's alertness."

• 11 • *The Cold May Night*

Type 1927, *The Cold May Night*. Compare Type 244**, *The Crow and the Titmouse*. IFC Vol. 1009, 289–98. Recorded in February, 1946, by Liam MacCoisdeala, collector, from Mícheál Ó Coileáin (70), Carn Mór, Claregalway, county Galway. Mícheál heard the story more than fifty years before from his father, Tomás (60), of the same townland.

Forty-three manuscript and published versions of this tale have been recorded in Ireland. For printed versions, see D. de Híde, *Celtic Review*, X (December, 1914–June, 1916), 116–43. It was republished by de Híde in *Legends of Saints and Sinners*, pp. 40–55, 56–62 and *Béaloideas* XIV (1944), 207–08. A study of the tale against its literary background has been made by E. Hull, "The Hawk of

Achill, or the Legend of the Oldest of the Animals," *Folk-Lore* XLIII (1932), 376–409.

Achill is a large island off the Mayo coast. Assaroe is the name of a waterfall on the River Erne in Co. Donegal. Old May Night has been the traditional name for the night of May 11, ever since the calendar was changed in 1752.

Motifs include B124.1, "Salmon as oldest and wisest of animals"; B841, "Long-lived animals"; R322, "Eagle's nest as refuge"; and X1620, "Lies about cold weather."

PART II

KINGS AND WARRIORS

· 12 · *The King Who Could Not Sleep*

IFC Vol. 168, 1–44. Recorded on July 5 and 27, 1934, by Liam Mac Meanman, collector, from Jimmy Cheallaigh (59), Cró na Duinne, parish of Glenfin, county Donegal. When he was young, Jimmy had heard the tale from his father, aged 80, of the same place.

Type No. 2412D (*The Man Who Never Slept*) has been suggested for this tale by S. Ó Súilleabháin and R. Christiansen, *The Types of the Irish Folktale*, p. 345. Twenty-five versions are listed in their book. A. Krappe, "The Celtic Provenance of the Lay of Tydorel," *Modern Language Review*, XXIV (1929), 200–204, gives a medieval French version, "Lai de Tydorel." See also W. G. Wood-Martin, *Traces of the Elder Faiths of Ireland*, II, 120–21; M. Dillon, *Cycles of the Kings*, p. 24; and S. O'Grady, *Silva Gadelica*, II, 286–89. For another tale-type of a sleepless mortal, son of a water-spirit, see *Béaloideas*, VIII (1938–1939), 77–79.

MacMeanman recorded other tales from this storyteller during 1935 and 1936, when Jimmy was bedridden.

Among the motifs which occur in the tale are F420.6.1.7, "Water-spirit surprises and rapes a mortal woman"; F564.1, "Person of diabolical origin never sleeps"; L111.2.4, "Future hero found in wolf den"; M92, "Decision left to first person to arrive"; J1170.2, "The Irish Solomon"; Q153, "Nature benign and fruitful during reign of good king"; Q552.3, "Failure of crops during reign of wicked king";

S334, "Tokens of royalty (nobility) left with exposed child"; and Z72.1, "A year and a day."

· *13* · Céatach

IFC Vol. 157; 215–51. Recorded by Ediphone in September, 1935, by Séamus Ó Duilearga from Éamonn a Búrc (62), Aill na Brón, Kilkerrin, Cárna, county Galway. The tale was later transcribed from the records by Liam Mac Coisdeala, collector. Éamonn had heard it forty years before from his father, a native of Ardmore, Cárna.

The storyteller, Éamonn a Búrc, was possibly the most accomplished narrator of folktales who has lived into our own time. His artistry is at once evident in any of the tales which fill the two thousand pages of manuscript recorded from him by Mac Coisdeala. One of his hero tales, Eochair, mac Rí in Éirinn, recorded in October, 1938, filled twenty-two Ediphone cylinders, that is, over 26,000 words. Five other tales from Éamonn are included in this volume; Nos. 26, 29, 32, 34, and 35. Mac Coisdeala, in the course of an article on his experiences as a collector, in *Béaloideas*, XVI (1946), 141–71, describes his work with Éamonn; and in the same journal, XII (1942), 210–14, he paid tribute to the storyteller on the occasion of his death on November 6, 1942.

In Ireland, this fine hero tale is found in two contrasting forms: (a) where Fionn mac Cumhaill is friendly toward the hero; and (b) where Fionn is hostile. The present version offers some examples, in translation, of the "runs" employed in hero tales by storytellers to impress their audience and to afford a rest to the narrator's memory. These "runs" fall into several classes, according to whether they describe the hero rising in the morning, or preparing for battle, or sailing over the sea, or anchoring his ship, or arriving home in the evening, and so on. Sometimes, the language of the "runs" is obscure or corrupt. Other interesting features of the present version are the inclusion of the Everlasting Fight motif, the series of quests on which the hero is sent, and the black-and-white-sails motif, which occurs in the Theseus story in ancient Greek literature. For the latter, see Gerard Murphy, *Duanaire Finn*, Part III, pp. 177–79, 192. The popularity of the tale is evidenced by the fact that the archives of the Irish Folklore Commission contain over one-hundred-and-fifty versions recorded during the past thirty years. Eight versions have been published in *Béaloideas*: III (1931–32), 304–307, 387–97; V (1935), 92–107; VI (1936), 61–71, 270–75; VII (1937), 121–24, 197–205. Ten versions have been published in various collections of tales and in Gaelic periodicals. Three versions have appeared in English translation: J. Curtin, *Myths and Folk-Lore of Ireland*, pp. 248–69; *Hero-Tales of Ireland*, pp. 463–83; W. Larminie, *West Irish Folk-Tales and Romances*, pp. 64–84. J. G. McKay gives Scottish references to the tale, *Béaloideas*, III (1931–32), 141.

Motifs include B871.1.6, "Giant cat"; D615, "Transformation combat"; D1005, "Magic breath"; D1244, "Magic salve (ointment)"; G263.5, "Witch revives dead"; G635.1, "Monster's returning head"; K1863, "Death feigned to learn how soldiers are resuscitated"; Z140.1, "Color of flag (sails) on ship as message of good or bad news."

• 14 • Fionn in Search of His Youth

IFC Vol. 984; 227–34. Recorded on Ediphone cylinders about 1930 by Dr. Robin Flower, Keeper of Manuscripts in the British Museum, from Peig Sayers (56), Blasket Islands, Dingle, county Kerry.

The present tale and many others recorded by Dr. Flower were transcribed in 1947 by Seosamh Ó Dálaigh, collector, by which time Peig had left the island and gone to live on the mainland near Dunquin. Peig helped the transcriber to fill in unintelligible gaps in the original recording. Peig died in December, 1958. For further examples of her tales, see Nos. 24 and 36 in this book.

The Irish Folklore Commission has thirty-three manuscript versions of this allegorical Fionn tale. For some of the eight published versions, see *Béaloideas* III (1931–32), 57–58, 129–30; VII (1937), 122; VIII (1938), 35–37, 87; XIV (1944), 215–16; de Híde, *An Sgéaluidhe Gaedhealach*, pp. 240–46. The last version was republished with a French translation by Ferdinand Lot, "Origine scandinave d'un conte irlandais," in *Annales des Bretagne*, XII (1896), 238–44. In a note in XIII (1897), 48–49, he suggests a Scandinavian origin for the tale. An early Irish version of the tale is found in the frame story, "Feis Tighe Chonáin," edited by Nicholas O'Kearney, *Transactions of the Ossianic Society*, II (1854), 146–57, with English translation, and again edited, under the same title, by Maud Joynt in *Medieval and Modern Irish Series*, VII (1936), 14–20.

Motifs include D1209.6, "Magic thong"; D1355.13, "Love-spot"; D1840, "Magic invulnerability"; D2061.2.1, "Death-giving glance"; F863.1, "Unbreakable chain"; K1886.2, "Mists which lead astray"; T466, "Necrophilism: sexual intercourse with dead human body"; Z111, "Death personified"; and Z126, "Strength personified."

• *15* • *The Coming of Oscar*

IFC Vol. 937, 418–48. Recorded December 2, 1944 by Seán Ó Cróinín, collector, from Amhlaoimh Ó Loingsigh (72), farmer, Cúil Aodha, Ballyvourney, county Cork. The storyteller had heard it over forty years before from some old people in Ballyvourney parish.

Oscar, the youthful hero of this tale, was the son of Oisín, whose father, Fionn mac Cumhaill, was leader of the Fianna, a legendary band of warrior hunters in ancient Ireland.

The poetic tales of the Fionn cycle in *Duanaire Finn* have been published by the Irish Texts Society, edited by Eoin Mac Neill, *Duanaire Finn*, Part I, Vol. VII (1908), and by Gerard Murphy, *Duanaire Finn*, Part II, Vol. XXVIII (1933). Volume XLIII (1953) of the series is devoted to a critical analysis by Murphy of both the manuscript and oral versions of these tales. Pages xii–lxx of his Introduction to that volume deserve close attention from students of the folklore content of the Fionn cycle.

For somewhat similar versions of the tale, see J. Curtin, *Hero Tales of Ireland*, pp. 489–90; *Béaloideas*, VI (1936), 11–13 (English summary, 30–31); and *An Claidheamh Soluis* (an Irish weekly newspaper), April 25, 1903, pp. 2–3. The inset story, "The Knight without a Laugh," was part of various frame-stories in Ireland, and over one-hundred-and-eighty versions of it are to be found in the Irish Folklore Commission's manuscripts and in print.

Motifs: D231, "Transformation: man to stone"; D315.5, "Transformation: hare (rabbit) to person"; D1791.2, "Withershins (countersunwise) circuit (for ill luck)"; H1381.2.2.1.1, "Boy twitted with illegitimacy seeks unknown father"; H1440, "The learning of fear"; P632.2.1, "The champion's portion"; P632.4.1, "Precedence shown by position of shield (flag)."

• *16* • *Cúchulainn and the Smith's Wife*

Type 1376A*, *Story-teller Interrupted by Woman*. IFC Vol. 142, 1312–34. Recorded November 23, 1935, by Seán Ó Heochaidh, collector, from Seán Mac Mriartaigh (70), fisherman, Iomaire Mhurnáin, Teelin, county Donegal. He had heard the tale about forty years before from Searlaí Mag Anna (70), of Teelin. Type 1376A* is used here as a frame-story.

Cúchulainn is said to have been the nephew of Conchobhar mac

Neasa, King of Ulster. The cycle of tales in which they are mentioned is known as the Ulster, or Red Branch cycle. Cúchulainn changed his name from Setanta after killing the hound of Culann, the king's smith, and guarding the smith's house in the animal's stead. His name signifies "the hound of Culann." This tale serves to explain how he acquired his nickname, Cú na Hadhairce (the hound of the horn).

The Irish Folklore Commission has twenty-four versions of the tale in manuscript recorded in Irish from oral narration. In a few of these versions, Oisín, son of Fionn mac Cumhaill, leader of the Fianna, takes the place of Cúchulainn. For published versions, see S. Mac Giollarnáth, *Loinnir mac Leabhair*, pp. 44–46; *Béaloideas*, IX (1939), 55–58, *Irisleabhar na Gaedhilge*, V (1882), 10–13.

Ó Heochaidh, the collector, describes his final call on this storyteller on April 7, 1936, (IFC Diary Vol. 421, pp. 151–67).

> This is probably my last visit to Seán. In all, he has filled more than a hundred Ediphone cylinders with tales. Each time I called to him, he told me that he had still other tales which I had not heard. Today, however, he said that he had no more. He was as generous with his stories as he was in his own house. It is a great pleasure to call to see a *seanchaí* like this, where you are sure of a welcome, and now, on my final visit, I was sad on parting with him. How many long pleasant nights I spent with Seán and his wife; how many times they made me laugh! I leave them now, well-satisfied with the work I have done and happy at the thought that Seán's stories and *seanchas* will be available when the scald-crows will be calling over his grave and mine.

Motifs include C181, "Tabu confined to women"; J1177.0.1, "None should interrupt or leave the room while story is told: treachery revealed."

• *17* • *Young Conall of Howth*

IFC Vol. 981, 106–73. Recorded on an Ediphone by Seosamh Ó Dálaigh, collector, in August, 1946, from Muiris Sheáin Connor (76), Baile Uí Bhoithín, parish of Márthan, Dingle Peninsula, County Kerry. The storyteller had heard it about forty years before from Pádraig Ó Mainnín (60), of the same townland.

The hero of this fine tale is more generally known as Conall Gulban. The tale itself was very popular in Ireland, and there are over sixty versions of it in the manuscripts of the Irish Folklore Commission. All are recorded in the Irish language. At least sixteen other versions have been published; two are in *Béaloideas*, VI (1936), 21–29, and XII (1942), 139–64. See also S. Laoide, *Fionn agus Lorcán*, pp. 11–17; S. Mac Giollarnáth, *Loinnir mac Leabhair*, pp. 16–17, 33–34; D. de Híde, *Ocht Sgéalta ó Choillte Mághach*, 104–24; and *An Stoc* (Iúl 1923), pp. 6–7. For versions in English, see J. Curtin, *Hero-Tales of Ireland*, pp. 58–92, 223–41.

The tale was well-known in Gaelic Scotland too. For a critical analysis of all the known versions from Ireland and Scotland, see Alan Bruford, "Eachtra Chonall Gulban," *Béaloideas*, XXXI (1963), 1 ff.

Another tale, "Art, King of Leinster," recorded from the same storyteller, is No. 18 in this volume. Muiris had a number of hero tales of this type in his repertoire. All of them have been recorded. He was also a fine singer.

Motifs: B552, "Man carried by bird"; D231, "Transformation: man to stone"; D1841.6, "Immunity from drowning"; G441, "Ogre carries victim in bag (basket)"; H1301, "Quest for the most beautiful of women"; P556, "Challenge to battle"; and Q501, "Unremitting torture as punishment."

• 18 •   Art, King of Leinster

IFC Vol. 980, 969–92, and Vol. 981, 1–62. Recorded on an Ediphone in July, 1946, by Seosamh Ó Dálaigh, collector, from Muiris (Sheáin) Connor (76), Baile Uí Bhoithín, parish of Márthan, Dingle Peninsula, county Kerry. The storyteller heard it about fifty years before from Seán Bán (Fíodóra) O'Connor, who was then fifty years old.

Another tale (No. 17) by this storyteller, "Young Conall from Howth," is included in this volume. Many "runs" in hero tales are found in both. Ó Dálaigh, the collector, describes Muiris's style in IFC Diary Vol. 1045, 374–77. Several songs have been recorded from him, as well as long tales and many pieces of *seanchas*.

This fine frame story contains many motifs: F531.1.1.1, "Giant with one eye in middle of forehead"; F833.3, "Sword extraordinarily bright, sharp"; H10, "Recognition through common knowledge"; H1301, "Quest for the most beautiful of women"; N121.1, "Child born with objects that indicate fate"; P556, "Challenge to battle"; and Q421.1, "Heads on stakes."

• 19 • The Speckled Bull

Type 425, *The Search for the Lost Husband*. Compare Type 707, *The Three Golden Sons*. IFC Vol. 990, 558–614. Recorded in June, 1946, by Seán Ó Heochaidh, collector, from Séamus Ó Beirn (45), shoemaker, Mín na Gaoithe, Teileann, County Donegal. Séamus had heard the tale thirty years before from his father (65), who lived in the same townland.

In a note at the end of the manuscript version of the tale, Ó Heochaidh remarked, "I think that this tale is one of the best I have recorded since I started working for the Commission. I had much difficulty in getting Séamus to tell it, not through his being unfriendly to me, but because he thought that a tale of this kind should not be written down—it was obscene! I don't think this is so, but nothing could change his opinion; so I had to coax him greatly before I got it from him. He has many other tales; I have recorded a good many of them from him. All his ancestors before him were famous as story-tellers in this district."

American versions of Type 425 are considerably shorter than the one given here. They often end when the animal husband is disenchanted, so that the search episode is not included. Emelyn Gardner in *Folklore from the Schoharie Hills, New York* (Ann Arbor, 1937), pp. 118–23, gives one such version, No. 5, "The Rosy Story"; and Marie Campbell in *Tales from the Cloud Walking Country* (Bloomington, Ind., 1958), pp. 228–30, records a similar text from Kentucky under the title "A Bunch of Laurel Blooms for a Present." In these American texts, the animal husband is a huge toad. Richard Chase gives a Virginia text, No. 5, "Whitebear Wellington," which includes the search episode, in his *Grandfather Tales* (Boston, 1948), pp. 52–64. The hero of this version is a bear. Versions and subtypes from other countries are given in companion volumes in this series: No. 58 in *Folktales of Israel*, No. 1 in *Folktales of England*, and Nos. 27 and 49 in *Folktales of Japan*. For a study of this tale-type, see J. Ö. Swahn, *The Tale of Cupid and Psyche* (Lund, 1955).

Motifs include D133.2, "Transformation: man to bull"; D231, "Transformation: man to stone"; D766, "Disenchantment by liquid"; F811.7.1, "Tree bearing all fruits"; K2115, "Animal-birth slander"; R131.2, "Miller rescues abandoned child"; S430, "Disposal of cast-off wife"; and T15, "Love at first sight."

PART III

SAINTS AND SINNERS

· *20* · *The Boy Who Became Pope*

IFC Vol. 277, 273–79. Recorded January 21, 1937, by Pádhraic Bairéad, collector, from Antoine Ó Catháin (66), Deibhleán, Clochar, Erris, county Mayo. Antoine was a native of the island of Inishkea off the coast of Mayo but migrated to the mainland with the rest of the islanders. He had heard the story about thirty-eight years before from Seán Ó Monacháin (68), a native of Inishkea.

The tale was published in its Irish version by Séan Ó Súilleabháin, "Scéalta Cráibhtheacha," *Béaloideas,* XXI (1951–52), 47–51, with a county Galway version, 43–47, of somewhat similar character. For the motif of the consecrated wafer which was lost, see A. Aarne, *Der reiche Mann und seine Schwiegerersohn,* p. 143. For miraculous manifestations at the choosing of a ruler, see V. Chauvin, *Bibliographie des ouvrages Arabes,* VI, 75 (239).

Motifs include D1825.3.4.1, "Ability to see angel of God"; D2064.1, "Magic sickness because girl has thrown away her consecrated wafer"; H171.6, "Pope selected by chair moving toward candidate"; and V510, "Religious visions."

· *21* · *The Man Who Struck His Father*

IFC Vol. 315, 194–226. Recorded 2/15/1937 by Seosamh Ó Dálaigh from Mícheál Ó Cinnéide (66), fisherman, Baile Uí Churráin, parish of Múrach, Dingle Peninsula, county Kerry. Mícheál had heard the story thirty years before from Diarmaid (Sheáin) O'Connor (60), who lived in Baile na bPoc, in the same parish.

Stories concerning severe penances for some wrong deed form a large part of Irish religious folktales. They are, in most cases, an amalgam of pagan and Christian beliefs. Six such stories were published in Seán Ó Súilleabháin, "Scéalta Cráibhtheacha," *Béaloideas,* XXI (1951–52), 106–26. This tale, in its Irish form, can be found there, pp. 113–20. J. F. Bladé, *Contes Populaires de la Gascogne,* II, 201–209, gives a tale which is very similar to the Irish version. See also J. Bolte and G. Polívka, *Anmerkungen zu den Kinder- und Hausmärchen der Brüder Grimm,* III, 167–69; R. Köhler, *Kleinere Schriften zur*

Märchenforschung, I, 473–77; and J. A. Herbert, *Catalogue of Romances*, III, 343.

Motifs include E754.1.3, "Condemned soul saved by penance"; H224.1, "Ordeal by kissing poisonous serpents"; S21, "Cruel son"; and V29.1, "Search for confessor."

• 22 • The Friar on Errigal

Type 756B, *The Devil's Contract*. IFC Vol. 224, 110–22. Recorded March 21, 1936, by Anna Ní Eigheartaigh, collector, from Mícheál Ó Heochaidh (68), Na Corra, parish of Kilcar, County Donegal. He had heard the tale about fifty-five years before, but could not remember from whom.

Two hundred and sixty-one Irish versions of this tale-type have been recorded. The present version was published in Irish, in S. Ó Súilleabháin, "Scéalta Cráibhtheacha," *Béaloideas*, XXI (1951–52), pp. 73–78. For studies of two related religious tale-types (756B and 756C), see N. P. Andrejev, *Die Legende von den zwei Erzsündern* and *Die Legende vom Rauber Madej*. For a study of the motif concerning the speaking picture, see J. Szövérffy, *Irisches Erzählgut im Abendland*, pp. 141–51.

Errigal Mountain and Anagry are both in county Donegal.

Motifs include D711.2, "Disenchantment by cutting person in two"; D1472.1.5, "Magic palace supplies food and drink"; F883, "Extraordinary writings (book, letter)"; H1273.1, "Quest to devil in hell for return of contract"; M201.1.2, "Pact with devil signed in blood"; N4, "Devil as gambler"; and T330, "Anchorites under temptation."

• 23 • How God's Wheel Turns

Type 759** (*How God's Wheel Turns*), has been suggested for this tale by S. Ó Súilleabháin and R. Th. Christiansen, *The Types of the Irish Folktale*. IFC Vol. 1052, 106–12. Recorded on April 18, 1948, by Tadhg Ó Murchadha, collector, from Mícheál Ó Fógartaigh (54), Sosa, parish of Prior, county Kerry. He had heard the story many years before from old people in the neighboring parish of Máistir Gaoithe, where he had been born and reared.

In his diary (IFC Vol. 522, 127–30) for March 1, 1938, Ó Murchadha says of this storyteller: "For a young man, he has an astonishing number of tales. He told me that when young, he preferred nothing to listening to the old people telling stories. As well as that, he has an amazing memory."

The tales were recorded by Ediphone, and in his diary for November 18, 1937, Ó Murchadha describes how the storyteller "used to stretch himself back, laughing, on hearing his own voice being repeated by the record." The storyteller had a sense of humor too. In his diary (IFC Vol. 582, 295–98), the collector describes Ó Fógartaigh as saying that the Ediphone took down the tale far more correctly than he himself had told it.

Forty-six versions of this *exemplum* tale have been recorded in Ireland. In many versions, the rich man is at first full of overweening pride; this is not so, however, in the present instance.

Motifs are L412, "Rich man made poor to punish pride"; and N111.3, "Fortune's wheel."

• 24 • *The Man Who Was Rescued from Hell*

Type 425J, *Service in Hell to Release Enchanted Husband*. IFC Vols. 965, 659–70; 966, 1–20. Recorded in November, 1944, by Seosamh Ó Dálaigh, collector, from Peig Sayers (71), Baile Viocáire, Dunquin, county Kerry, who heard the story often from her father.

Thirty versions of this subtype are included among the 275 versions of Type 425 *The Search for the Lost Husband* which have been recorded in Ireland. Other versions of this tale are to be found in S. Ó Súilleabháin, "Scéalta Cráibhtheacha," *Béaloideas*, XXI (1951–52), 141–47 (translation in *European Folktales*, ed. L. Bødker, C. Hole, and G. D'Aronco, pp. 136–42) and in *Imtheachta an Oireachtais*, III (1899), 121–32, the latter, submitted under a pen name, has the title "Sgéal na Mná a Chuaidh go hIfreann." Jan-Öjvind Swahn (*The Tale of Cupid and Psyche*, pp. 329–33), has a note on this taletype, which Swahn recognizes as a subtype of 425. He says that the tale in this form is entirely limited to Irish-Gaelic tradition. Compare this tale with the version of 425 given in this volume, No. 19 "The Speckled Bull." Robert L. Morris gives an American version of Type 425J in "Told in Ozarkia," *Folk-Say*, III (1931), 94–102, in which a woman serves in hell to release her child whom she had unwittingly promised to the devil. Like her Irish counterpart, she takes many other souls with her when she leaves the netherworld.

The narrator, Peig Sayers, who died in December, 1958, was one of the greatest Irish women storytellers of recent times. Some of her tales were recorded on the Ediphone in the late 'twenties by Dr.

Robin Flower, Keeper of Manuscripts in the British Museum, and again recorded from her own narration by Seosamh Ó Dálaigh twenty years later. Both recordings are available in the archives of the Irish Folklore Commission and are evidence of the changes (if any) which a storyteller makes in her telling of a tale after some years. In all, the Commission has in its collections many hundreds of items (tales, songs, prayers, proverbs, and many types of local lore) recorded from her—more than 5,000 manuscript pages. For references to her published tales, see *Béaloideas*, VIII (1938–39), 85.

Motifs include C211.2.2, "Tabu: eating in hell (hades)"; E474, "Cohabitation of living person and ghost"; E754.1.3, "Condemned soul saved by penance"; H94.4, "Identification by ring dropped in glass (cup) of wine"; and P241, "Parents descend to hell instead of sons."

• 25 • *The Hour of Death*

IFC Vol. 31, 136. Recorded on August 4, 1933, by Seán Ó Súilleabháin, from Muircheartach Ó Sé, Adrigole, Bantry, county Cork.

Premonitions of death are commonplace in the folklore of most peoples. In Ireland, they are often mentioned in the lives of saints. The present etiological legend is not common in Ireland.

Motif: D1812.0.1, "Foreknowledge of hour of death."

PART IV

PEOPLE OF THE OTHERWORLD

• 26 • *The Fairy Frog*

Compare Type 476*, *In the Frog's House*. IFC Vol. 155, 121–25. Recorded October 5, 1935, by Liam Mac Coisdeala, collector, from Éamonn a Búrc (62), tailor, Aill na Brón, Kilkerrin, Carna, county Galway. Éamonn had heard the story from his father forty years before.

Thirty-six versions of this tale in various forms have been collected by the Irish Folklore Commission. For two published versions in English, see J. Curtin, *Tales of the Irish Fairies*, pp. 43–45, and

P. Kennedy, *Legendary Fictions of the Irish Celts*, pp. 106–10. For a version of Type 476 from Kurdistan as well as for Jewish literary references to the tale, see *Folktales of Israel*, a companion volume in this series, pp. 24–27. See also "The Frog's Midwife," in *Folktales of Hungary*, p. 351.

Dealings between fairies and mortals form the theme of thousands of Irish tales. Malignity or gratitude is shown by the fairies, according to the case.

Motifs: F234.1.6, "Fairy in form of frog"; F235.4.1, "Fairies made visible through use of ointment"; and F361.3, "Fairies take revenge on person who spies on them."

· 27 · The Fairy Wife

IFC Vol. 1033, 246–52. Recorded February 4, 1948, by Seán Ó Heochaidh, collector, from Seán Mac an Bhaird (68), Cruach Thiobraid, Na Cruacha, county Donegal.

Tales about marriages between mortals and fairies or mermaids are to be found in early Irish literature. In later folklore, the motif is comparatively rare.

Motifs include F211.1, "Entrance to fairyland through door in knoll"; F302.3.3.1, "Fairy avenges herself on inconstant lover (husband)"; F302.5.3, "Man loses luck when he leaves fairy wife for mortal"; and F342, "Fairies give mortal money."

· 28 · Fairy Money

IFC Vol. 1034, 47–51. Recorded in October, 1946, by Seán Ó Heochaidh, collector, from Diarmaid Mac Seáin (55), Ceapach, Teelin, county Donegal.

The basic motif, D1602.11, "Self-returning magic coin," is loosely related to Type 580*, *The Inexhaustible Purse*. A more common Irish tale of fairy money deals with coins which turn into leaves or something useless when one parts with them.

In No. 19, the version of Type 580* given in *Folktales of Israel*, a companion volume in this series, a gift of an inexhaustible purse comes from God; still another version of this type is No. 80 in *Folktales of Norway*.

Other motifs include D813, "Magic object received from fairy"; and D871, "Magic object traded away."

• 29 • *The Children of the Dead Woman*

IFC Vol. 156; 141–48. Recorded August 7, 1935 by Liam Mac Cois-deala, collector, from Éamonn a Búrc (62), tailor, Aill na Brón, Kilkerrin, Carna, county Galway, who had heard the story from his grandfather.

"My grandfather saw one of the dead woman's children," said the storyteller.

It was a common belief in Irish oral tradition that the fairies were continually trying to abduct newborn children (usually males) to re-plenish their own fairy population, and that they also took young mothers into fairyland to suckle such abducted children.

The Irish Folklore Commission has thousands of tales illustrating this belief. In many of them, attempts to rescue the abducted woman failed at the last moment through lack of courage. More rarely, the attempt succeeded, as in this version, but the rescued woman was struck dumb.

For another version of this tale from county Galway, see *Béaloideas*, V (1935), 243–44. There are hundreds of printed versions about fairy abduction of women in Ireland. See S. Laoide, *Trí Torpáin*, pp. 28–33; *Irisleabhar na Gaedhilge*, VIII (May, 1897–July, 1898), 11–13; J. M. Synge, *The Aran Islands*, pp. 60, 210; J. Curtin, *Tales of the Irish Fairies*, pp. 60–66; R. Shaw, *Carleton's Country*, pp. 57–59; and E. Andrews, *Ulster Folklore*, pp. 26–27.

Motifs: E323.1.1, "Dead mother returns to suckle child"; F322, "Fairies steal man's wife and carry her to fairyland"; and F322.2, "Man rescues his wife from fairyland."

• 30 • *The Three Laughs of the* Leipreachán

Type 670, *The Animal Languages*. IFC Vol. 451, 71–78. Recorded on December 20, 1937, by Brian Mac Lochlainn, collector, from Seán Ó Conaola (84), Doire Gimleach, Ballyconneely, county Galway. Seán had heard the story from the old people of the area.

The *leipreachán* of this story was traditionally said to be the shoe-maker of the fairies. Many tales are told about attempts made by humans to get him to reveal the hiding place of his treasure. A mermaid, whom a mortal marries, takes the place of the *leipreachán* in most Irish examples of this tale. Elsewhere, the *leipreachán* may be replaced by animals.

Seventy-eight versions of the tale have been recorded in Ireland. See A. Aarne, *Der tiersprachekundige Mann und seine neugierige Frau*.

Motifs include F244, "Fairies' treasure"; F451.0.1, "Luchrupáin (leprechauns)"; N456, "Enigmatical smile (laugh) reveals secret knowledge"; and X1424, "The great mushroom."

· *31* · The Man Who Had No Story

Type No. 2412B (*The Man Who Had No Story*) has been suggested for this tale by S. Ó Súilleabháin and R. Christiansen, *The Types of the Irish Folktale*, pp. 343–44. It is not listed by A. Aarne and S. Thompson, *The Types of the Folktale*. IFC Vol. 47, 8–15.

This tale was recorded on May 18, 1933, by Proinsias Ó Ceallaigh, collector, from Conchobhar Pheadair Uí Chéilleachair (83), Cúl an Bhuacaigh, parish of Ballyvourney, county Cork. The storyteller had heard it seventy years before from his mother.

The popularity of this tale-type is evident since one hundred and thirty-seven versions of it have been recorded in Ireland. It belongs to the genre of fantastic nightmarish adventures and was generally told as a humorous tale.

Motifs vary a good deal in the different versions. Motifs here include F990, "Inanimate objects act as if living"; and F771.6, "Phantom house: disappears at dawn."

· *32* · Doctor Lee and Little Aran

IFC Vol. 447, 376–86. Recorded February 9, 1938, by Liam Mac Coisdeala, collector, from Éamonn a Búrc (65), tailor, Aill na Brón, Kilkerrin, Carna, county Galway. Éamonn had heard the story forty years before from his father, who was then 58.

There are many traditional stories of islands that appear and vanish off the Irish Coast as well as of sunken towns: Little Aran, in this story; Cill Stuifín, off the coast of Clare; Cathair Tonn Tóime, in Dingle Bay; and Bannow, off the coast of Wexford. There was a belief that fire lighted by human hands could remove the enchantment from these places.

See T. J. Westropp's article, "Brasil and the Legendary Islands of the North Atlantic: Their History and Fable. A Contribution to the 'Atlantis' Problem," *Proceedings of the Royal Irish Academy*, XXX

(1912–13), Section C, 223–63. For Welsh lore on the subject, see F. J. North, *Sunken Cities*.

The Irish Folklore Commission has recorded one-hundred-fifty versions of the story of the knife thrown against the wave. A Hungarian text in which the knife is thrown into a whirlwind is given in *Folktales of Hungary*, a companion volume in this series, p. 317.

Archer Taylor has discussed Motif D2121.8, "Magic journey by throwing knife into whirlwind," in *The Black Ox*. For the medical fame of the Lees, see *Béaloideas*, IV (1933–34), 78; X (1940), 21–23, and *An Stoc* (Series 3) I, No. 5 (June, 1930), 3.

Motifs: D784, "Disenchantment by lighting fire"; D1500.1.22, "Magic healing book"; D1976.1, "Transportation during magic sleep"; D2121.8, "Magic journey by throwing knife into whirlwind"; and F379.2.1, "Book (medical) brought back from otherworld."

• 33 • The Child from the Sea

IFC Vol. 589, 603–604. Recorded February 1, 1939, by Liam Mac Coisdeala, collector, from Val Ó Donnchadha (36), Bántrach Ard, Carna, county Galway. He had heard the story from the old people.

According to Irish folk belief, the world under the sea was populated by beings who resembled those on earth and life below the waves corresponded in some ways with that above. Stories were told of fishermen who brought up on their fishing lines a pot of boiling potatoes or a sprig of heather on which bees sucked the flowers. Many stories were told of the seals, which were regarded as having human speech and other similar characteristics. Also, underwater houses visited by mortals have been mentioned.

Motif: F725.5, "People live under sea."

• 34 • The Big Cat and the Big Rat

IFC Vol. 388, 258–67. Recorded August 31, 1938, by Liam Mac Coisdeala, collector, from Éamonn a Búrc (65), Aill na Brón, Kilkerrin, Carna, county Galway. Éamonn had heard the story forty years before from his father.

Stories of abnormal rats are common in Irish folklore; the rat which sucks a woman's breast at night (cf. Motif A2435.6.2.1, "Snake sucks milk from woman's breast"); the rat which follows a man everywhere, even to America, until finally killed by two weasels, and so on.

Motifs include B524.1.3, "Cat kills attacking rat"; and B871.1.6, "Giant cat."

• 35 • *The March Cock and the Coffin*

IFC Vol. 529, 241–43. Recorded by Ediphone, September 23, 1938, by Liam Mac Coisdeala, collector, from Éamonn a Búrc (65), Aill na Brón, Kilkerrin, Carna, county Galway.

This tale was widely known in Ireland. In some versions, a black cloud, which is seen by a sea captain descending over a house on shore, is banished by the house cock. The captain buys the cock and takes him away. That night, the cloud again descends on the house. Next morning the man of the house and his wife are found dead in bed. In olden times, fowl were kept in the dwelling house, and the people believed that a March cock (born from an egg laid on the first Tuesday in March and hatched out on a Tuesday of the same month) could protect the house against evil. In Irish, the name for such a cock is *coileach Mhárta*. The similarity of the word *Márta* (March) with the words *Máirt* (Tuesday) and *Mártan* (Saint Martin) have caused confusion regarding the original etymology of the name.

Motifs include B122.7, "Cock advises of coming enemy"; and E538.1, "Spectral coffin."

• 36 • *Seán na Bánóige*

Type 726*, *The Dream Visit*. IFC Vol. 965, 628–58. Recorded by Ediphone in October, 1944, by Seosamh Ó Dálaigh, collector, from Peig Sayers (1873–1958), then 71, in Baile Viocáire, Dún Chaoin, county Kerry. She had often heard the story from her father. Dr. Robin Flower, Keeper of Manuscripts in the British Museum, had recorded the same tale from Peig about fourteen years before, and the transcript of this is to be found in IFC Vol. 983, 145–61. Two other tales from Peig with a note about her life as a storyteller are Nos. 14 and 24 in this volume. For her life story, see Peig Sayers, *An Old Woman's Reflections* (London, 1962).

Two hundred and twenty-four versions of this tale have been recorded in Ireland.

In many of the Irish versions, the magic vision of the hidden treasure of the Lochlannaigh (Danes or Vikings) in Ireland is brought about by the drinking of the soup of the mouse; this power is lost when the flesh is tasted.

The Vikings held power in Ireland for a few hundred years. They were ultimately defeated by Brian Boru's army in 1014 at the Battle of Clontarf. Their sway declined after that time, but Irish tradition still tells of old Danes bequeathing some land in Ireland to their sons to the present day. They were said to have left much treasure behind them in Ireland.

R. Christiansen has studied this tale ("The People of the North," *Lochlann*, II [1962], 137–64) and has indicated that it is not an international type, but rather an Irish legend to illustrate a facet of folk belief and that it is of fairly recent origin. He gives a Norwegian version in No. 34 in *Folktales of Norway*, a companion volume in this series. A Kerry version of the tale has been published by M. L. Sjoestedt, "Seán Ó Sé na Bánóige," *Revue Celtique*, XLIX (1932), 424–30.

Motifs include B183.1, "Magic mouse"; B576.2, "Animals guard treasure"; B871.1.6, "Giant cat"; D1825.2, "Magic power to see distant objects"; D1880, "Magic rejuvenation"; D1822, "Loss of magic sight"; and G635.1, "Monster's returning head."

· 37 · The Queen of the Planets

Types 461, *Three Hairs from the Devil's Beard*; and 947B*, *Goddess of Fate Allots Fate to People*. IFC Vol. 2, 122–39. Recorded January 1, 1930, by Seán Ó Dubhda from Seán Mac Criomhthain (55), Cill Mhaolchéadair, Dingle Peninsula, county Kerry.

"The storyteller never spent a day in school," the collector says.

The introduction to this tale is very common in Irish versions of Type 461 in which the quest for answers to certain questions is the main feature. For a study of the tale, see A. Aarne, *Der reiche Mann und seine Schwiegersohn*, No. 23. This Irish version was published with a short summary in English by S. Ó Súilleabháin, "Scéalta Cráibhtheacha," *Béaloideas*, XXI (1951–52), 128–32, 318. See also S. Thompson, *The Folktale*, pp. 79, 122, 140, 147, 444, and *Folktales of China*, a companion volume in this series, where type 461 forms part of tale No. 20.

The collector recorded many tales from Mac Criomhthain, as did Seosamh Ó Dálaigh, who, in IFC Vol. 1294, 87–104, lists four hundred and thirty-nine items recorded from him.

Motifs include E501.4.1, "Dogs in wild hunt"; F813.1.4, "Brass apple"; H1291, "Questions asked on way to other world"; and N111, "Fortuna."

• *38* • *Seán Palmer's Voyage to America with the Fairies*

This extraordinary story illustrates the grafting of twentieth-century experience onto the sanctioned themes of Irish fairy lore. The Irish migration to the United States in the last century established a network of kinships across the Atlantic that embraced virtually every Irish family. Seán Palmer's wish to see his well-to-do relatives, friends, and old sweetheart in America could properly be satisfied by the traditional transporters of Irish folk to remote, exotic places, that is, the fairies.

Familiar Irish motifs are F320, "Fairies carry people away to fairyland"; F341, "Fairies give fulfillment of wishes"; and F379.2.2, "Tokens brought back by mortal returning from fairyland." Visits of mortals to fairyland are discussed in detail by E. S. Hartland in *The Science of Fairy Tales* (London, 1891).

Tadhg Ó Murchadha (Murphy), a fieldworker for the Irish Folklore Commission, resident in county Kerry, obtained this tale from William Bradley, who heard Seán Palmer tell it in June, 1933. Bradley, then 75, is described by Tadhg as "a small farmer and water-keeper, a grand step-dancer, gay, light-hearted, and possessing an inexhaustible fund of Gaelic stories, anecdotes, and songs." Rineen Bán, Seán's home, is a little village on the southwest side of Ballin-skelligs Bay in county Kerry, in southwest Ireland, facing toward America.

Reprinted from R. M. Dorson, "Collecting in County Kerry," *Journal of American Folklore*, LXVI (1953), 36–42, as translated by Tadhg Ó Murchadha (Murphy).

A rich legend complex lies behind Seán Palmer's narrative. The theme of a visit to a foreign country with the fairies is represented in a separate file of the archives of the Irish Folklore Commission, classified as the "Hie Over to England (London, Dublin, Paris, Spain, Scotland, etc.)" type. An early chapbook version, "Manus O'Mallaghan and the Fairies", is reprinted in "The Royal Hibernian Tales," *Béaloideas*, X (1941), 172–75. Manus visited both Spain and Rome and was granted a request by the Pope. Other printed texts are in B. Hunt, "The Voice at the Door," *Folk Tales of Breffny* (London, 1912), 137–42, in which an Irish youth, abducted by the fairies because of his fine singing voice, says he has seen America, France, and Spain; Seumas MacManus "The Adventurer," *Bold Blades of Donegal* (London, n.d.), chap. 13, pp. 138–50, in which the fairies take an Irish lad to Philadelphia (where he buys tobacco), then to China and Spain; Philip Dixon Hardy, "Hie Over to England," *Legends, Tales, and Stories of Ireland* (Dublin, 1837), pp. 134–48, where an Irish mason flies with the fairies to Lancashire and as in the preceding tale, saves himself from hanging by putting on his red cap, which transports him home; Patrick Kennedy, *Legendary Fictions of the Irish Celts* (London, 1891), pp. 148–50, condensed version of the above; P. Kennedy, "Tom Kiernan's Visit to France," *The Fireside Stories of Ireland* (Dublin, 1870), pp. 144–45, where an Irish servant boy brings back a goblet from a French wine cellar.

PART V

MAGICIANS AND WITCHES

• *39* •   *The Sailor and the Rat*

IFC Vol. 160, 211–13. Recorded February 26, 1936, by Liam Mac Coisdeala, collector, from Pádhraic Mac an Iomaire (67), Coillín, Carna, county Galway, who had heard the story from his uncle, Seán Ó Laoidh, of the same townland.

The story is illustrative of the folk belief, common in Ireland in former times, that certain individuals were possessed of unusual powers. Plagues of rats could be banished by poets who wrote a charm on a piece of paper that was then laid at the entrance to the hole where the rats lived. Soon after, according to the many stories about it, the leader of the rats emerged from the hole, bearing the paper in its mouth, followed by all the other rats, and all made their way to the location indicated on the paper—usually the farm of some-body against whom the poet had a grudge. This custom was also known in the United States; see William W. Newell, "Conjuring Rats," *Journal of American Folklore*, V (1892), 23–32.

Mac Coisdeala recorded over 1300 pages of manuscript material from this storyteller.

In his field diary on September 9, 1935, the collector says of him, "Pádhraic is most willing to give me what he knows. He is a fine, fluent speaker, tells his tales slowly and clearly, is especially suited for the Ediphone, and has a great many tales."

IFC Vol. 850, 432 ff. has a long account by Mac Coisdeala of the storyteller and his ancestors.

Motif: Q421.3, "Punishment: cutting throat."

· 40 · *The Girl and the Sailor*

IFC Vol. 1051, 138–43. Recorded March 20, 1948, by Tadhg Ó Murchadha, collector, from Mícheál Ó Siochfhradha (79), Clochán na n-Uagha, parish of Prior, county Kerry. The storyteller recorded this and many other tales while lying ill in bed.

"He thinks it too long until I call to see him," remarks the collector (IFC Diary Vol. 1049, 546). "He improves immediately, the moment I arrive."

An account of this collector is given by R. M. Dorson in "Collecting in County Kerry," *Journal of American Folklore*, LXVI (1953), 19–42.

Tales of men who had the power of making women fall in love with them were common in Ireland. The best known is the story of Diarmaid Ó Duibhne, a member of the Fianna, whose love spot (Motif D1355.13) caused Gráinne to fall in love with him. Other stories of this type tell of the use of a love philtre (Motif D1355.2) or of some other love-producing object (D1355). The present story is told in many forms in Ireland.

Motifs are D1355.3, "Love-charm"; and K2259.4, "Treacherous sailor."

· 41 · *The Four-leafed Shamrock and the Cock*

IFC Vol. 272, 415–19. Recorded on December 7, 1936, by Seosamh Ó Dálaigh, collector, from Seán Ó Muircheartaigh (50), Gleann Loic, Dunquin, county Kerry.

The three-leafed shamrock has become one of the national emblems of Ireland. The four-leafed variety is much rarer and is said to be found only where a mare drops her first foal. It was supposed to have special powers, including the ability to float against the current of a stream.

For instances of the present story (there are hundreds of Irish versions), see Mrs. S. C. Hall, "The Orangeman," *Dublin and London Magazine*, III (1827), 251; J. Curtin, *Tales of the Irish Fairies*, pp. 154–56; P. Kennedy, *Legendary Fictions of the Irish Celts*, p. 114; and T. Crofton Croker, *Legends of the Lakes*, II, 14. The story is at

least as old as the thirteenth century. It was recorded by Etienne de
Bourbon (d. 1261), *Anecdotes historiques*, No. 233. See also J. Bolte
and G. Polívka, *Anmerkungen zu den Kinder- und Hausmärchen der
Brüder Grimm*, III, 203.

Motif: D2031.2, "Thread made to appear as a large log carried by
a cock."

• *42* • *The Black Art*

IFC Vol. 1034, 56–60. Recorded in October, 1946, by Seán Ó
Heochaidh, collector, from Diarmaid Mac Seáin (55), Ceapach,
Teelin, county Donegal.

Stories of women who were supposed to possess supernatural
powers are very common in Irish folklore. The witches which form
such a large part of Scandinavian and Germanic folk-belief were
unknown to native Irish tradition. The women (and men) who were
supposedly endowed with special powers were mortals. Stories of the
sinking of boats and ships at sea by evily disposed persons usually
took two forms: (*a*) the violent movement of water in a vessel, by
boiling or otherwise, caused a similar storm at sea; or (*b*) the raising
of a small stone castle (*caisleán Phléimeann*, Fleming's castle?) on
land caused the sea to become storm tossed. There are, of course,
many stories in Irish oral tradition of storms raised at sea by supernatural beings.

Motif: G269.8, "Ship wrecked by witch."

PART VI

HISTORICAL CHARACTERS

• *43* • *Daniel O'Connell and the Trickster*

IFC Vol. 12, 333–35. Recorded in the spring of 1933 by a pupil of
Brother P. T. Ryan, Dingle, from Seán Bruic, Ceathrú an Phúca,
Dingle Peninsula, county Kerry.

Daniel O'Connell, who died in 1847, was a great Irish political
leader as well as a famous lawyer. Apart from the large body of lore
about him and his ancestors and contemporaries that the Irish Folklore Commission has collected, the archives also contain hundreds of

versions of stories illustrative of O'Connell's cleverness as counsel. He has thus become a folktale character. For example, Type 1585, *The Lawyer's Mad Client*, as well as Type 155, *The Ungrateful Serpent Returned to Captivity*, are often associated with him in Ireland. He was born at Carhan, near Caherciveen, in county Kerry, where one of the men in the present tale was said to have lived.

Published versions of this tale can be found in *Béaloideas*, V (1935), 257–58, and *An Stoc* (New Series), III (July, 1926), 7. For other folktales of O'Connell's cleverness as a lawyer and adviser, see *Béaloideas*, V (1935), 259–61.

Motifs include K475, "Cheating through equivocation"; and K493, "Dupe betrayed by asking him ambiguous questions."

· *44* · O'Connell Wears His Hat in Parliament

Published in *Béaloideas*, XI (1941), 116. Recorded in May, 1937, by Seán Ó Dubhda, collector, from Seán Mac Criomhthain (61), Cill Mhaolchéadair, Dingle Peninsula, county Kerry.

For many years, members of the Irish Party sat in the British House of Commons as representatives of Ireland. This apocryphal story concerns that period.

Motif: J1161, "Literal pleading: letter of law has been met."

· *45* · The Smell of Money for the Smell of Food

Published in *Béaloideas*, XI (1941), 122–24. Recorded in March, 1937, by Seán Ó Dubhda, collector, from Seán Mac Criomhthain (61), Cill Mhaolchéadair, Dingle Peninsula, county Kerry.

This is another example of the cleverness attributed to Daniel O'Connell as a lawyer. The tale has been recorded also in Italy, Japan, India, and Indonesia. For the tale as told by American Negroes, see R. M. Dorson, *Negro Folktales in Michigan*, pp. 60–61 and note 30, p. 212.

Motif: J1172.2, "Payment with the clink of the money."

· *46* · The Heather Beer

Type No. 2412E (*The Heather Beer*) has been suggested for this tale by S. Ó Súilleabháin and R. Christiansen, *The Types of the Irish Folktale*, pp. 345–46, where one hundred and eighty-three Irish versions, from manuscript and printed sources, are listed. IFC Vol. 1094, 87–88. Recorded December 27, 1947, by Niall Mac Suibhne, teacher, from Antoin Ó Gallchobhair (81), Mín na Mánrach, Clochán Liath, county Donegal.

For some printed versions, see *Béaloideas*, V (1935), 28–51. C. W. von Sydow, "Niebelungendiktningen och sägen om 'An bheoir lochlannach,'" *Festskrift till Professor E. A. Kock*, p. 377, has studied the basic motif (unrevealed secret) as found in an old Germanic story. For the Danes, see introductory note to tale No. 36 in this book.

Motif: C420, "Tabu: uttering secrets."

· 47 · *The Man Who Lost His Shadow*

IFC Vol. 1093, 159–60. Recorded in January, 1943, by Labhrás Ó Cadhla, Cappoquin, county Waterford. It was one of his own stories as heard from the old people.

R. S. Boggs, *Index of Spanish Folktales*, p. 47, lists this tale under Type 325A*.

The motif of the lost shadow is more usually associated with the devil, who is cheated by a clever mortal.

Motifs are F1038, "Person without shadow; and K525.2, "Man steps aside so that only his shadow is caught."

· 48 · *Cromwell and the Friar*

IFC Vol. 157, 176–83. Recorded in August, 1935, by Liam Mac Coisdeala, collector, from Marcus Ó Neachtain (29), Aird Mhór, Carna, county Galway. Marcus had heard the story from his father, Eoghan, who in turn had heard it from his father, Marcus. Both Eoghan and old Marcus were renowned storytellers, and Mac Coisdeala recorded much lore from Eoghan.

Cromwell's reign of terror in Ireland in the middle of the seventeenth century has insured him an unenviable place in Irish popular tradition. Many stories are told about him, some based on history, others told to illustrate some trait of his character. The present story was very common in Ireland. In many versions, the friar's role is played by a prophet named Mac Amhlaoimh and the King of France is the gentleman who was accidentally shot by Cromwell. Other versions describe how Cromwell died in Ireland and was buried there, but the Irish soil rejected his body and the coffin was found on top of the grave each morning. Finally, it was thrown into the sea and sank down between Dublin and Holyhead, thereby causing that part of the Irish sea to be very turbulent ever since.

Motifs include M306, "Enigmatical prophecy"; M301.5, "Saints (holy men) as prophets"; Q211.5, "Suicide punished"; and R11.2.1, "Devil carries off wicked people."

· 49 · Damer's Gold

Type 1305A, *Workman Looks at Miser's Gold*. IFC Vol. 404, 147–54. Recorded on September 9, 1937, by Seán Ó Flannagáin, collector, from Seámus Ó Ceallaigh (47), Killeen, parish of Behy, Kiltartan, county Galway.

Joseph Damer (1630–1720), who is mentioned in this story, was born in England, served in Cromwell's army, and in 1662 acquired an estate at Shronell in County Tipperary. He became a banker and usurer, and his wealth, as well as stories about how he acquired it, became part of Irish folklore. "As rich as Damer" is still a popular saying in Ireland. One version of the present story says that it was the church plate and ornaments from Hore Abbey, in county Tipperary, that formed the nucleus of Damer's riches. Among other apocryphal stories about him was Type 1130, *Counting out Pay*.

For a published version of this tale, see *Béaloideas*, XXIX (1961), 27.

Motifs: K1872, "Camouflage"; and W153, "Miserliness."

PART VII

THE WISE, THE FOOLISH, AND THE STRONG

· 50 · Secret Tokens Prove Ownership

Type 1532A (*Proof of Ownership by a Trick*) has been suggested by S. Ó Súilleabháin and R. Christiansen for this story in *The Types of the Irish Folktale*. IFC Vol. 1009, 311–17. Recorded on Ediphone in February, 1946, by Liam Mac Coisdeala, collector, from Mícheál Ó Coileáin (70), Carn Mór, parish of Oranmore, county Galway.

Mícheál had heard the story over fifty years before from his father, Tomás, then aged sixty.

Twenty-one versions of the story have been collected in Ireland.

Motifs: D1712, "Soothsayer (diviner, oracle, etc.)"; H80, "Identification by tokens"; and M302.4, "Horoscope taken by means of stars."

· 51 · *The Cow That Ate the Piper*

Type 1281A, *Getting Rid of the Man-eating Calf.* IFC Vol. 702, 167–69. Recorded May 26, 1940, by Seosamh Ó Dála, collector, from Seán Bruic (84), fisherman, Tír Íochtarach, parish of Cloghane, county Kerry.

Until the early decades of the present century, it was customary for men from the western seaboard of Ireland to go to midland and eastern counties as seasonal laborers (*spailpíní*). They were hired at fairs and near the churches on Sundays by the farmers who required help with the farm work, especially harvesting. When the season's work was ended, they returned home again. There is a very large body of lore about these *spailpíní*, many of whom were also storytellers who carried tales from place to place.

Forty versions of the tale have been recorded in Ireland. A text from Maine is in R. M. Dorson, *Buying the Wind*, pp. 87–88.

The Motifs are J1815, "Did the calf eat the man?"; and X422, "Corpse with his feet cut off."

· 52 · *Seán na Scuab*

Type 1284, *Person Does Not Know Himself.* Compare Type 1383, *The Woman Does not Know Herself.* IFC Vol. 32, 57–59. Recorded on Ediphone, December 23, 1932, by Seán Ó Súilleabháin, from Mícheál Ó Súilleabháin (Uaithne) (75), Doire an Locha, Tuosist, Kenmare, county Kerry.

Béara is a peninsula in West Cork, and until the end of the last century, it was customary for the people in such outlying parts of Munster to send their butter to the butter market in Cork City. Cork was at that time, as it still is, the main commercial center of the southern province of Ireland.

Scuaba (brushes) were mainly of home manufacture at that time, and men like the Seán of this story had ready sales for their goods.

Thirty-six versions of this story have been recorded in Ireland. A

Norwegian version appears as No. 70 in *Folktales of Norway*, a companion volume in this series.

Motifs: J2012.4, "Fool in new clothes does not know himself"; and M92, "Decision left to first person to arrive."

• *53* • *The Great Liar*

Types 852, *The Hero Forces the Princess To Say, "That Is a Lie"*; 1911A, *Horse's New Backbone*; and 1960D, *The Great Vegetable*. IFC Vol. 143, 2093–2104. Recorded on Ediphone, February 7, 1936, by Seán Ó Heochaidh, collector, from Seárlaí Ó Baoighill (40), Mín an Chearbhaigh, parish of Glencolmkille, county Donegal. He had heard the story twenty years before from an old man (unnamed) of the same place.

Two hundred and fifty-five versions of Type 852 have been recorded in Ireland, 108 versions of Type 1911A, and 80 versions of Type 1960D. An American example of Type 1911A is given by June Clark, "Big Lies from Grassy," *Journal of American Folklore*, XLVII (1934), 390–91, and Vance Randolph devotes an entire chapter of his book *We Always Lie to Strangers* (New York, 1951) to lies about vegetables of extraordinary size. This motif is popular in American folklore; for additional references see Ernest W. Baughman, *A Type and Motif-Index of Folktales of England and North America* (The Hague, 1965).

Motifs: X1401, "Lie; the great vegetable"; and X1721.1, "New backbone for the horse made from a stick."

• *54* • *The Uglier Foot*

Type 1559B*, *The Uglier Foot*. IFC Vol. 211, 216–20. Recorded by Máire de Brún in 1936 from her grandmother, Mrs. Sweeney (83), Gortnafunshin, Ballymakeera, county Cork.

Wagers having amusing results are the theme of many humorous Irish stories. For example, a man goes into a shop. The shopkeeper says he has every possible kind of article for sale. A wager ensues and it is won by the customer who asks for such things as saddles for frogs, a yard of buttermilk, and so on.

Thirteen versions of this story have been recorded in Ireland.

Motifs: F517.1, "Person unusual as to his feet"; N72, "Wager on second marvelous object"; and X137, "Humor of ugliness."

· *55* · *The Blacksmith and the Horseman*

IFC Vol. 966, 313–16. Recorded November 26, 1944, by Seosamh Ó Dála, collector, from Seán Mac Criomhthain (67), Kilmaelkedar, Dingle Peninsula, county Kerry. Seán had heard the story from his father.

The blacksmith held a unique place in Irish social life in earlier times. His magical and curative powers derived from the metal which he used for his craft. His curse was feared by all. Many stories were told in Ireland to also illustrate his physical strength.

Motif: H1562, "Test of strength."

Glossary

báinín Flannel. A white coat or jacket.

banbh A young pig.

barra bua A kind of musical instrument (trumpet?) used by the Fianna to call for help when in danger.

ben Irish for mountain, e.g., Ben Bulban, Co. Sligo.

caisleán Phléimeann A small stone castle built for magical purposes.

cess Luck.

coileach Mhárta A March cock; one born from an egg laid on the first Tuesday in March and hatched on a Tuesday of the same month. It is believed to have the power of protecting the house.

dearg-laoch A kind of spurge that grows in wet bogs.

dripping of the royal candle (sileadh na rí-choinle) A form of torture mentioned in folktales in which hot candle grease was dripped on an enemy as he lay bound.

Domhnall na Gréine "Daniel of the Sun." The name of a humorous Irish song.

Eight-legged Dog (Madra na nOcht gCos) The name of an Irish tale in which the hero is sent on many quests.

fabaíneach fubaíneach An alliterative, adjectival phrase (untranslatable).

fiannaíocht Romancing. Telling stories about the Fianna. Storytelling in general.

Fíodóra (nom. *Fíodóir*) (Son) of the weaver.

Fú fá féasóg An alliterative phrase similar to "fee faw fum." *Féasóg* means beard or whisker.

garron A small horse or gelding.

garsún (cf. French *garçon*) A young boy.

geasa Solemn injunctions of a magical kind. In folktales, the hero was often placed under *geasa* by his opponent so that he was forced to perform certain tasks.

grianán   A sunny upper chamber in a castle.

gruagach   In folktales, an enchanter, magician, or champion.

gruagaigh   Plural of the preceding word.

gurnet   A deep-sea fish.

handspikes   A handbarrow or litter carried by hand.

keelers   Broad, shallow cream tubs cut from the bottom of casks or barrels.

leipreachán   A fairy shoemaker or cobbler.

lios   An ancient Irish steading or dwelling place which, when abandoned was popularly regarded as a "fairy fort."

Lochlainn   Scandinavia in general.

moryah (*mar dheadh*)   As it were. By way of pretence.

naggin   A variant of noggin; a wooden milk pail.

oscartha   Heroic, mighty, active. A pun on the name of the hero (Oscar).

peelers   Policemen. So nicknamed after their founder, Sir Robert Peel.

piast (cf. Latin *bestia*)   A monster or serpent.

pits   Elongated mounds of earth within which potatoes, turnips, etc., were stored in the open during the winter months.

poor scholar   An itinerant student. Many such men acted as unofficial teachers in rural districts of Ireland until the middle of the nineteenth century when the people were denied formal education.

redden   Translation of the Irish word *deargadh*. To "redden" or light a pipe of tobacco.

seanchaí   A tradition-bearer or storyteller.

seanchas   Ancient lore or traditional knowledge.

smiortán   The inner core of marrow in a bone.

spalpeens   Anglicized form of the Irish word *spailpíní*. Migratory laborers.

station   Ireland is one of the few countries in the Catholic world in which Mass may be offered in a private house. Twice a year, in spring and autumn, the priests of each parish offer Mass in one house in each townland of their parish and the neighbors attend the service. The "station" rotates from house to house year by year. The custom, which is still widespread in Ireland, is said to have originated in penal times, when Mass had to be celebrated in secret.

strapaire A vigorous, well-built "strapping" fellow.

turf bog An area in which deposits of peat (turf) are found. Turf has been used as fuel in Ireland for a long time, and is now being produced commercially on a large scale.

Bibliography

AARNE, ANTTI. *Der tiersprachkundige Mann und seine neugierige Frau.* ("Folklore Fellows Communications," No. 15.) Helsinki, 1914.

———. *Der reiche Mann und sein Schwiegersohn.* ("Folklore Fellows Communications," No. 23.) Hamina, 1916.

———. See THOMPSON, STITH.

ANDREJEV, N. P. *Die Legende von den zwei Erzsündern.* ("Folklore Fellows Communications," No. 54.) Helsinki, 1924.

———. *Die Legende vom Rauber Madej.* ("Folklore Fellows Communications," No. 69.) Helsinki, 1927.

ANDREWS, ELIZABETH. *Ulster Folklore.* London, 1913.

BAUGHMAN, ERNEST W. *A Type and Motif-Index of the Folktales of England and North America.* The Hague, 1965.

Béaloideas. Journal of the Folklore of Ireland Society. Vols. I–XXXI. Dublin, 1927–.

BLADÉ, J. F. *Contes populaires de Gascogne* ("Les Littératures Populaires des toutes les nations," Nos. 19–21.) 3 vols. Paris, 1886.

BOLTE, JOHANNES, and POLÍVKA, GEORG. *Anmerkungen zu den Kinder- und Hausmärchen der Brüder Grimm.* 5 vols. Leipzig, 1913–31.

BØDKER, L.; HOLE, C.; and D'ARONCO, G. *European Folk Tales.* Copenhagen, 1963.

BOGGS, R. S. *Index of Spanish Folktales* ("Folklore Fellows Communications," No. 90.) Helsinki, 1930.

BRUFORD, ALAN. "Eachtra Chonall Gulban," *Béaloideas,* XXXI (1963), 1 ff.

CAMPBELL, MARIE. *Tales from the Cloud Walking Country.* Bloomington, Ind., 1958.

CHASE, RICHARD. *Grandfather Tales.* Boston, 1948.

CHAUVIN, VICTOR. *Bibliographie des ouvrages arabes.* 12 vols. Liège and Leipzig, 1892–1922.

CHRISTIANSEN, REIDAR TH. (ed.). *Folktales of Norway.* Chicago, 1964.

———. "The People of the North," *Lochlann*, II (1962), 137–64.

———. *See* Ó SÚILLEABHÁIN, SEÁN.

Claidheamh Soluis, An. Irish weekly paper. Dublin, 1899–.

CRANE, T. F. *The Exempla of Jacques de Vitry.* ("Publications of the Folklore Society," Vol. 26.) London, 1890.

CROKER, T. C. *Legends of the Lakes.* 2 vols. London, 1829.

CROSS, TOM PEETE. *Motif-Index of Early Irish Literature.* ("Indiana University Folklore Series," No. 7.) Bloomington, Ind., n.d.

CURTIN, JEREMIAH. *Myths and Folklore of Ireland.* London, 1890.

———. *Hero-Tales of Ireland.* London, 1894.

———. *Tales of the Irish Fairies.* London, 1895. (Also titled *Tales of the Fairies and of the Ghost World.*)

DE BOURBON, ETIENNE. *Anecdotes historiques.* Paris, 1877.

DE HÍDE, DUBHGLAS (Hyde, Douglas). *An Sgéaluidhe Gaedhealach.* Dublin, 1895, 1901.

———. "The Adventures of Léithín," *The Celtic Review*, X (December, 1914–June, 1916), 116–43.

———. "Mar fuair Dairmuid a bhall-seirc," *Annales de Bretagne,* XII (1896), 238–44.

———. *Legends of Saints and Sinners.* Dublin, 1915.

———. *Ocht Sgéalta ó Choillte Mághach.* Dublin, 1936.

DÉGH, LINDA (ed.). *Folktales of Hungary.* Chicago, 1964.

DELARGY, JAMES H. *The Gaelic Storyteller.* ("Rhŷs Memorial Lecture," Proceedings of the British Academy.) London, 1945.

DILLON, MYLES. *The Cycles of the Kings.* Oxford, 1946.

DORSON, RICHARD M. *Buying the Wind.* Chicago, 1964.

———. "Collecting in County Kerry," *Journal of American Folklore*, LXVI (1953), 19–42.

———. *Negro Folktales in Michigan.* Cambridge, Mass., 1956.

Dublin and London Magazine. Dublin and London, 1825.

EBERHARD, WOLFRAM (ed.). *Folktales of China.* Chicago, 1965.

FFC Folklore Fellows Communications. Helsinki, 1910–.

GARDNER, EMELYN E. *Folklore from the Schoharie Hills, New York*. Ann Arbor, Mich., 1937.

HALL, MRS. S. C. Anna Maria. "The Orangeman," *Dublin and London Magazine*, III (1827), 251.

HERBERT, J. A. *A Catalogue of Romances in the Department of Manuscripts in the British Museum*, III. London, 1910.

HULL, ELEANOR. "The Hawk of Achill, or the Legend of the Oldest of the Animals," *Folk-Lore*, XLIII (1932), 376–409.

Irisleabhar na Gaedhilge, V (1882), 10–13; VIII (May, 1897–July, 1898), 11–13.

JOYNT, MAUD. (ed.). *Feis Tighe Chonáin* ("Medieval and Modern Irish Series," No. 7). Dublin, 1936.

KENNEDY, PATRICK. *Legendary Fictions of the Irish Celts*. London, 1866.

KÖHLER, REINHOLD. *Kleinere Schriften*, ed. J. BOLTE. 3 vols. Weimar, 1898–1900.

KRAPPE, A. H. "The Celtic Provenance of the Lay of Tydorel," *Modern Language Review*, XXIV (1929), 200–204.

LAOIDE, SEOSAMH. *Fionn agus Lorcán*. Dublin, 1903.

———. *Trí Torpáin*. Dublin, 1911.

LARMINIE, WILLIAM. *West Irish Folk-Tales and Romances*. London, 1893.

LOT, F. "Origine scandinave d'un conte irlandais," *Annales de Bretagne*, XIII (1897), 48–49.

MACGIOLLARNÁTH, SEÁN. *Loinnir mac Leabhair*. Dublin, 1936.

MACNEILL, EOIN. (ed.). *Duanaire Finn*, Part I. ("*Irish Texts Society*," No. 7.) London, 1908.

MACLYSAGHT, E. *Irish Life in the Seventeenth Century*. Dublin, 1939.

MCKAY, J. G. "Scottish Gaelic Parallels to Tales and Motifs in *Béaloideas*, Vols. I and II," *Béaloideas*, III (1932), 139–48.

MURPHY, GERARD (ed.). *Duanaire Finn*, II, III. ("*Irish Texts Society*," Nos. 28 and 43.) Dublin, 1933, 1953.

NEWELL, WILLIAM W. "Conjuring Rats," *Journal of American Folklore*, V (1892), 23–32.

NORTH, F. J. *Sunken Cities*. Cardiff, 1957.

NOY, DOV (ed.). *Folktales of Israel*, Chicago, 1963.

O'GRADY, STANDISH (ed.). *Silva Gadelica, a Collection of Tales in Irish.* 2 vols. London, 1892.

O'KEARNEY, N. (ed.). *Feis Tighe Chonáin.* ("Transactions of the Ossianic Society," No. 2.) Dublin, 1855.

Ó SÚILLEABHÁIN, SEÁN. "Scéalta Cráibhtheacha," *Béaloideas,* XXI (1951–52).

Ó SÚILLEABHÁIN, SEÁN, and CHRISTIANSEN, R. *The Types of the Irish Folktale.* ("Folklore Fellows Communications," No. 188.) Helsinki, 1963.

Our Boys. Dublin, 1914–.

RANDOLPH, VANCE. *We Always Lie to Strangers.* New York, 1951.

SAYERS, PEIG. *An Old Woman's Reflections.* London, 1962.

SEKI, KEIGO (ed.). *Folktales of Japan.* Chicago, 1963.

"Sgéal na Mná a Chuaidh go hIfreann," *Imtheachta an Oireachtais,* III (1899), 121–32.

SHAW, ROSE. *Carleton's Country.* Dublin, 1930.

SJOESTEDT, M. L. "Seán Ó Sé na Bánóige," *Revue Celtique,* XLIX (1932), 424–30.

STEPHANUS. *See* DE BOURBON, ETIENNE.

Stoc, An, I (1930), 36–7, and New Series, III (1926), 7.

SWAHN, J-Ö. *The Tale of Cupid and Psyche.* Lund, 1955.

SYDOW, C. W. VON. "Niebelungendiktningen och sägnen om 'An bheoir lochlannach'," *Lunder germanische Forschungen. 1. Studia Germanica tillägnade Ernst Albin Kock.* Lund, 1934.

SYNGE, J. M. *The Aran Islands.* London, 1921.

SZÖVÉRFFY, J. *Irisches Erzählgut im Abendland.* Berlin, 1957.

TAYLOR, A. *The Black Ox* ("Folklore Fellows Communications," No. 70). Helsinki, 1927.

THOMPSON, STITH. *The Folktale.* New York, 1946.

———. *Motif-Index of Folk Literature.* 6 vols. rev. ed. Copenhagen and Bloomington, Ind., 1955–58.

THOMPSON, STITH, and AARNE, ANTTI. *The Types of the Folktale: A Classification and Bibliography.* ("Folklore Fellows Communications," No. 184.) Helsinki, 1961.

WESTROPP, T. J. "Brasil and the Legendary Isles of the North Atlantic: Their History and Fable. A Contribution to the

'Atlantis' Problem," *Proceedings of the Royal Irish Academy,* XXX (1912–13), Section C, 223–63.

Wood-Martin, W. G. *Traces of the Elder Faiths of Ireland.* 2 vols. London, 1902.

Index of Motifs

(From Stith Thompson, *Motif-Index of Folk Literature*. [6 vols.; Bloomington, Ind., 1955–58]). For further references, see T. P. Cross, *Motif-Index of Early Irish Literature* (Bloomington, Ind., n.d.).

B. ANIMALS

C. TABU

D. MAGIC

E. THE DEAD

F. MARVELS

G. OGRES

H. TESTS

J. THE WISE AND THE FOOLISH

P. SOCIETY

Q. REWARDS AND PUNISHMENTS

R. CAPTIVES AND FUGITIVES

S. UNNATURAL CRUELTY

T. SEX

V. RELIGION

X. HUMOR

Index of Tale Types

(Type numbers are from Antti Aarne and Stith Thompson, *The Types of the Folktale* [Helsinki, 1961]. For type numbers whose titles are in parentheses, as well as for Irish versions of all types, see Ó Súilleabháin and Christiansen, *The Types of the Irish Folktale* [Helsinki, 1963]).

I. ANIMAL TALES (1–299)

II. ORDINARY FOLKTALES

A. Tales of Magic (300–749)

B. Religious Tales (750–849)

General Index

Swimming: tabu, 21
Sword: 39, 61, 66, 67, 82, 93; fatal
    thrust of, 48; magic, 62; screams,
    62, 113; broken, 74; of light, 109,
    113, 116

Tablecloth: self-spreading, 182
Tabu: swimming in lake, 21; eating
    while in hell, 159; opening book
    for seven years, 187; mentioning
    name, 259
Tailor: advises miser to spend, 241;
    as hero, 252; wins bet, 253
Tale: told to king, 31; told as true,
    188, 192, 273; saves man from
    hanging, 251; humorous, 274;
    introduction to, 277; apocryphal,
    282; dissemination of, 285
Tallow: used to conceal treasure,
    240
Task: fetch sword, 25; to narrate
    tales, 33; to recover magician's
    daughter, 38; borrow hound
    from magician, 42; borrow honey
    dish from king, 44; bring head
    of warrior, 100; bring most
    beautiful princess, 108; find magic
    objects, 109; remove Geasa, 125,
    126. See also Quest
Terror. See Fear
Theft, 4; of game, 6; by fox, 7;
    of honey dish, 45; from giant, 77;
    of cattle, 77; of food from feast,
    91; of money, 181; by rat, 189; of
    food, 189; of straw, 209; of horse,
    245; of shoes from corpse, 247;
    of church treasures, 284
Threat: by grandson, 26; to get
    confession, 36; of beheading, 44;
    from hero, 66, 68, 69; by devil,
    146; of death, 181; to friar, 238
Tobacco: craving for, 209; obtained
    from fairies, 211; a part of
    deception, 231

Token: of royalty, 27, 29, 98; of
    recognition, 163; concealed coin,
    245; proves ownership, 247; of
    office, 249
Tongs: self-moving, 182
Towel: magic, 198, 201
Transformation, human to animal:
    prince to dragon, 47; prince to
    poisonous lion, 47; prince to
    bird, 47; prince to fish, 48; man
    to horse, 111; man to bull, 115,
    125; man to dog, 115
        human to object: man to
    stone, 95; woman to stone, 119;
    woman to jelly, 209
        object or animal to human:
    stool to man, 69; bull to man,
    125; stone to woman, 129
        object to object: ring to ship,
    39, 45; ship to stone, 39, 45;
    straw to bagpipes, 45; hovel to
    house, 203
Treasure: demanded from leip-
    reachán, 180; hidden by Danes,
    180; unwittingly given away,
    181; loss of brings madness, 181;
    magic sight of, 196, 276; guarded
    by cat, 197; promised, 197; three
    jars of gold, 198; found in fairy
    fort, 201; concealed, 240, 241;
    unwittingly purchased, 240; of
    leipreachán, 273; of Danes, 276;
    taken from church, 284
Tree: from grave of murdered
    child, 120; magically destroyed,
    170; grows from horse's back,
    252
Turf, 226; as fuel, 182, 197, 200;
    thrown into wave, 185

Uí Chéilleachair, Conchobhar Phea-
    dair (narrator), 274
Uí Choinghialla, Áine (narrator),
    260
Ulster cycle, 265